System Performance Tuning

System Performance Tuning

Mike Loukides

O'Reilly & Associates, Inc.
103 Morris Street, Suite A
Sebastopol, CA 95472

System Performance Tuning

by Mike Loukides

Editor: Tim O'Reilly

Printing History:

November 1990:	First Edition.
March 1991:	Minor corrections.
October 1991:	Minor corrections.
December 1992:	Minor corrections.

This book is printed on acid-free paper with 50% recycled content, 10-15% post-consumer waste. O'Reilly & Associates is committed to using paper with the highest recycled content available consistent with high quality.

ISBN: 0-937175-60-9

[1/95]

TABLE OF CONTENTS

Figures

Tables

Preface

Audience
Organization
UNIX Versions
Conventions Used in This Handbook
We'd Like to Hear From You
Acknowledgements

Several years ago I believed that it was virtually impossible to tune UNIX for better system performance. Everything you could do to improve performance involved customizing the kernel, which was forbidden territory. Working for a supercomputer company for several years changed my attitude completely. Kernel customization is possible, though difficult, and may be a very effective way to help your system along. And before you resort to kernel customization, you can use many simple tricks and techniques to improve your system's behavior.

Unfortunately, many UNIX users and system administrators have succumbed to a general despondency about system performance. They are still under the impression that UNIX won't let them do anything about system-wide performance or that the mechanisms available for tuning the UNIX system are so inscrutable that they'd better not try. Of course, this attitude is a recipe for failure. UNIX is not as easily tunable as other large operating systems, which often allow you to change major system parameters on the fly, but it is possible to do a lot to improve your system's performance. The most important changes involve building a custom UNIX kernel, which is a daunting and sometimes perilous task. But a lot of the tuning you can do is no more than implementing good management policies for your system: keeping watch over how it is used, running large jobs at night if possible, and so on.

This book provides a basic introduction to system performance tuning: optimizing the performance of a UNIX system as a whole. We don't mean making an individual program run faster, although if the system as a whole is working better, your individual jobs will run faster. We mean structuring the system to maximize its total throughput. We mean structuring the system so that its resources are used efficiently and distributed fairly among the users. We mean finding out which part of the system is overloaded, understanding how to lessen the load, and knowing which part of the system to upgrade when an upgrade is necessary.

One large topic we won't cover is the performance of an individual job. Getting an individual job to run faster is a matter of improving or changing algorithms, ensuring that the program is optimized properly, and so on. Particularly with the supercomputers and near-supercomputers currently on the market, the right way to optimize a program depends a lot on the system's architecture. And the use of faster algorithms is a subject far beyond the confines of this book.

If you are interested in scientific programming, we recommend that you take a look at *Numerical Recipes: The Art of Scientific Computing* by William H. Press et. al. (Cambridge University Press). There are separate versions of this book for FORTRAN, C, and PASCAL programmers. The examples and algorithms discussed in the book are all available electronically, so you can use them and then develop your own programs. For more general programming topics, read Donald Knuth's classic three-volume series *The Art of Computer Programming* (Addison Wesley).

Audience

This book should be of interest to:

- Administrators of UNIX systems or networks of UNIX systems.
- Users of personal computers or standalone workstations (i.e., single keyboard systems) that run UNIX. If there is no system administrator responsible for your system (and there won't be if you're running a large PC at home) you are responsible for your own tuning.

We assume you are already familiar with basic UNIX system administration; therefore, we won't tell you how to perform basic tasks such as adding a new user, nor will we explain basic concepts such as file ownership. We will give a lot of attention to the concepts that underlie performance management. As far as system performance is concerned, understanding the problem is three-quarters of the battle.

We aren't aiming this book at UNIX wizards. I have chosen to omit tuning techniques that require patching the UNIX kernel with *adb*, looking at kernel tables that aren't accessible through standard utilities, and so on. There are a number of things that you can tweak this way, and some of them may even improve your system's performance. But you are much more likely to create a kernel that is broken in very mysterious ways, that cannot be reproduced when the next software upgrade comes out, and that can't be understood three days after you have made the change. In short, patching the kernel may be an interesting wizard's trick, but it produces software that is completely non-maintainable. Speed may be important, but reliability and maintainability are even more important.

Organization

We have organized this book according to the major components of the UNIX operating system:

Chapter 1, *Introduction to System Performance*, gives a basic introduction to performance tuning, summarizes the issues involved and points to some of the solutions.

Chapter 2, *Monitoring System Activity*, focuses on measuring and analyzing the system's load. In order to make intelligent tuning decisions, you must know what your system does: what programs it runs and what resources it uses. We therefore spend some time looking at basic tools such as *ps* and the accounting system.

Chapter 3, *Managing the Workload*, discusses techniques for managing your system's load. It begins with some tricks that will help users to improve their interactive response. It then discusses more weighty CPU configuration issues: how to eliminate unnecessary work, how to reset priorities, and how to tailor the UNIX kernel's configuration for your system's needs.

Chapter 4, *Memory Performance*, discusses how contention for memory affects the system's overall performance. This chapter describes how to tell whether your system has enough memory for its workload and discusses some ways of freeing additional memory.

Chapter 5, *Disk Performance Issues*, discusses how disk use (i.e., contention for file access) affects overall performance. This chapter describes how to organize your filesystem so that it will be as efficient as possible. It also describes some other techniques behind disk optimization.

Chapter 6, *Network Performance*, discusses how network usage affects overall performance. This chapter describes how to detect faulty and overloaded networks, both of which cause poor performance.

Chapter 7, *Terminal Performance* discusses the role played by terminal I/O in overall performance. This chapter describes how to detect and eliminate noisy terminal lines.

Chapter 8, *Kernel Configuration*, discusses the kernel configuration process for Berkeley UNIX (including SunOS), XENIX, 386/ix, and System V.4.

Appendix A, *Real-time Processes in System V.4*, discusses the System V.4 real-time facility.

Appendix B, *A Performance Tuning Strategy*, summarizes a strategy for approaching performance problems. You can use it as a quick-reference or a checklist for analyzing your system.

The *Glossary* defines many of the technical terms used throughout the book.

UNIX Versions

This book is based on the Berkeley implementation of UNIX (BSD Version 4.3); we have used Berkeley UNIX for most of the general discussions. We refer to this implementation as BSD UNIX. However, BSD 4.3 is only part of the Berkeley UNIX story. SunOS (Versions 4.0 and following) has added several kinks: new facilities such as in-memory filesystems and changes in the way filesystem buffering works.

We also discuss AT&T's version of UNIX, System V, which adds another level of complexity to the game. Not only are the System V administrative tools completely different from Berkeley, System V implementations are far from uniform among themselves—in fact, significantly less uniform than Berkeley implementations. System V versions of UNIX can be divided into several significant groups:

• **Descendants of System V, Release 2 (V.2).** XENIX (the first version of UNIX to run on a personal computer) is the most important system in this class, although it isn't a true port of V.2. XENIX is a descendant of Version 7 (a late-1970s version) that has been converted to. V.2 over time. Because BSD 4.3 UNIX is also an heir of Version 7, XENIX and BSD UNIX have some tools in common.

- **Descendants of System V, Release 3 (V.3).** Many manufacturers, including Hewlett-Packard and NCR, provide implementations of V.3. Many of these implementations freely mix features from BSD UNIX with standard System V.3. Versions of V.3 for 8086-series personal computers (80286, 80386, and so on) are available from Interactive and SCO, among others. Interactive's version is called 386/ix, while SCO's goes under the name SCO UNIX.

- **Descendants of System V, Release 4 (V.4 or SVR4).** V.4 integrates many of the most important features of Berkeley UNIX (including networking) and the SunOS network filesystem. It promises to bring some uniformity to the confusing world of UNIX implementations. Unfortunately, V.4 is still in the wings as of this writing. Our discussion covers the 3B2 (AT&T) version of V.4. Information about the 8086-series implementation was not available as of publication.

Unfortunately, System V versions differ radically from each other. Furthermore, there are many processor- and vendor-specific features within any version. For example, Interactive's version of 386/ix differs from SCO's. Both are different from HP's UNIX (HP-UX) in many ways. In turn, HP-UNIX incorporates many BSD features, plus several of its own tools. To make the situation worse, HP-UNIX isn't completely uniform itself. The versions that run on different processors have significantly different tools.

The moral of this story is simple: when you read this book (or any other book on UNIX administration), don't take anything for granted. Check your manufacturer's documentation before doing anything you may regret. We can give you a lot of help with the principles behind performance tuning and will tell you as many details as possible. We can show you how different factors interrelate and where to go to find more information. And we can give you as much information as possible about the most important UNIX versions on the market. But we can't be comprehensive about the different UNIX implementations that are available.

In this book, we use these implementations:

- **For BSD UNIX:** Multiflow Computer's TRACE/UNIX Version 4.1. Multiflow is no longer in business but their port of BSD 4.3 was almost completely standard. We have, of course, omitted Multiflow-specific features.

- **For SunOS:** SunOS 4.1, running on a Sun 3/60.

- **For System V.3:** Interactive 386/ix Release 2.2, running on an 80386-based system.

- **For XENIX:** SCO XENIX for the 80386, Release 2.3.3.

If you don't have one of these systems, you will still find a lot of valid principles in this book. The concepts discussed here are valid for any UNIX system and probably apply to other time-sharing virtual memory operating systems as well.

Given the broad range of UNIX systems, the difference in personal tastes, and the differences between UNIX implementations, it is best to take any recommendations with a grain of salt. Tuning parameters that would be appropriate for a PC runing 386/ix would be inappropriate for a CRAY or a CONVEX system, even though the same concepts may apply. Furthermore, I certainly have my own tastes, and haven't hesitated to reveal them. For example, I really believe that systems shouldn't spend time paging, and won't hesitate to tell you so. I'll admit that I am an extremist in this respect—it probably comes from doing time at a supercomputer company. But paging is the first sign of more serious problems. The point at which it becomes serious depends on how much paging takes place, how fast your disks are, what kinds of applications you are running, and so on. Likewise, I like to see my system humming along with zero idle time—it makes me think that lots of work is getting done. But I will admit that this is a good sign that your CPU is overloaded. I'll try to inform you of "minority opinions" (by definition, opinions that differ from my own). Even if I could force you to follow my recommendations, I wouldn't. But don't ignore the principles behind them. Above all, performance tuning means knowing what your system is doing and why. The point at which paging or CPU workload becomes a problem is very subjective, but the factors that create these problems, the tools for detecting them, and the techniques for solving them are not.

Conventions Used in This Handbook

The following conventions are used in this book:

Italic   is used for the names of all UNIX utilities, directories, tuning parameters, and filenames and to emphasize new terms and concepts when they are first introduced.

`Constant Width`   is used in examples to show the contents of files or the output from commands.

`Constant Italic`   is used in examples to show variables for which a context-specific substitution should be made. (The variable `filename`, for example, would be replaced by some actual filename.)

Constant Bold	is used in examples to show commands or text that would be typed in literally by the user.
Quotes	Surround a reference in explanatory text to a word or item used in an examples or code fragment.
%, $, #	When we are demonstrating commands that you would give interactively, we normally use the default C shell prompt (%). We use the default Bourne shell prompt ($) if the commands we are demonstrating must be executed from the Bourne shell. We use the default superuser prompt (#) if the commands must be executed as root. Note that the superuser prompt can easily be confused with the comment character for shell scripts.

We'd Like to Hear From You

We have tested and verified all of the information in this book to the best of our ability, but you may find that features have changed (or even that we have made mistakes!). Please let us know about any errors you find, as well as your suggestions for future editions, by writing:

```
O'Reilly & Associates, Inc.
103 Morris Street, Suite A
Sebastopol, CA 95472
1-800-998-9938 (in the US or Canada)
1-707-829-0515 (international/local)
1-707-829-0104 (FAX)
```

You can also send us messages electronically. To be put on the mailing list or request a catalog, send email to:

info@ora.com	(via the Internet)
uunet!ora!info	(via UUCP)

To ask technical questions or comment on the book, send email to:

bookquestions@ora.com	(via the Internet)

Acknowledgements

Many people have helped this book along the way. My thanks go to NCR and Elizabeth Pearson for providing the initial idea and some drafts of material they had developed. Tan Bronson (Microvation Consultants) and Greg Benjamin

(LaserLab) gave me access to XENIX and 386/ix systems. Mike Frisch and Ray Ellis (Gaussian) gave me access to a Stardent system, for another perspective on System V. Tan Bronson, Pat Clancy (Em, Inc.), Doug Gilmore (Scientific Computing Associates), Paul Wellens (Interactive), Jim Browning (NCR), Hal Stern (Sun), Clem Cole (Cole Computer Consulting), Eric Ahlberg (Interactive), and John Coleman (Interactive) answered many questions and solved many problems. Hal Stern, Dave Curry (SRI International), Clem Cole, Dave Lennert (Sequent), Ken Fullett (Comsat), Tim O'Reilly (ORA), and Doug Gilmore read the finished manuscript; this book has profited greatly from their comments. My thanks also go to the production group of O'Reilly and Associates for putting the finishing touches on this book.

1

Introduction to
System Performance

System Performance Issues
System Resources
User Communities

System performance is easy to talk about but difficult to understand. Everyone knows when a computer system is slow, but it's much more difficult to get the most out of any given configuration. Many different factors play a role in determining your system's response. Usage patterns, I/O configuration, CPU configuration, and software configuration all contribute to your system's behavior. Changing any of these variables can make an apparently slow system much faster or make an apparently fast system yield significantly worse performance. A system that is well-configured and used appropriately will give better performance than one that is not. But this statement tells you absolutely nothing about how to analyze a system, determine whether or not it's running well, and take steps to correct any problems you might find.

This book has three goals: to help you understand system performance, to give you the tools needed to monitor performance and determine what system components (if any) are not performing optimally, and to discuss the actions you can take to improve the performance of your system as a whole. With an understanding of the issues involved, you will be able to make informed decisions about how to tune your system. Above all, optimizing system performance is a matter of making tradeoffs. You can't optimize one aspect of performance without compromising some other aspect; therefore, it is important to understand what basic performance measurements mean and how they relate to each other.

1.1.1 How Users Perceive Performance

To a user, performance means: "How much time does it take to run my job?" For a system manager, this question is much too simple: a user's job may take a long time to execute because it is badly written or because it doesn't really use the computer appropriately. Furthermore, a system manager must optimize performance for all system users—which is much more complicated than optimizing performance for a single user. But listening to the problems of individual users is an excellent place to start. Complaints from users indicate that something may be wrong with your system's configuration, particularly if there is a sudden change in the system's perceived performance. It is worthwhile understanding exactly what a user is complaining about.

The UNIX utility */bin/time* reports the amount of time required to execute a program, breaking down the total time into several important components. For example, consider the report below:

```
% /bin/time application
  4.8 real      0.5 user       0.7 sys
```

This report shows that the program ran in roughly 4.8 seconds. This is the *elapsed* or *wall-clock* time: it is the actual time that the program runs as it would be measured by a user sitting at the terminal with a stopwatch. The amount of time that the system spent working on your program is much smaller. It spent 0.5 seconds of *user time*, which is time spent executing code in the user state, and about 0.7 seconds of *system time*, which is time spent in the system state (i.e., time spent executing UNIX system code) on behalf of the user. The total amount of CPU time (actual execution time on the main processor) was only 1.2 seconds, or only one-quarter of the elapsed time.*

Where did the rest of the time go? Some time was spent performing I/O operations, which */bin/time* doesn't report. Handling I/O requires some computation, which is attributed to system time. But time that is spent by disk drives, network

---

*Note that BSD and System V versions of */bin/time* have different output formats but provide the same information. */bin/time* also differs from the C shell's *time* command, which provides a more elaborate report.

interfaces, terminal controllers, or other hardware isn't accounted for; most of the time was spent running jobs on behalf of other users. This entails its own performance overhead (context-switch time, swapping time, etc.).

Many different components contribute to a program's total running time. When you understand the role these components play, you will understand the problem. Here is a summary of the different components:

- **User-state CPU time.** The actual amount of time the CPU spends running the user's program in the user state. It includes time spent executing library functions but excludes time spent executing system calls (i.e., time spent in the UNIX kernel on behalf of the process). User-state time is under the programmer's control and won't be discussed except as an administrative issue. Your system's programmers should know how to write well-optimized code. They should know which library routines are efficient and which aren't, and they should know how to use *prof* and *gprof* to find out where a program is spending its time.

- **System-state CPU time.** The amount of time the CPU spends in the system state (i.e., the amount of time executing kernel code) on behalf of the program. This includes time spent executing system calls and performing administrative functions on the program's behalf. The distinction between time spent in simple library routines and time spent in system services is important and often confused. A call to *strcpy*, which copies a character string, executes entirely in the user state because it doesn't require any special handling by the kernel. Calls to *printf, fork*, and many other routines are much more complex. These functions do require services from the UNIX kernel so they spend part of their time, if not most of it, in the system state. All I/O routines require the kernel's services.

  System-state CPU time is partially under the programmer's control. Although programmers cannot change the amount of time it takes to service any system call, they can rewrite the program to issue system calls more efficiently (for example, to make I/O transfers in larger blocks).

- **I/O time.** The amount of time the I/O subsystem spends servicing the I/O requests that the job issues. Under UNIX, I/O time is difficult to measure; however, there are some tools for determining whether the I/O system is overloaded and some configuration considerations that can help alleviate load problems.

- **Network time.** The amount of time that the I/O subsystem spends servicing network requests that the job issues. This is really a subcategory of I/O time and depends critically on configuration and usage issues; however, the issues are different, so we will consider it separately.

- **Time spent running other programs.** As system load increases, the CPU spends less time working on any given job, thus increasing the elapsed time required to run the job. This is an annoyance, but barring some problem with I/O or virtual memory performance, there is little you can do about it. Some policy decisions can make life more pleasant for most users. We will discuss these policy decisions later.

- **Virtual memory performance.** This is by far the most complex aspect of system performance. Ideally, all active jobs would remain in the system's physical memory at all times. In practice this is impossible, even on systems with large memory configurations. When physical memory is fully occupied, the operating system starts moving parts of jobs to disk, thus freeing memory for the job it wants to run. This takes time. It also takes time when these disk-bound jobs need to run again and therefore needs to be moved back into memory. When running jobs with extremely large memory requirements, system performance can degrade significantly.

If you spend most of your time running standard utilities and commercial applications, you can't do much about user-state or system-state time. To make a significant dent in these, you have to rewrite the program. But you can do a lot to improve your memory and I/O performance, and you can do a lot to run your big applications more efficiently.

Keyboard response is an extremely important issue to users, although it really doesn't contribute to a program's execution time. If there is a noticeable gap between the time when a user types a character and the time when the system echoes that character, the user will think performance is bad, regardless of how much time it takes to run a job. In order to prevent terminal buffers from overflowing and losing characters, most UNIX systems give terminal drivers very high priority. As a side effect, the high priority of terminals means that keyboard response should be bad only under exceptionally high loads. If you are accessing a remote system across a network, however, network delays can cause poor keyboard response. Network performance is an extremely complex issue which is covered in Chapter 6.

1.2 System Resources

We have just discussed the various components that make up a user's perception of system performance. There is another equally important approach to this issue: the computer's view of performance. All system performance issues are basically resource contention issues. In any computer system, there are three fundamental resources: the CPU, memory, and the I/O subsystem (e.g., disks and networks). From this standpoint, performance tuning means ensuring that every user gets a fair share of available resources.

Each resource has its own particular set of problems. The biggest challenge of a system administrator is figuring out which subsystem is really in trouble. Resource problems are complicated because all resources interact with each other. If you spend enough time working on performance problems, your instincts will eventually become pretty reliable. Barring a good set of instincts, your best approach is to consider carefully what each system resource does: CPU, I/O, and memory. Later chapters of this book discuss each resource in detail. To get you started, here's a quick summary of each system resource and the problems it can have. In many respects this summary is an overview of the entire performance tuning process.

1.2.1 The CPU

On any time-sharing system, even single-user time-sharing systems (such as UNIX on a personal computer), many programs want to use the CPU at the same time. Under most circumstances the UNIX kernel is able to allocate the CPU fairly; however, each process (or program) requires a certain number of CPU cycles to execute and there are only so many cycles in a day. At some point the CPU just can't get all the work done.

There are a few ways to measure CPU contention. The simplest is the UNIX load average, reported by the BSD *uptime* command. Under System V, *sar -q* provides the same sort of information. The load average tries to measure the number of active processes at any time (a *process* is a single stream of instructions.) As a measure of CPU utilization, the load average is simplistic, poorly defined, but far from useless. As long as you realize its limitations, the load average provides a good way to start thinking about system activity. You can get a much better picture of your CPU's utilization by using various versions of the *ps* command repeatedly or by using your accounting system to provide long-term summaries.

Before you blame the CPU for your performance problems, think a bit about what we *don't* mean by CPU contention. We don't mean that the system is short of memory or that it can't do I/O fast enough. Either of these situations can make your system appear very slow. But the CPU may be spending most of its time idle; therefore, you can't just look at the load average and decide that you need a faster processor. If the CPU already spends a lot of time idle, buying an even faster processor will only increase its idle time. It will be even quicker at not doing any work. Your programs won't run a bit faster. You have bought more of a resource you don't need. Before you understand your system, you also need to find out what your memory and I/O subsystems are doing. In a way, CPU problems are the gap between memory problems and I/O problems. It's important to ensure that you determine which subsystem is really in trouble. Users often point their fingers at the CPU, but I would be willing to bet that in most situations memory and I/O are equally (if not more) to blame.

Given that you are short of CPU cycles, you have three basic alternatives:

• You can get users to run jobs at night or at other low-usage times (i.e., ensuring the computer is doing useful work 24 hours a day).

• You can prevent your system from doing unnecessary work.

• You can get users to run their big jobs at lower priority.

If none of these options is viable, you may need to upgrade your system.

1.2.2 The Memory Subsystem

Memory contention arises when the memory requirements of the active processes exceed the physical memory available on the system; at this point, the system is out of memory. To handle this lack of memory without crashing the system or killing processes, the system starts *paging*: moving portions of active processes to disk in order to reclaim physical memory. At this point, performance decreases dramatically. Paging is distinguished from *swapping*, which means moving entire processes to disk and reclaiming their space. Paging and swapping indicate that the system can't provide enough memory for the processes that are currently running, although under some circumstances swapping can be a part of normal "housekeeping." Under BSD UNIX, tools such as *vmstat* and *pstat* show whether the system is paging; *ps* can report the memory requirements of each process. The System V utility *sar* provides information about virtually all aspects of memory performance.

To prevent paging, you must either make more memory available or decrease the extent to which jobs compete. To do this, you can:

• Reduce the amount of memory that is devoted to filesystem buffers and other kernel data structures. If you take this approach, you are always giving up something. If you make the buffer cache smaller, you will sacrifice I/O performance. If you make the kernel tables smaller, you sacrifice your system's ability to support many users.

• Change the paging algorithm's characteristics so it starts paging earlier. Making paging begin earlier may sound strange; after all, we have said that paging is an indicator of memory trouble. Paging isn't really a problem when the shortage of memory is relatively small. It only becomes a problem as the memory shortage gets more serious. By configuring the system to start paging earlier, you reduce the likelihood that the memory shortage will become severe.

- Terminate the jobs with the largest memory requirements. This extreme approach to performance optimization is recommended only in drastic situations.

If your system has a lot of memory, the size of the data structures may not be an issue. The kernel's memory requirements will be relatively small. On systems with a lot of memory, the typical antagonists are very large application programs. If this is your situation, your only recourse may be to buy even more memory or to motivate users to write programs that use memory more efficiently.

1.2.3 The I/O Subsystem

The I/O subsystem is a common source of resource contention problems. A finite amount of I/O bandwidth must be shared by all the programs (including the UNIX kernel) that currently run. The system's I/O buses can transfer only so many megabytes per second; individual devices are even more limited. Each kind of device has its own peculiarities and, therefore, its own problems. Unfortunately, UNIX has poor tools for analyzing the I/O subsystem. Under BSD UNIX, *iostat* can give you information about the transfer rates for each disk drive; *ps* and *vmstat* can give some information about how many processes are blocked waiting for I/O; and *netstat* and *nfsstat* report various network statistics. Under System V, *sar* can provide voluminous information about I/O efficiency, and *sadp* (V.4) can give detailed information about disk access patterns. However, there is no standard tool to measure the I/O subsystem's response to a heavy load.

The disk and network subsystems are particularly important to overall performance. Disk bandwidth issues have two general forms: maximizing per-process transfer rates and maximizing aggregate transfer rates. The per-process transfer rate is the rate at which a single program can read or write data. The aggregate transfer rate is the maximum total bandwidth that the system can provide to all programs that run. By maximizing the per-process transfer rate, we allow one program to take maximum advantage of the system, possibly to the detriment of other programs that are running at the same time. Setting up a filesystem with a very large block size helps to maximize the per-process transfer rate. Maximizing the aggregate transfer rate is a more egalitarian approach to computing. It allows the largest number of programs to get the most benefit from the system but may compromise the performance of jobs with particularly large I/O requirements. As a system administrator you must decide which situation is more important to you. If your system is used to run large programs that make a lot of demands on the I/O subsystem, you should optimize the per-process transfer rate. In this situation, helping individual jobs to complete as quickly as possible will be of more use than maximizing the total I/O throughput. If your system runs many smaller jobs, maximizing the aggregate throughput makes the most sense. Of course, there is no reason you can't have it both ways, provided that you have several disks. You can optimize some filesystems for per-process bandwidth and optimize others for aggregate throughput.

Network I/O problems have basically two forms: a network can be overloaded or a network can lose data integrity. When a network is overloaded, the amount of data that needs to be transferred across the network is greater than the network's capacity; therefore, the actual transfer rate for any task is relatively slow. Network load problems can usually be solved by changing the network's configuration. You can divide a single network into several smaller networks, called *subnets*, or if you have already done this, you can reorganize the computers that belong to each subnet. Integrity problems occur when the network is faulty and intermittently transfers data incorrectly. In order to deliver correct data to the applications using the network, the network protocols may have to transmit each block of data many times. Consequently, programs using the network will run very slowly. The only way to solve a data integrity problem is to isolate the faulty part of the network and replace it.

From the perspective of system resources, there is a fundamental solution to all resource contention problems: buy more of whatever resource you lack. That is, buy more computers, more memory, more disks and disk controllers. This is an expensive and, therefore, painful approach to system performance problems. The fundamental motivation behind system tuning is to get the most you can out of the hardware you already own. But even if you decide that an upgrade is your only solution, you will find that your investment in performance tuning pays off. Your work will show you exactly how the system should be upgraded. If you have done your homework, you will know whether you need more memory, faster disks, or a completely new processor.

1.3 User Communities

So far we have discussed the different factors that contribute to overall system performance. But we have ignored one of the most important factors: the users who submit the jobs to your system.

In talking about the relationship between users and performance, it is easy to start seeing users as problems: the creatures who keep your system from running the way it ought to. Nothing is further from the truth, and no attitude can be a bigger hindrance to effective administration. Computers are tools: they exist to help users do their work and not vice versa.

It is particularly important for a UNIX system administrator to maintain good user relations. More than most operating systems, UNIX requires good will between the administrator and the users. Because a clever user can evade almost any limitation you impose, effective administration is only possible when you have the cooperation of your users. Limitations on memory requirements, file size, job priorities, etc., are only effective when everyone cooperates. Likewise, you can't force people to submit their jobs to a batch queue. Most people will cooperate when they understand a problem and what they can do to solve it. Most people will resist a solution that is imposed from above, that they don't understand, and that seems to get in the way of their work. In managing a UNIX system, good communication is your most important tool.

The nature of your system's users has a big effect on your system's performance and an even greater effect on the tactics you can use to improve performance. We can divide users into several classes:

- Users who run a large number of relatively small jobs: for example, users who spend most of their time editing or running UNIX utilities.

- Users who run a small number of relatively large jobs: for example, users who run large simulation programs with huge data files.

- Users who run a small number of CPU-intensive jobs that don't require a lot of I/O but do require a lot of memory and CPU time. Program developers fall into this category. Compilers tend to be large programs that build large data structures and can be a source of memory contention problems.

All three groups can cause problems. Several dozen users running *grep* and accessing remote filesystems can be as bad for overall performance as a few users accessing gigabyte files. However, the types of problems these groups cause are not the same. For example, setting up a "striped filesystem" will help disk performance for large, I/O-bound jobs but won't help (and may hurt) users who run many small jobs. Setting up batch queues will help reduce contention among large jobs, which can often be run overnight, but it won't help the system if its problems arise from users typing at their text editors and reading their mail.

Modern systems with network facilities complicate the picture even more. In addition to knowing what kinds of work users do, you also need to know what kind of equipment they use: a standard terminal over an RS-232 line, an X terminal over Ethernet, or a diskless workstation? The X window system requires a lot of memory and puts a heavy load on the network. Likewise, diskless workstations place a load on the network. Similarly, do your users access local files or remote files via NFS or RFS?

System administrators should know which users fall into each class and should be able to characterize a typical job mix for the site. It is not enough to know what system components are overloaded. You must also know why they are overloaded (i.e., what programs and users account for the load) before you can make appropriate decisions about optimization.

1.3.1 Performance Agreements

Performance agreements can be an important element in managing your system's users. A performance agreement is nothing more than a definition of what you and your users consider acceptable performance. The concept of a performance agreement originated with large IBM systems (all diehard UNIX users may now groan) but it's really very useful. If you and your system's users haven't made some sort of pact about what is acceptable and what isn't, you will be forever arguing about whether performance is good or bad. Defining good and bad performance as precisely as possible will help to prevent petty wars and let you concentrate on providing performance where it's really needed.

A performance agreement serves one other purpose. It gets you thinking about performance before it becomes an issue. All too often systems run for months without anyone looking to see what the I/O system or memory is doing. Sooner or later a crisis appears and everyone starts worrying about performance. *vmstat* shows that you are paging, *iostat* shows that your disk load looks unbalanced, and so on. But you are missing one crucial piece of information: you have no idea what the system looks like when it is running normally and, therefore, you don't really know what any of these statistics mean. Maybe your system is paging all the time but for some reason it hasn't been a problem; maybe your disk workload has always been unbalanced. Making a performance agreement is one way to structure your quest for optimized performance. It forces you to look at your system before it gets sick.

Unfortunately, it's hard to come up with good performance agreements under UNIX. No matter what else you might say about IBM's huge and ancient operating systems, you have to agree that they had the tools needed to manage performance. UNIX is very weak in this area. Furthermore, it is easier to define acceptable performance in a batch or transaction-processing environment than in the typical UNIX environment; however, that just means that UNIX users and administrators need to exercise a little more thought and creativity. You can certainly make an agreement such as: "Group A should be able to make X runs of the WYZ application on Q megabyte data files in a day." If group A doesn't get this performance, you start tuning; if tuning doesn't solve the problem, you start looking into system upgrades. If you and the users of your system can agree about acceptable performance and if you know how to use the tools available to determine whether performance is acceptable, you will be way ahead of the game.

2

Monitoring System Activity

Tools of the Trade: What Your System
   is Really Doing
System Load Average
Process Summary and Status
Idle Time
The cron Facility
Accounting
Administrative Setup for sar
SunOS Performance Meters
Benchmarks

How do you know when system performance is poor? This is a difficult question and in many ways more amenable to impressionistic analysis than to data: system performance is poor when the system feels sluggish to the users. When the system seems slow, when jobs seem to take longer to complete than they ought, you should start considering ways to improve the situation, particularly if the system suffers a sudden change in performance. We won't, and you shouldn't, deny the validity of an impressionistic analysis. Users' impressions are particularly important because, in practice, there is always some degree of "acceptable badness" that should be tolerated; if there weren't, you would buy new equipment whenever anyone reported the slightest problem. However, acceptable badness is absolutely impossible to quantify. It has altogether too much to do with personalities, frustration levels, corporate culture, and other factors that can't be scientifically analyzed. For this reason it is important for a system manager to be a system user and to know personally how the computer responds under different circumstances.

But the system's feel is obviously not the whole picture. It's difficult to say precisely what constitutes poor performance, and it's easy to get into long arguments about whether any particular feel is acceptable. The only way to avoid these long and painful arguments is to take a close and rigorous look at what your system is doing. Users who complain that the system is too slow know only one thing: they can't get their work done fast enough. You have to figure out why the system is too slow. Is the processor swamped by a workload too large for it to handle? Is the CPU wasting time, idle, when there is work to be done? Is there enough memory to handle the workload effectively? In this chapter we will discuss how to answer these questions and how to identify particular system utilization problems. In the next chapter we'll start looking at solutions.

The trick to identifying system usage problems is realizing how closely the different problems are intertwined. Any program requires all of the system's resources: CPU, memory, and I/O. If you're short on one, you're likely to be short on all. If there are simply not enough cycles to handle your system's workload effectively, it's a good bet that you're also short on memory. If you're short on memory, the additional disk activity caused by paging has probably placed a heavy burden on the I/O system, and so on. Simply reducing the number of jobs you are running is bound to help, but a thorough analysis of the system's situation will help you to decide the best way to solve any problems. For example, you may notice that you are running a lot of jobs that require a lot of memory and that your system's performance is fine except when it's running these jobs. Once you've made this observation, you can start thinking about solutions. Building a more memory-efficient kernel may solve your problem. Buying more memory will definitely help. Running the memory-intensive jobs at night is another possible solution. You still may not have enough memory, but if no one else is using the system, you might not care as long as the job is finished in the morning.

2.1 Tools of the Trade: What Your System is Really Doing

Many tools are available for taking your system's pulse. In this chapter we'll discuss the general purpose tools that provide general system information. You will use these tools to get yourself headed in the right direction. We'll discuss tools that are designed to work with one subsystem (for example, tools that are primarily relevant to memory) in the appropriate chapter. The general purpose tools are:

cron   Runs specified commands at regular intervals. Strictly speaking, this has nothing to do with performance; however, you will use *cron* to gather data regularly, clean up your filesystems, and accomplish many other important tasks. You won't get far without it. (All UNIX systems.)

uptime   Reports the system's load average. This is a crude but useful measure of the total system load. (BSD and XENIX. All systems with TCP/IP have *ruptime*, a related tool.)

ps   Reports information about processes running on the system. *ps* doesn't provide any summary information, but you can easily get an accurate picture of what's going on.

iostat   Provides information about disk usage. In this chapter, though, we'll focus on a slightly different aspect of *iostat*. In addition to disk data, *iostat* gives some important information about CPU usage. (BSD only.)

sar   Provides information about CPU usage (percentage of idle time, etc.). *sar* produces an incredible number of useful reports. It requires some administrative setup, which we'll discuss at the end of the chapter. (System V, except XENIX.)

sa   Generates a set of accounting reports showing what commands have been executed and what CPU resources they required. (BSD only.)

prdaily   Generates a set of daily accounting reports; the System V equivalent to *sa*. (System V only.)

perfmeter   Generates a visual report that can describe several significant statistics. You can run *perfmeter* on your own system, or you can run it over the network to get data about some other system. (SunOS only.)

home-grown benchmarks
      Programs you write to test performance in ways that are important to you. Developing a good set of benchmarks is absolutely crucial to performance tuning.

Of these tools, *ps* is undoubtedly the most important. Using it, you can quickly get a feel for what the system is doing and what is causing performance problems. It also provides the most accurate information about the system's workload.

This is only a partial list. Many other utilities provide different pieces of the performance puzzle. In particular, there are a dozen or so different *sar* reports, each telling you about some different aspect of the system. This chapter focuses only on the tools that give you the best overall picture of what your system is doing. We will discuss more specialized tools later.

2.2 System Load Average

The *system load average* provides a convenient way to summarize the activity on a system. It is the first statistic you should look at when performance seems to be poor. UNIX defines the load average as the average number of processes in the kernel's run queue during an interval. A *process* is a single stream of instructions.* Most programs run as a single process, but some spawn (UNIX terminology: *fork*) other processes as they run. A process is in the run queue if it is:

- Not waiting for any external event (e.g., not waiting for someone to type a character at a terminal).

- Not waiting of its own accord (e.g., the job hasn't called *wait*).

- Not stopped (e.g., the job hasn't been stopped by CTRL-Z). Processes cannot be stopped on XENIX and versions of System V.2. The ability to stop processes has been added to System V.4 and some versions of V.3.

While the load average is convenient, it may not give you an accurate picture of the system's load. There are two primary reasons for this inaccuracy:

- The load average counts as runnable all jobs waiting for disk I/O. This includes processes that are waiting for disk operations to complete across NFS. If an NFS server is not responding (e.g., if the network is faulty or the server has crashed), a process can wait for hours for an NFS operation to complete. It is considered runnable the entire time even though nothing is happening; therefore, the load average climbs when NFS servers crash, even though the system isn't really doing any more work.

- The load average does not account for scheduling priority. It does not differentiate between jobs that have been *nice*d (i.e., placed at a lower priority and therefore not consuming much CPU time) or jobs that are running at a high priority. Under V.4 the load average cannot account for real-time processes. They are the same as everything else, even though they place a much greater load on the CPU.

---

*This is a better definition of a "thread," but it will suffice until the MACH kernel becomes more popular. A better definition of a "process" is a single set of virtual system resources, but it is harder to think in these terms. Bach's definition of a process ("an instance of a program in execution," *The Design of the UNIX Operating System*, Prentice-Hall, p.10) is acceptable provided that you realize that one program can create many processes.

The BSD command *uptime* reports the system load average over the last minute, the last 5 minutes, and the last 15 minutes. It produces the following report:

```
% uptime
mysystem  up  6 days, 1:27, load average: 1.34, 2.18, 2.51
```

This report tells you the system's name and how long it has been running. It then reports three load averages. The first load average (1.34) is measured over the last minute. Over the last 5 minutes, the load average was 2.18, while the 15-minute load average was 2.51. It is often useful to note whether the load average is climbing or falling. In this case it is falling (the 1-minute load average is smaller than the 15-minute load average). If a system appears to be slow but the load average is falling, you may not want to take action immediately. Wait and see whether the problem resolves itself with time.

NOTE

Some details of this report depend on your implementation, but all versions of *ruptime* provide the same three load averages.

If your system has TCP/IP networking, you can use *ruptime* to produce similar reports for each host on the local network. These reports also tell you which remote systems appear to be dead and how long they have been dead. You should be aware that *ruptime* summarizes data from a local database. Its reports are never quite up to date but are accurate enough for most purposes. *rup* is another useful variant of *uptime*. The command *rup host* queries the named *host* and produces an *uptime* report for it. Its reports are always accurate. Both *rup* and *ruptime* have one big drawback: they require the remote system to run the daemon *rwhod*, which can be a performance problem in itself.

By running *uptime* and observing the load average from time to time, you will get a feeling for what usage is typical and what indicates a problem. How your system tolerates any given load depends on a lot of configuration issues. Systems with a lot of memory tolerate heavy CPU loads much more gracefully than systems with underconfigured memory. Likewise, systems with a well-balanced I/O system and several swapping areas on different disks tolerate heavy loads better than systems with a single swapping area and an underconfigured I/O system. As a rough rule of thumb, a load average of more than 10 is extremely high for a mainframe or some other large computer system. If a system is regularly working under this kind of load, you should take some steps to distribute CPU usage more evenly. A load average of between 4 and 7 is fairly heavy. At this level most users will notice that the computer feels sluggish and that their commands are taking longer to execute. You may want to suggest that users run big jobs at night. If the load average is below 3, you have no cause for concern: the system's workload is relatively light. If you are dealing with a workstation or a personal computer, you should downgrade these figures considerably. Most workstations are designed as single-user systems and don't tolerate load averages much more than 1 or 2 gracefully.

If you are running System V but don't have the TCP/IP tools, or have chosen not to use them, the closest equivalent to *uptime* is *sar -q*. This gives you information about the system's run queue: the list of jobs that are ready to run at any time. Here's a typical report from *sar -q*:

```
% sar -q
ora ora 3.2 2 i386      05/21/90

00:00:01     runq-sz %runocc swpq-sz %swpocc
01:00:03       1.2     45       0       0
02:00:02       1.5     70      .4      15
03:00:01       2.1     95     1.1      53
```

The fields in this report are:

runq-sz The average length of the run queue during this interval. The run queue lists jobs that are in memory and runnable. It doesn't include jobs that are waiting for I/O or sleeping.

%runocc The percentage of time that the run queue is occupied.

swpq-sz The average length of the swap queue during the interval. This queue lists jobs that are ready to run but can't because they have been "swapped out." Many systems (and all V.4 systems) don't report this statistic.

%swpocc The percentage of time that the swap queue is occupied.

The length of the run queue is similar to the BSD load average. AT&T states that the run queue should always be less than 2. Depending on the size of the system, this may be too conservative. Whatever the critical threshold, longer run queues mean heavier load. Ideally the run queue would be occupied (nonzero) 100 percent of the time, minimizing the system's idle time. Of course, this is not likely when the load is low. If the load is high and the run queue spends a lot of time empty, you should look for I/O or memory problems. In our example we show a system under moderately heavy load. The load is increasing with time, and the last interval shows fairly heavy swapping. This system needs to be watched closely; it could be in trouble.

The *sar* data collection machinery isn't enabled by default. Later in this chapter we discuss how to start collecting statistics for *sar* and give a quick overview of its capabilities.

2.3 Process Summary and Status

If the system has a high load average, you should look more closely at the jobs that it is running. The *ps* command will provide the information you need. The *ps* report will help you to differentiate between virtual memory problems, I/O problems, and other problems. The report will also tell you which jobs and which users are responsible for the system's load. This information may help you to determine whether you should reconfigure your system.

ps has many options, most of which correspond to different output formats. We won't discuss these options exhaustively here; for this kind of information, refer to the reference page for *ps*. We will discuss the most useful displays, focusing on how to analyze the data in them.

2.3.1 ps Under BSD UNIX

Under BSD UNIX the most useful set of *ps* options is *ps -au*. The *-a* option requests information about all processes with a controlling terminal. It omits daemons and other system processes; if you want to include these, use the command *ps -aux*. The *-u* option requests a *user-oriented display* showing user names, command names, and the CPU and memory usage of each process. Here is a typical report:

```
% ps -au
USER     PID %CPU %MEM    SZ   RSS  TT STAT  TIME  COMMAND
boss    6565 22.6 22.0 16072 13304 p7  R     0:05  ccom /tmp/cpp06562a
root    6588 13.4  0.7   504   400 pd  S     0:00  sched -M mysystem
boss    6562  1.0  0.6   392   344 p7  IN    0:00  brep
bob     6583  1.0  0.2  1728    96 pd  S     0:00  sleep 120
ted     6511  0.4  2.0  5352  1184 q6  S     0:00  az
bob    21225  0.2  0.4  2488   208 pd  S     2:09  lop2 (lop2)
boss    5927  0.1  1.1  2432   664 p7  I     0:03  make -f Makefile
alice  13597  0.0  0.0  1768   120 p5  SW   21:41  tail -f om
```

The report can be quite long, especially if your system has many users. Processes are listed in order of decreasing CPU usage. Because you are often most interested in the first few lines, it is convenient to pipe the report into *more* or *head*.

This report shows:

USER   The user who started the process. The report in the previous example includes processes started by *root* (superuser), *boss*, *bob*, *ted*, and *alice*.

PID   The process identification (PID) number assigned by the system when the process started running. No two processes can share the same PID. More often than not, when you invoke *ps* you are looking for a process ID number.

%CPU   The percentage of the CPU time used by this process. Because of inaccuracies, the sum of all CPU percentages may not equal 100. It should be easy to spot which processes are consuming most of the CPU time. Three or four processes usually account for 90 percent (or more) of the total CPU time. If you always see the same processes at the top of the *ps* report, you have some data to work with. These programs are probably commonly used and certainly CPU-bound. Do whatever is necessary to get these jobs out of the way.

%MEM   The percentage of the system's physical memory used by this process. Again, the total may be more than 100. It should be fairly easy to spot the processes that have large physical memory requirements. If the system is paging, this statistic will show you which processes are responsible.

SZ   The amount of nonshared virtual memory, in kilobytes, currently allocated to the process. This does not include the program's text size, which is normally shared; it does include the program's statically and dynamically allocated data areas. Knowing the virtual memory requirements of different jobs can help you to decide what the system's memory capacity should be. When you look at the report above, some alarms should go off: *ccom* (a part of the C compiler) has allocated more than 16 MB of memory. You can't do anything to reduce *ccom*'s memory requirements, and this might not even be a problem if your system has enough memory; but it's certainly worth knowing.

RSS   The *resident set size* of the process, in kilobytes; the amount of physical memory that is currently allocated to the process. *ccom* has gathered a lot of the system's physical memory: more than 13 MB. This may be normal, but you should be aware of all programs that require a lot of memory to run.

TT   The controlling terminal for the process. Prefix the two characters in this field with *tty* to get the terminal name. For example, the first process shown above was started from *ttyp7*.

STAT   One to four letters indicating the process's status. The first letter is the most important; it indicates whether the process is runnable and, if not runnable, why not. It can be one of these:

R   The process is currently runnable.

T   The process is currently stopped (i.e., it has received a signal).

P   The process is currently waiting for a page-in.

D   The process is waiting for disk I/O.

S   The process has been sleeping for less than 20 seconds.

I   The process is idle (it has been sleeping for more than 20 seconds).*

Z   The process has terminated but has not died. These are called *zombies* or *defunct processes*.

Sleeping and idle processes are usually waiting for keyboard input. For example, an interactive program such as an editor will be listed as idle if the user has walked away from the terminal. Idle processes are candidates for being swapped out. Under UNIX, only rarely will you see processes waiting for a page-in or for disk I/O. This does not mean that disk I/O or memory performance are not a problem; rather, it means that even in worst-case situations, disk waits are relatively short. It is difficult for *ps* to catch a process in the instant that it is waiting for a disk. If you do see a lot of processes in the **P** or **D** state, check disk performance and memory usage: both subsystems may be overloaded.

Zombie processes are an interesting but unimportant special case. A zombie is a process that has terminated but won't die—at least temporarily. Zombies are waiting for their parent process to call *wait*, at which point they will disappear nicely. Some will stick around until the system reboots. In either case they are inactive. They don't consume any resources other than an entry in the kernel's process table. Unless you have a severely underconfigured kernel or a tremendously large number of zombies, you don't need to worry about them.

---

*The amount of time after which a process is declared idle is defined by the configuration parameter *MAXSLP*, which is defined in the header file *vmparam.h*. You can change this during configuration, although Sun (and other BSD vendors) strongly recommends that you leave it untouched.

The second letter indicates the process's status with respect to memory management. It can be one of these:

W   The process has been swapped out.

>   The process has exceeded a soft limit on memory imposed by the *limit* command.

blank The process is not swapped out and has not exceeded a memory limit.

While swapped-out processes are an important symptom of memory problems, you unfortunately can't gather any relevant information from *ps*. Idle processes are eventually swapped out just to neaten up the system's tables; therefore, you'll always see a large number of **W** processes. These will be editors, shells, and other interactive programs. Swapping only becomes important when the system is swapping processes that are otherwise runnable.

The third letter indicates the process's scheduling priority. It can be one of these:

N   The process is running *nice*d (i.e., a lowered priority).

<   The process is running at a high *nice* level (i.e., a raised priority).

blank The process is running at a normal priority.

The *brep* process started by *boss* is running at a *nice* priority and therefore cannot consume a large percentage of the CPU's time. Later we will discuss ways of manipulating the scheduling priority.

The fourth letter in the **STAT** field shows any special memory requirements. The program can inform the kernel about its special needs by calling *vadvise* or *madvise*. Possibilities are:

blank The process has no special requirements. This should almost always be the case.

S   The process has informed the system that it tends to access memory sequentially.

A   The process has informed the system that its memory requirements are large and that its memory references are highly random. This tells the system that it can't trust its normal algorithms for paging. Programs that do a lot of "garbage collection" on large address spaces (such as the BSD LISP interpreter) usually set this flag.

TIME   The total amount of CPU time that the program has consumed.

COMMAND   The command that is being executed. For security reasons, processes are allowed to obscure the command name and any arguments, so this field may be blank or filled with garbage. This field may list some zombie processes as "<defunct>" or "<exiting>".

2.3.2 ps Under System V

Compared to BSD, System V's version of *ps* is anaemic. It doesn't have as many options, and the ones it has are less useful. The most useful report is *ps -el*, which is similar to the BSD report *ps -xl*. Here's some sample output, taken from a 386/ix system:

```
% ps -el
 F S UID   PID PPID C PRI NI   ADDR SZ    WCHAN TTY       TIME COMD
19 S   0     0   0 0   0 20 40256c  2 d0158de8 ?         0:01 sched
10 S   0     1   0 0  39 20 40256c 15 e0000000 ?         6:30 init
19 S   0     2   0 0   0 20 40256c  0 d0071a8c ?         0:00 vhand
19 S   0     3   0 0  19 20 40256c  0 d006af98 ?         4:31 bdflush
10 S   0   107   1 0  28 20 40256c 29 d1020000 console 0:01 csh
10 S   0  4398   1 0  28 20 40256c 15 d1020064 vt01      0:00 getty
10 S   0    81   1 0  26 20 40256c 20 d011e32a ?         0:40 cron
19 S   0    92   1 0  20 20 40256c 10 d004313c ?         4:33 netsched
10 S   0    94   1 0  39 20 40256c 21 e0000000 ?         0:00 netd
10 S   0   105   1 0  26 24 40256c 21 d0111a08 ?         0:20 syslogd
10 S   0   103   1 0  26 24 40256c 18 d0111a08 ?         0:03 inetd
10 S  13 23873   1 0  30 20 40256c 29 d00c353c ttyi1j   0:01 csh
10 S   0   121   1 0  30 24 40256c 44 d00c37b8 ?        10:02 sendmail
```

The worst aspect of this display is that processes are ordered by age, not by anything that's useful. From the standpoint of performance tuning, the important fields are:

F   A set of flags. This is a hexadecimal number that indicates the process's current state. The value for this field is formed by adding these hexadecimal flags:

    0   The process has terminated. Its place in the process table is free.

    1   The process is a system process and is always in memory.

    2   The process is being traced by its parent.

    4   The process is being traced by its parent and has been stopped.

8	The process cannot be awakened by a signal.
10	The process is currently loaded into memory.
20	The process cannot be swapped.

S   A letter indicating the process's state. This is similar to the **stat** field from the BSD *ps* report. You may see these letters here:

O	The process is currently running on the processor.
S	The process is sleeping; it is waiting for an event to complete. This includes processes waiting for terminal I/O.
R	The process is currently runnable.
I	The process is currently idle.
Z	The process is a zombie: it has terminated but is still in the process table.
T	The process is stopped because its parent is tracing it.
X	The process is waiting for more memory.

UID   The identification number of the user who created the process (i.e., the process's owner).

PID   The process identification (PID) number.

PPID   The process identification (PID) number of the process's parent.

C   The process's CPU utilization (i.e., an estimate of the percentage of the CPU time used by this process).

PRI   The process's scheduling priority: lower numbers indicate higher priorities. This changes dynamically, according to many factors including CPU utilization. This number usually grows as a program's CPU utilization increases. This means that the scheduler, trying to allocate CPU time fairly, reduces the scheduling priority of processes that require a lot of time.

NI   The process's *nice* number; this is one factor used in computing the scheduling priority.

SZ   The amount of virtual memory (in pages) required by the process. Although you would like to know the resident set size (which isn't available), a process's virtual memory requirements are still an accurate indication of how much stress it places on the memory system.

TTY   The terminal that started the process (or the process's parent). A process with a question mark in this field doesn't have a controlling terminal; these are usually system processes.

TIME   The total amount of CPU time used by the process so far.

COMD   The actual command.

2.3.3 Some Quick Remedies

You can tell a lot about your system just by looking at the commands that are running. No matter what version of UNIX you are using, it should be easy to identify which processes are consuming most of the system's CPU time and memory. Whether you should do anything about them is another issue: after all, the problem is not that people are using the system, but that CPU load is preventing users from getting enough work done. Here are some quick fixes for some fairly obvious problems:

- Occasionally you will see that the system is clogged by many identical jobs created by the same user. Depending on the situation, it may be acceptable to terminate some of these jobs using *kill*. Always let the user know why you are taking this action. This situation usually arises because the user doesn't understand how to use the system properly. Early in my career, a user wrote a shell script that started 30 or so background jobs without waiting for any of the jobs to terminate. The load average skyrocketed and was in the mid-20s when the system (a VAX 11/750) crashed. He needed, and got, a quick lesson in proper shell programming.

- A process may have accumulated an abnormally large amount of time. This may indicate that the process is in an infinite loop or that something else has gone wrong. After consulting with the user, you may want to terminate the job. Of course, to make this kind of a judgement you must know how long it is reasonable for the program to run. Before killing the job, you may want to get a core dump by using the command *gcore process-id*. A core dump may help the user to figure out what went wrong.

- A process you don't consider important is consuming a large percentage of CPU. If you are using BSD UNIX, you may want to use *renice* to force this job to a lower priority. Log in as superuser and enter the command *renice 4 -p pid*, where *pid* is the process ID number listed in the second column. Four is a typical low priority (0 is the default priority; under UNIX, higher numbers mean lower priorities). *renice* isn't available under System V; your only recourse is to kill the offending job.

- A process is consuming an unexpectedly large percentage of the system's memory. Consult the user and try to find out if anything has changed since the last time he or she ran the job. If necessary, *kill* the job. Don't try to *renice* programs that are running into memory problems. Reducing the priority of a memory pig only guarantees that it will stay around even longer. You're better off hoping that it terminates quickly, freeing its memory.

- A user who knows the superuser password may have figured out how to increase his job's scheduling priority. Use *renice* to undo this. *renice* isn't available under System V; your only recourse is to kill the offending job.

- If the system is running several large jobs that appear to be progressing normally, you may want to suggest that users run them at low priority (*nice*) or at night (*at*). *nice* is only effective for CPU-bound jobs.

Beyond quick fixes, there are some other things you should look for. In general, you only need to worry about jobs that are runnable, blocked for disk I/O, or paging. Sleeping or stopped processes are waiting for an external event and don't affect overall performance. If the memory sizes (**RSS** or **SZ**) of the runnable processes are very large, check for memory usage problems. Your system may have insufficient memory for the current job mix and may be paging; this is discussed at length in Chapter 4, *Memory Performance*.

Under UNIX, it is rare for *ps* to catch a process while it is waiting for disk I/O or waiting for paging. If you should see several processes in this state, your I/O workload may be unbalanced; check to see whether your I/O configuration can be improved. A process is also considered waiting for disk I/O if it is trying to read or write across NFS and the file server is not responding. This usually means that the network is faulty or that the file server has crashed. If this is the case, the process will wait until the file server becomes accessible. You cannot do anything about this situation because you can't even kill a job while it is waiting for disk I/O.* The program will continue running normally as soon as the server returns to life.

2.3.4 Other Options and Ideas

Some other useful *ps* options are:

tcc Print information about processes associated with terminal *cc* (i.e., with */dev/ttycc*).

l Print a long report. We previously showed System V's version of the long report.

w Print a report that is 132 columns wide, rather than the standard 80-column report. This lets you see more of the command name. (BSD only.)

---

*This isn't quite true. If the remote filesystem is mounted with the option *intr*, you can stop it with *kill* or CTRL-C. But it may take a long time—minutes or even tens of minutes—for the *kill* to take effect.

ww Print an arbitrarily wide report. This report shows the entire command, no matter how long it is. (BSD only.)

k Look at a kernel crash dump (usually named */vmcore*) and show what the system did when it crashed. This might help you to figure out why the crash occurred. To get the most information, invoke *ps*:

```
% ps -alkx vmunix-name core-dump
```

where *vmunix-name* is the name of your UNIX executable and *core-dump* is the name of your kernel crash dump. (BSD only.)

v Produce a different report showing virtual memory statistics. (BSD only.)

c A modifier to System V.4's *f* and *l* options. Show the process's scheduling class in an additional field, labeled **CLS**. The scheduling class is either real-time or time-sharing. Several other fields change with this option. The C and **NI** fields are omitted and the **PRI** field gets redefined so that higher numbers mean higher priorities. In the standard *ps -l* report, lower numbers mean higher priorities. Note that CPU-intensive real-time process will destroy a system's performance. (System V.4 only.)

One final note: The reference page for *ps* always warns you that its output only represents a snapshot of the system's activity, that it is invalid by the time you read it, that it is fraught with inaccuracies, and so on. This is all true, but in practice none of these concerns is worth worrying about. The worst that can happen is that you may try to *kill* a process and find out it no longer exists.

However, there's a bigger hole in *ps* that is worth worrying about and it's not mentioned at all. *ps* is an excellent example of the Heisenberg principle. Taking a *ps* report distorts the data you want to see. When you invoke *ps*, you will almost always see the command *ps* at the top of the report, grabbing a quarter to a half of your CPU and a fair portion of your memory. There is no way to escape this distortion. The *ps* command for System V.4 is said to be much more efficient, but I am reserving judgement.

2.4 Idle Time

The data available from *ps* is often too microscopic. You don't want to know about every process; you want to know about the system as a whole. There are a number of ways to get a much more global picture of CPU usage. If you're using BSD UNIX, you can use *iostat* or *vmstat* to give you a quick picture of CPU utilization. XENIX users can use *vmstat*, whose output (in this respect) is similar to *iostat*. Other System V users must use *sar -u*.

The tool *iostat* provides a measure of the CPU's *idle time*: the time it spends doing nothing, waiting for some external event to happen. We won't discuss *iostat* much here; its primary purpose is to analyze the I/O system. A typical report looks like this:

```
% iostat 5
          tty            dk0           dk1        cpu
   tin tout bps tps msps  bps tps msps  us  ni  sy  id
     1   32  16   2  0.0   14   1  0.0  14   1  10  74
     0    0  17   2  0.0   11   1  0.0   1  47  13  40
     0    0  87   7  0.0   12   1  0.0   0  96   4   0
     0    0  36   3  0.0    0   0  0.0   0  97   3   0
     0    7  28   2  0.0    0   0  0.0   1  97   1   0
     1    5  25   2  0.0    0   0  0.0   0  95   5   0
     7    7  25   2  0.0    0   0  0.0   0  90  10   0
```

The first argument, *5*, tells *iostat* to print statistics every five seconds. Ignore the first line of the report, which attempts to report statistical averages since the system was booted. This average is unreliable on most systems. For the time being, ignore all but the four columns on the right. The interesting columns are:

us The percentage of time that the system spent in the user state running processes at or greater than the default scheduling priority.

ni The percentage of time that the system spent in the user state running processes at *nice* (i.e., low) scheduling priority.

sy The percentage of time that was spent in the system state (i.e., executing system calls, UNIX kernel code, scheduling overhead, etc.).

id The percentage of time that the system spent idle.

When we took this report, the CPU was spending almost no time idle. It was spending almost no time executing system calls. Almost all of the system's time was spent running user state code at a low priority. A quick check with *ps* revealed that there was only one runnable job, which was at a low priority. Because there were no other active jobs, this one program was able to grab virtually all of the CPU's time.

When combined with information about the load average, this data can give you a good global picture of what's happening on the system. Ideally you want the idle time to be relatively low. You can expect the idle time to be high when the load average is low. The computer may not have any runnable processes when the current process waits for I/O. If the idle time and load average are both high, you are probably facing a memory problem (the system doesn't have enough physical memory and is paging). In the worst case, you may also have disk- or network-related I/O trouble.

I consider zero idle time while the system is under load to be a sign of health, though some system administrators disagree. These administrators argue that if the idle time is always zero, you may have an overloaded CPU: you are probably running many CPU-bound jobs and should consider upgrading to a faster system. In this situation, though, the important criterion isn't how much time the CPU spends idle: it is the system's total throughput. Are users getting their work done fast enough? If so, don't worry about 100% CPU utilization. Idle time does tell you whether or not upgrading to a faster CPU will help your performance. If your system is idle 25 percent of the time even when it is under load, a faster CPU may not help a tremendous amount. Faster disks and more memory may be what you need. If the idle time is usually close to 0 percent, it's a good bet that a faster CPU will be helpful.

The ratio of system time to *user-state time* (the sum of **us** and **ni**) varies widely, depending on the actual job mix. A system that is spending more than 50 percent of its time in the system state is probably doing a lot of disk I/O—not necessarily a problem but something you should be aware of. To confirm that the system is spending a lot of time doing disk I/O, look at the **bps** and **tps** columns for each disk drive. The **bps** column reports the number of kilobytes per second transferred by the system's disk drives; **tps** reports the average number of transfers per second for each drive. If you see a lot of transfers but relatively little data, start investigating the programs that are running and figure how they are doing I/O. Are they doing I/O one character at a time when they should be transferring large blocks of data? Are they inefficient in other ways? If the developers are at hand, you may want to encourage them to write more efficient code. If the I/O activity is concentrated on one or two disk drives, think about how the file system is organized. By rearranging the filesystem, you may be able to spread the disk activity around more equitably.

If you are using System V (except for XENIX), *sar -u* provides general activity information. Here's a typical report:

```
% sar -u
ora ora 3.2 2 i386      05/21/90

00:00:01    %usr    %sys    %wio    %idle
01:00:03     25       6       2      67
02:00:02     22       6       3      69
03:00:01     20       6       2      72
04:00:01     15       5       2      79
```

For each time period, *sar* reports the percentage of time spent in four states:

usr   The amount of time spent executing code in the user state (i.e., executing code on behalf of the user).

sys   The amount of time spent executing code in the system state (i.e., the amount of time spent in system calls, handling I/O, etc.). If the system is spending an exorbitant amount of time in the system, you may be running a lot of programs that use the system inefficiently (i.e., programs that use character I/O to access a large file).

wio   The amount of time spent waiting for blocked I/O (i.e., disk, NFS, or RFS operations) to complete. If this is a significant portion of the total, the system is I/O-bound: investigate your I/O performance.

idle   The amount of time that the CPU was idle. If the system is lightly loaded, you expect the percentage of idle time to be fairly high. If the system is working under a heavy load and the idle time is high, you certainly have problems: possibly I/O problems, more likely memory problems.

The report in our example shows a light load throughout the entire period. The percentage of idle time is high, but this is consistent with the light workload. If we also saw a lot of **wio** time, there would be cause for concern.

If you are using the System V RFS (Remote File Sharing) facility, *sar -Du* will split the **sys** field into two subcategories: *local* (system call time on behalf of local processes) and *remote* (system time on behalf of RFS requests from remote machines). If your system is spending a lot of time servicing remote requests, you may want to consider rearranging your network.

2.5 The cron Facility

As we've said, the *cron* facility has absolutely nothing to do with performance; however, it is essential to almost any kind of administration, including performance monitoring. You will need *cron* to set up the accounting system and the System V performance monitoring machinery, which will be discussed shortly.

2.5.1 BSD cron

BSD UNIX and System V have slightly different versions of *cron*. If you are using a BSD-based system, the files */usr/lib/crontab* and */usr/lib/crontab.local* control the *cron* facility. Use any editor you wish to edit the *crontab* file. Each entry in the file is a single line with the form:

minute hour dayofmonth month dayofweek username command

where:

minute   Specifies the minute (or minutes) within the hour at which the command will be executed. It is a number between 0 and 59.

hour   Specifies the hour (or hours) within the day at which the command will be executed. It is a number between 0 and 23.

dayofmonth Specifies the day (or days) of the month on which the command will be executed. It is a number between 1 and 31.

month   Specifies the month (or months) in which the command will be executed. It is a number between 1 (January) and 12 (December).

dayofweek Specifies the day of the week on which the command will be executed. It is a number between 1 (Monday) and 7 (Sunday).

username   Specifies which user should execute the command. For administrative commands, this field is most often *root*: the command is executed by the superuser.

command   Is the command you want to execute.

For the five numeric fields, an asterisk (*) is a wildcard. For example, the *crontab* line below executes a complicated *find* command as the user *root* at midnight (minute 0 of hour 0) every day (all other fields wildcarded):

```
0 0 * * * root find / -name core -atime +1 -exec rm {} \;
```

You can specify a group of times (i.e., of minutes, hours, months, or days) by using several numbers separated by commas. For example, this entry runs the same command at noon and at midnight:

```
0 0,12 * * * root find / -name core -atime +1 -exec rm {} \;
```

Finally, you can specify a range of times by using two numbers separated by a dash (-). For example, assume you want to execute this command on weekdays at noon and midnight. Here's the appropriate line:

```
0 0,12 * * 1-5 root find / -name core -atime +1 -exec rm {} \;
```

The *find* command is executed at hours 0 and 12 on days 1 through 5 or Monday through Friday.

Any changes you make to the *crontab* files take effect on the next minute.

2.5.2 System V cron

The *cron* facility for System V is almost identical to the BSD *cron* facility; how-ever, it's a bit more structured. Each user has an individual *cron* file which he or she edits using some specialized utilities. Unlike the older *cron* facility, you aren't allowed to edit the *cron* files on your own.

Display the current *crontab* file for *root* with the command:

```
# crontab -l root
```

To edit the *crontab* file for *root*, use the command:

```
# crontab -e root
```

This creates a temporary *crontab* file and invokes an editor (by default, *vi*) to let you modify it. When you save the file and exit the editor, the new file is automat-ically installed. The format of the *crontab* file itself is identical to the BSD-style *crontab* file, except that it doesn't include the **username** field. Because there is a separate file for each user, the **username** field isn't necessary. Here are the Sys-tem V versions of the three *crontab* examples we showed above:

```
0 0     * * *     find / -name core -atime +1 -exec rm {} \;
0 0,12 * * *     find / -name core -atime +1 -exec rm {} \;
0 0,12 * * 1-5   find / -name core -atime +1 -exec rm {} \;
```

NOTE

SunOS 4.0 (and following) uses a System V-style *crontab*. Earlier ver-sions use the BSD-style *crontab*.

Versions of System V prior to V.3 may use the BSD-style *crontab*.

2.6 Accounting

On any operating system, accounting tools provide an important part of the over-all performance optimization picture. This is no less true of UNIX which has often been criticized for having a weak accounting package. Many systems don't even run the accounting software. A lot of history is involved here. UNIX evolved on small systems in fairly informal academic environments, whereas issues such as billing and connection-time accounting are most important on large systems embedded within a corporate bureaucracy. Mention accounting to many UNIX users and you will get fear and loathing in response.

Rest assured—we aren't going suggest that you implement some sort of billing policy. Penalizing users for using their tools may make your computer look more productive but it's a great way to stifle real productivity. There are many valid reasons for billing, but performance optimization is not one of them. We do suggest that you enable the accounting system and pay the slight penalty in performance and the somewhat larger penalty in disk requirements that it entails.

Why do we think accounting is important? The accounting system provides the easiest way to gather some very important information. Anyone interested in system performance needs to know accurately what the system does. You should know what applications users run, how much system time is spent running these applications, how much system time is spent running general utilities, which users use the system most heavily, and so on. Once you know which programs are eating up your system's time and memory, you can start developing a tuning strategy. If the most important programs at your site were developed locally, you can suggest that the developers tune their algorithms. If the most important programs use a lot of memory, you should think about ways to conserve memory. If your system runs many programs that stress the I/O system, you should think about faster disks, and so on. When you are dealing with global problems, you can't do without good global summaries.

The BSD and System V accounting packages differ in a number of respects. BSD accounting has a few simple commands that produce two or three standard reports. System V accounting has many more features: a large number of shell scripts cooperate with several basic utilities to produce daily reports, monthly summaries, connection-time billing, and all the trappings of a large system. Because these systems are so different, we'll discuss each of them at length.

2.6.1 BSD Accounting Utilities

The accounting system is enabled by the *accton* command, which is usually given by the system startup script */etc/rc*. You will almost always find the line:

```
/etc/accton /usr/adm/acct
```

present in your */etc/rc* script, though it may be commented out. After executing *accton*, your system will perform accounting if it meets the following conditions:

- */usr/adm/acct* exists. The accounting system won't create this file if it doesn't exist.

- The filesystem on which */usr/adm* resides is less than 95 percent full. If this filesystem is more than 95 percent full, accounting will automatically stop. */usr/adm* either belongs to the *root*, */usr*, or */var* filesystem, depending on your installation.

- If you are using SunOS, the *SYSACCT* configuration option is included in your kernel. *SYSACCT* and other configuration options are discussed in Chapter 8, *Kernel Configuration*.

The first of these conditions places a special constraint on administrators. */usr/adm/acct* grows without bound and will become large quickly. However, you can't just delete it periodically, because deleting it will stop accounting. The right way to handle this file is to truncate it:

```
# cp /dev/null /usr/adm/acct
```

Truncating the accounting file destroys all of your accounting data. Subsequent reports from *sa* will include only statistics gathered after you truncated the file. If you don't want to discard your old accounting records, there's an alternative. Invoking *sa* with the -s option compresses the contents of */usr/adm/acct* and merges them into a summary file */usr/adm/savacct*. This file will always be reasonably small.

NOTE

SunOS 4.1 calls the raw accounting file *pacct* rather than *acct*.

Once you have enabled accounting, you need to gather reports regularly. Under BSD UNIX, the *sa* program is the focal point of the accounting system. By default, it prints a summary of all commands that the system has executed. Here are the first few lines from a typical *sa* report:

```
% /etc/sa
 5426051   49700735.77re   3650685.91cp       63avio   -11k
     756     172065.06re     70989.36cp     2531avio   196k  bp
    5237      81820.60re     31071.74cp     3966avio    45k  rout
      66     654740.28re     29512.48cp  1198265avio     1k  nfsd*
   11838      99708.97re     20197.14cp     4857avio   462k  nx
    1181      55891.37re     18255.60cp      745avio   119k  tim
   32709    2592026.01re     10303.77cp      167avio    63k  gmacs
    3478      21172.05re      9712.48cp       11avio   208k  ccom
     263      24742.86re      8789.88cp     1039avio   204k  dms
   99043   15770676.25re      8725.54cp       42avio     9k  csh
   10060    8395749.60re      7038.05cp       14avio     3k  rlogind
   21953      76449.35re      5666.62cp      690avio     7k  find
     719      17340.93re      5594.43cp     4808avio    55k  aid
```

The different fields in this report are:

leftmost; unlabeled
> Total number of times the command was executed.

re   Total real time (elapsed time in minutes) spent executing the command.

cp   Total CPU time (both system time and user time in minutes) spent executing the command. The default display is sorted in order of CPU time.

avio   Average number of I/O operations per invocation of the command.

k   Average physical memory usage, in kilobytes. The average is based on the program's CPU time. More formally, this average is the integral of physical memory used over time, divided by the total CPU time. The storage interval (integral of memory used over time) is an important statistic in its own right. We'll discuss it a bit later.

rightmost; unlabeled
> Command name.

The first line of the report summarizes all the commands that have been executed. We haven't found it useful, though it could help you to compute your own averages and percentages. The rest of the report lists all of the commands that have been executed, in order of decreasing total CPU time. For example, the report above shows that the command *bp* (a local program, not a standard utility) was executed 756 times and used almost 71,000 CPU minutes; on the average, each run took roughly 90 minutes of CPU time. This program was a fairly heavy memory user, occupying an average 196 KB of physical memory while it was running. Its I/O requirements were modest for a program this large, averaging roughly 2500 I/O operations per run. The best way to get a sense for relative I/O requirements is to look at *sa -d*, which we'll discuss shortly.

Looking down the report, we find that *rout* only requires five minutes per run, but was invoked much more often. The network filesystem (NFS) daemons also took a lot of CPU time and accounted for a huge amount of I/O. Aside from reorganizing the network, we can't change this. *nx* requires about two minutes of CPU time per run but is used more often than any of the other programs we have seen. It also requires of lot of memory—several simultaneous invocations may cause memory problems. *tim* takes about 15 minutes per run; *gmacs* (the gnu-emacs editor) only uses about 20 seconds of CPU time per invocation, although its elapsed time is huge, since programmers spend most of their time sitting in front of their terminals and thinking, rather than typing. The C compiler (*ccom* is the major component of the UNIX C compiler) also accounted for a lot of time. As expected, the compiler does relatively little I/O and requires a lot of memory.

Another useful report is *sa -d*. This produces a report that shows the average number of I/O operations for each invocation of the program. Here are the top few lines from a report:

```
% /etc/sa -d
      66   654740.28re    29512.48cp    1198264avio        1k   nfsd*
    1600     8459.59re     1393.13cp      11326avio        22k   messy
    2633    24003.80re     5432.82cp       7418avio       108k   flat
   11838    99708.97re    20197.14cp       4857avio       462k   nx
    5237    81820.60re    31071.74cp       3965avio        45k   rout
```

The new field here is **avio**, which reports the average number of I/O operations per invocation of the command. As we would expect, the NFS daemons are at the top of the list. More surprising is that *bp* isn't near the top of the list at all. We cut off the listing well before it appeared; it was almost at the bottom. While *bp* consumes a lot of CPU time, it evidently is not a major user of I/O services. Just as surprising is that *flat* and *messy* are among the heaviest I/O users but are nowhere near the top of the CPU usage list. *messy* also has modest memory requirements.

Once you have this information, what do you do with it? You know which programs are the major users of CPU time, memory, and I/O. This will help you to plan a filesystem layout; you may want to dedicate additional I/O resources to the groups that stress the I/O subsystem. If you choose to implement a queueing system, you may want to create separate queues for CPU-bound jobs and I/O-bound jobs. You would like to avoid running two or three invocations of *bp* at once, since it would choke a system that was already struggling. Likewise, running several simultaneous invocations of *messy* could bring the I/O system to its knees. The system should be able to run *bp* and *messy* at the same time without trouble, since both jobs stress different components of the system.

The standard BSD 4.3 version of *sa* has 20 different options, most of which produce different kinds of reports or different ways of sorting the report. The sidebar "*sa* in a Nutshell" summarizes the different reports that you can produce.

Here are a few hints about how to use the BSD accounting reports:

- Sometimes you'll see a command whose name is followed by an asterisk (*). These are "daemon" processes. If a command is invoked both "by hand" and by a daemon, you'll see two entries: one with an asterisk and one without it.

- Programs such as daemons and shells accumulate a huge amount of elapsed time, even though they usually aren't doing anything. Some of these programs also accumulate a lot of CPU time. This distorts any averaging *sa* does. For example, *sendmail* needs a lot of memory to process a long mail queue. But when it runs as a daemon, it gradually accumulates CPU time even when it isn't doing anything significant; therefore, its average memory usage appears to be small.

sa In A Nutshell

/etc/sa *options datafile*

By default, the *datafile* is */usr/adm/acct* for BSD ; */usr/adm/pacct* for SunOS.

"options"

-a   Show all commands, instead of omitting commands that are only used once.

-b   Sort by average CPU time per invocation. The report shows you the system's heaviest CPU users.

-c   Show percentages, in addition to absolute figures.

-d   Sort the average number of disk operations per invocation. This report shows the heaviest disk I/O users.

-D   Sort the listing by the total number of disk operations per all invocations of the program.

-i   Ignore the summary file (*savacct*). With this option, *sa* reports usage since the last time you ran *sa -s*.

-j   Report average CPU and elapsed time (in seconds) per invocation.

-k   Sort by average memory usage. This report identifies big memory users.

-K   Sort by the "storage integral," or the integral of memory usage over time, in kilobyte-seconds.

-l   Report system-state CPU time and user-state CPU time separately.

-m   Print the number of processes, total CPU time, total I/O operations, and storage integral for each user.

-n   Sort by the number of executions. This report identifies frequently used programs.

-r   Print the report in reverse order.

-s   Merge the current accounting records into the *savacct* file.

-t   Report the ratio of elapsed time to total CPU time. This report identifies programs with a lot of idle time.

-u   Print the ID number of the user who gave each command. This report shows who uses which commands.

-v*n*   Prompt to see whether or not each command that has been run fewer than *n* times should be added to the ** junk ** category.

-Saltsav
    Get past data from the file *altsav* rather than *savacct*.

-Ualtusracct
    Get user data from the file *alturacct* rather than *usracct*.

- The *savacct* file can contain a lot of ancient history which distorts your current data. The report may contain data about commands from the report. These commands are added to a special category called `**junk**` and are summarized by a single line in the report.

- You can write a shell script to gather a set of accounting reports and then you can run this script regularly through *cron*. This report-gathering strategy simulates the behavior of System V.

A Script to Collect Accounting Data

The following script collects a series of accounting reports:

```
#!/bin/sh
filename=`date | awk '{ print $2 $3 $6}' - `
                          # typical filename: Oct161990
sa=/usr/etc/sa           # SunOS; Other BSD uses /etc/sa
recorddir=/usr/adm/localacct  # directory to keep reports in
if [ ! -d $recorddir ]   # does the directory exist?
then                     # make the directory if it
    mkdir $recorddir     # doesn't already exist
fi
pathname=$recordir/$filename
date > $pathname
echo "Day's Activity (command summary)" >> $pathname
$sa -i >> $pathname
echo "Total activity (command summary)" >> $pathname
$sa >> $pathname
# this time, also compress reports into savacct
echo "Per-user activity" >> $pathname
$sa -ms >> $pathname
```

This script labels each report and puts them all into a file named *mmmddyyyy*, where *mmm* is the month, *dd* is the day of the month, and *yyyy* is the year. For example, the file for September 18, 1990, is named *Sep181990*.

Once you have written and tested a script like this, you can run it nightly via *cron*. Here's an appropriate *crontab* entry:

```
0 0 * * * root /usr/local/bin/my-custom-acct-program
```

Our accounting script is only a framework. It is trivial to modify it to include any reports that interest you. For example, you could easily modify it to invoke *sa -Ki* to find out which programs were the heaviest memory users during the previous day.

2.6.2 System V Accounting Utilities

The System V accounting system is also enabled by *accton*; however, you don't invoke *accton* directly. Instead, you run the shell script */usr/lib/acct/startup*. This command should be entered into the startup script */etc/init.d/acct*:*

```
/bin/su - adm -c /usr/lib/acct/startup
```

This command assumes that *adm* is a valid user name on your system. Add an entry for *adm* to */etc/passwd* if an entry isn't already there.

To disable accounting cleanly, execute the shell script */usr/lib/acct/shutacct*. The *shutacct* command should be executed whenever you execute a normal shutdown.

Day-to-Day Management

A number of shell scripts generate accounting reports for System V. These are usually run via the *cron* facility. The most important commands are:

runacct   Generates a set of five daily reports. These are placed in the directory */usr/adm/acct/sum* in a file named *rprtmmdd*, where *mm* indicates the month and *dd* indicates the day.

dodisk   Gathers disk usage statistics, which are summarized by *runacct*.

ckpacct   Prevents the main accounting file (*/usr/adm/acct/pacct*) from growing excessively; suspends accounting if there are less than 500 free blocks in the filesystem.

monacct   Converts all daily reports into a monthly report. This is placed in the directory */usr/adm/acct/fiscal*, in the file *fiscrptnn*, where *nn* indicates the month.

prdaily   Gets the accounting statistics for the current date and send them to standard output.

For tuning, we are primarily interested in the reports generated by *runacct* and *prdaily*. However, you should set up the entire system if you're going to set up any of it: *monacct* will prevent your daily reports from growing too

---

*For System V.3, this file should be linked to */etc/rc2.d/S22acct*. Under System V.4, both files are located in */sbin* rather than */etc*. If your system doesn't follow this model, put the *accton* command into whatever initialization file contains your site-specific startup commands.

large and also give you the ability to detect long-term changes in your system's usage. To set up automatic accounting, add the following lines to the *crontab* file for the user *root* (*/usr/spool/cron/crontabs/root*):

```
# generate daily accounting reports (1 a.m.)
0 1 * * * /usr/lib/acct/runacct
# update disk usage statistics weekly (2 a.m. Monday)
0 2 * * 1 /usr/lib/acct/dodisk
# manage accounting file size hourly (on the half-hour)
30 * * * * /usr/lib/acct/ckpacct
# generate monthly summaries (2 a.m. on the 1st of the month)
0 2 1 * * /usr/lib/acct/monacct
```

NOTE

Strange things happen if the system crashes while *runacct* is running. Your system administrator's manual will discuss how to restart *runacct* properly.

Accounting Reports

To get a set of accounting reports, either look directly at the files in */usr/adm/acct/sum* (the most recent file will be yesterday's report) or use the *prdaily* command:

```
% /usr/lib/acct/prdaily mmdd
```

where *mmdd* indicates the month and day for which you want a report. The report is sent to standard output. If you omit *mmdd*, *prdaily* generates the results for the current day.

Unlike BSD UNIX, which overwhelms you with a huge number of reports and options, the System V accounting system produces five reports. You always get all five reports: there's no way to select one without the others.

- **Terminal activity.** Reports the usage for each terminal. This report is useful for isolating chattering terminal lines. We'll discuss this report in Chapter 7, where we discuss terminal problems.

- **Usage report.** Reports system usage on a per-user basis. The report summarizes the total amount of CPU time, disk blocks, etc. This report shows you who your system's heaviest users are—important background material for understanding performance complaints.

- **Command summary.** Reports the number of times each command was used and statistics about its CPU usage. This is the most important report for finding CPU problems.

- **Monthly command summary.** Same as the previous report, but summarizes usage since the last time *monacct* was run.

- **Last login.** Reports the last time each user logged in. On a large system, this report may help you find users who are no longer active but who are still listed in */etc/passwd*. Eliminating inactive users may make it faster to log in.

If you want different reports, you can write your own programs. Most of the System V accounting tools are just shell scripts, so it is relatively easy to accommodate them to your own taste; however, the standard set of reports is more than adequate for performance tuning.

The Usage Report

The usage report is an elaborate summary of system usage by user. By reading this report, you can identify your system's heaviest users in terms of CPU and disk usage.

The usage report distinguishes between prime and nonprime usage, where prime time is defined by the file */usr/lib/acct/holidays*. This file lets you charge for nonprime usage at a lower rate; you can specify certain nonprime hours and holidays (which are all nonprime). If you don't want to establish billing policies, the distinction between prime and nonprime time is usually superfluous. You may be interested in nonprime usage if you are trying to get users to run large jobs at night. A summary of nonprime usage will tell you whether your admonitions are succeeding.

Here's a sample usage report:

	LOGIN	CPU (MINS)		KCORE-MINS		CONNECT(MINS)		DISK	# OF	# OF
UID	NAME	PRIME	NPRIME	PRIME	NPRIME	PRIME	NPRIME	BLOCKS	PROCS	SESS
0	TOTAL	313	12	16	2	4100	116	123434	522	27
0	root	...								
101	mike	50	2	1	0	500	30	1234	52	1

We've omitted a few fields at the end of the report which aren't relevant to our discussion. The quantities reported are:

UID
The user's ID number (assigned in /etc/passwd).

LOGIN NAME
The user's login name.

CPU (MINS)
The total amount of CPU time, in minutes, required by this user. This field shows how much of the system's time each user requires. It shouldn't be hard to identify the heaviest users.

KCORE-MINS
The user's *storage integral*, in kilobyte-minutes. This figure is the integral of physical memory usage over time for the given user or, much less precisely, the amount of physical memory the program needs multiplied by the amount of time it ran. The storage integral is a way of measuring memory requirements that accounts for both absolute memory and the time for which the memory is needed. A program that requires a 1-MB resident set for an hour is significantly harder on your system than a program that requires 4 MB for a minute. The storage integral allows you to take this time factor into account.

CONNECT (MINS)
The total amount of time the user was logged in.

DISK BLOCKS
The total amount of disk storage that the user is occupying. This field will show you if any users have accumulated an excessively large amount of disk space. It changes only on days when *dodisk* runs.

OF PROCS
The total number of processes the user executed.

OF SESS
The number of times the user logged in during the day.

AT&T warns against users who log in and do little work (i.e., they accumulate a lot of connect time but execute very few processes). These users may be a management problem but aren't an issue for system performance. Don't worry about them. You are interested in knowing which users accumulate a lot of CPU time and memory, and whether they accumulate it by running a lot of programs (many **PROCS**) or by running a few programs (few **PROCS**). Users who accumulate a lot of time or memory even though they run relatively few jobs must obviously be running large jobs. Knowing who is running large jobs and why is crucial to developing a tuning strategy.

The Command Summaries

The command summaries provide you with important information about how your system is being used. These reports tell you what programs run, how often they run, the amount of CPU time they require, the amount of memory they require, etc. Here's a sample command summary:

COMMAND NAME	NUMBER CMDS	TOTAL KCOREMIN	TOTAL CPU	TOTAL REAL	MEAN SIZE	MEAN CPU	HOG FACTOR	CHARS TRNSFD	BLOCKS READ
TOTALS	111	202.56	0.77	15.65	262.02	0.01	0.05	812907	147
nroff	4	163.79	0.48	0.50	339.85	0.12	0.97	569216	43
col	4	4.42	0.03	0.51	151.39	0.01	0.06	55656	12
sh	24	3.30	0.04	5.08	77.59	0.00	0.01	8115	16
man	3	2.44	0.02	4.77	159.85	0.01	0.00	24872	12

...

COMMAND NAME

The name of the program.

NUMBER CMDS

The number of times the program was executed during the period that the report covers (typically one day or one month).

TOTAL KCOREMIN

The total storage integral, in kilobyte-minutes, for all invocations of this program. The storage integral is the integral of resident set size over time. Programs that occupy a lot of memory for a long time have a higher storage integral than programs that occupy the same amount of memory for a short time. From a performance standpoint, programs that occupy memory for a long time are a much bigger load on the system and should be weighted more heavily.

TOTAL CPU

The total amount of CPU time that all invocations of the command accumulated, in minutes.

TOTAL REAL

The total amount of elapsed time (i.e., wall-clock time) that all invocations of the program required, in minutes.

MEAN SIZE

The average amount of memory that the program required, in KB.

MEAN CPU

The average amount of CPU time required to execute the program, in minutes.

HOG FACTOR

The program's *CPU efficiency*: the program's total CPU time divided by its total elapsed time. This statistic measures the ability of any program to grab the CPU's attention. It is misnamed and is virtually useless.

CHARS TRNSFD

The total number of characters transferred by this program (i.e., the number of characters read plus the number of characters written). This figure accounts only for character devices: terminals, network interfaces, tape drives, and so on. It does not take into account block I/O (i.e., file operations).

BLOCKS READ

The total number of disk blocks read and written by this command. This figure measures the program's filesystem usage.

It should be simple to figure out which programs require the most CPU time and memory. In this report, *nroff* (part of the UNIX typesetting package) was by far the worst offender. Running *nroff* typically required about 7 seconds and roughly 262 KB of memory. It's not surprising, or even particularly important, that *nroff* would be the biggest CPU user on a small system. After all, it is a relatively large program that runs whenever users invoke the *man* command. But if your system is having problems, knowing that it spends a lot of time running *nroff* can be very important. Once you know the culprit, you can take steps to resolve the problem. For example, if *nroff* really is at fault, you can look to see whether the */usr/man/catman.** directories exist. These serve as a cache for preprocessed reference pages, saving the system from running *nroff* repeatedly for the same file. If the *catman* directories don't exist, creating them will significantly reduce the time spent running *nroff*, but they could require up to 8 MB of disk space.

nroff isn't likely to be a problem on most systems. But the line of reasoning we are following is basic: once you know which programs account for a lot of CPU time, ask whether you can reduce the load by changing the program's setup, installation, typical usage, etc.

Last Login

The last login report shows the date that every user listed in */etc/passwd* last logged in to your system. Its format is very simple; here's a fragment from a typical report:

```
90-06-12   judy
90-06-12   mikel
90-06-12   root
90-06-12   tan
```

All four of these users last logged in on July 12, 1990. This information has virtually no impact on performance tuning. Unless you plan to improve system performance by eliminating active users (which isn't usually feasible), the fact that someone hasn't used his or her account recently is meaningless. This report may tell you who is on vacation or who is temporarily working on another project, but that's not going to help you particularly.

The last login report can help you to spot users who have left your organization but who still have accounts (i.e., users who shouldn't have accounts but still do). Ideally, the *passwd* entries for these users should be deleted as soon as they leave, but this isn't always the case, especially on large systems. Purging old users from your password file is a good idea for two reasons:

- These accounts are obvious security holes. Even if you trust your former associates, each valid login name is a weak spot in your armor.

- An excessively long password file can slow down the login process. Login time is a meaningless indicator of system performance, but it is one that users notice.

2.7 Administrative Setup for sar

For System V, performance monitoring is based on the *sar* utility, which reads and interprets data about system activity. The data files are generated by the *sadc* command, which periodically collects system statistics and saves them for later analysis. If you want to use *sar*, you have to set up the system to run *sadc* at appropriate intervals. It's surprisingly difficult to find discussions of *sadc*, even in the System V reference manuals. The material is there but you might miss it if you blink; therefore, we'll take some time to describe the statistics collection mechanism in detail. If you're interested only in BSD UNIX or XENIX, you can skip this section; there is no equivalent to *sar* or *sadc*.

sadc (the data-collection program) normally runs once an hour, plus whenever the system boots. Its data files are placed in the directory */usr/adm/sa*. Files in this directory are named *sadd*, where *dd* is the current date (a two-digit number). Therefore, at any time */usr/adm/sa* should include one file for every day in the past month. It's important to obey this naming convention. By default, *sar* uses these rules to find the data file for the current day.

Because there are at most 31 files in this directory, each containing one day's worth of data (24 sets of records if you run *sadc* hourly), the disk space required for *sadc* shouldn't be extremely large. If you don't want to spend that much disk space on data collection, decrease the frequency with which you run *sadc*, write a script to periodically delete the oldest file (or files) in *lusr/adm/sa*, or stop collecting data when the system isn't heavily used. Unfortunately, the one time you need to collect data is during peak hours, when a heavily loaded system is least able to tolerate additional load. But that's life.

2.7.1 Running sadc at Startup

You must run *sadc* whenever the system is booted to record the current time. If you don't, system statistics can be distorted. To guarantee that *sadc* is run, make sure that the following command is in *letclinit.d/perf*:*

```
su sys -c "/usr/lib/sa/sadc /usr/adm/sa/sa'date +%d'"
```

The *date* command produces the current day of the month as a one- or two-digit number and is used to generate the filename. When invoked this way, *sadc* just places a time marker in the file; it does not record any statistics.

2.7.2 Running sadc Periodically

To collect records, you need to run *sadc* periodically. Rather than running *sadc* directly, use the shell script *sa1* (in *lusr/lib/sa*). This script can be invoked by *cron* to run *sadc* on a regular basis. To collect hourly statistics, put the following line into the *crontab* file for *root* or *sys*.

```
0 * * * * /usr/lib/sa/sa1
```

The name of the *crontab* file will be *lusr/spool/cron/crontabs/sys* or *lusr/spool/cron/crontabs/root*, depending on how your system is set up. *sa1* always observes the file-naming conventions we discussed earlier.

An hourly report is the most basic way to collect data, but it's not necessarily the best. *sa1* takes two arguments: the length of time (in seconds) over which it will sample data, and the number of samples to take. For example, to take samples every 20 minutes, use this *crontab* entry:

```
0 * * * * /usr/lib/sa/sa1 1200 3
```

---

*For Systems V.3 and V.4, the organization of the initialization files is confusing and version-dependent. *letc/init.d/perf* is linked to *letc/rc2.d/S21perf*. Under System V.4, both of these files are in the directory *lsbin* rather than *letc*. If your system doesn't follow this model, put the *sadc* command into whatever file holds your site-specific startup commands.

This line tells *cron* to run *sa1* every hour; every time it runs, it should take three samples, each lasting 20 minutes (1200 seconds). If you want to collect statistics three times per hour during peak activity periods, use this *crontab* entry:

```
0 8-17 * * 1-5 /usr/lib/sa/sa1 1200 3
```

This line collects data every 20 minutes from 8 a.m. to 5 p.m., Monday through Friday.

The shell script *sa2* (also in */usr/lib/sa*) automatically produces *sar*-style reports, rather than binary data files. You should know that this facility is available, but we really think you can live without it. You are better off generating reports when you need them and as you need them. It is too easy to clutter the system with a lot of meaningless data. Remember, you can always use *sar* to generate a report for any date in the past, provided that the *sadc* statistics are still available.

2.7.3 Some sar Basics

sar is a complicated tool that can be used in several different ways to produce many reports. There are three basic ways to get *sar* reports:

```
% sar -keys interval number    Report current activity; doesn't require sadc
% sar -keys -f file            Summarize statistics from sadc data
% timex -s command             Report statistics gathered as command executes
```

The first of these commands samples system activity every *interval* seconds, for a total of *number* samples. If you omit *number*, sampling continues indefinitely. You can use it even if you aren't running *sadc*. It is good for gathering short-term reports at times when the system is under load.

The second command gathers data collected by *sadc*, interprets it, and prints a report. The *file* argument tells *sar* which data file to use. If you omit it, *sar* reads the data file for the current day. Data files are named */usr/adm/sa/sadd*, where *dd* indicates the day of the month. This command lets you find out long-term trends in system usage. For example, you can find out if system performance degraded as a deadline approached and users started working more frantically.

The third command, *timex*, is a *sar* command in disguise. It runs the given *command*, collects data while the command is running, and prints all possible *sar* reports when the command is finished. It is a good way to find out if any particular program is responsible for performance problems, especially if you have any hypotheses about which programs are critical. It is also an ideal way to collect statistics from benchmark programs.

In each command except *timex*, the *keys* are a sequence of letters that control which reports *sar* produces. Table 2-1 summarizes the different reports available from *sar*, together with their key letters.

Table 2-1: Reports Available from sar

Key	Function
a	Report usage of file access system calls.
b	Report buffer cache usage and hit rate.
c	Report system calls.
d	Report block device activity. (Probably 3B2 only.)
g	Report paging activity (V.4 only).
k	Report kernel memory allocation activity. (V.4 only.)
m	Report message and semaphore activity.
p	Report paging activity.
q	Report average queue length.
r	Report unused memory pages and disk blocks.
u	Report CPU utilization.
v	Report status of system tables.
w	Report swapping and paging activity.
x	Report RFS operation. (V.4 only.)
y	Report terminal activity.
A	Report all data (same as *-udqbwcayvmprgkxSDC*).
C	Report RFS buffer caching overhead.
D	Report CPU utilization by RFS and local activity (same as *Du*).
Db	Report buffer cache usage for RFS and local activity.
Dc	Report system calls separately for RFS and local activity.
Du	Report CPU utilization by RFS and local activity.
S	Report RFS server and request queue status.

We'll discuss the actual format of these reports in the coming chapters, as they turn up in our discussions. If you use System V and are interested in performance, you'll see *sar* a lot: there's nothing you can do without it.

Here are a few samples of useful *sar* commands. The first command prints the *b* and *a* reports (file access system calls and buffer cache usage) for the current day, as recorded by *sadc*:

```
% sar -ba
```

The next command reports the swapping, paging, and free memory statistics (*w*, *s*, and *r*) for current activity, taking ten samples separated by an interval of 1 minute (60 seconds). You can gather current statistics with this command even if you haven't enabled the data collection machinery.

```
% sar -wsr 60 10
```

Finally, the command below runs *make* and generates a complete set of *sar* statistics covering the time that *make* is running:

```
% timex -s make bigprogram
```

sar can easily give you a quick series of reports about the system's status. It provides an easy mechanism (*timex*) for assessing one program's impact on the system's behavior. And once you have set up the data collection machinery, it can show you long-term trends in your system's usage, making it easy to find out whether your system spends the better part of its day paging. In the long run, *sar*, with all its complications and variations, provides better information than the BSD tools.

2.8 SunOS Performance Meters

SunOS has developed a set of *performance meters* that provide a simple graphical representation of system performance. A performance meter can monitor your own system or some other system on the network, provided that the other system is running the statistics daemon, *rstatd*. You can set up a few performance meters to watch the system and then sit back and enjoy the show. They're actually mildly entertaining.

Sun's native window system, SunView, has a mouse-based way to set up performance meters. There's also a command line interface, which is more important: if you want a performance meter for some remote system, you need to use the command line interface. A performance meter has two forms: a graphical form and an iconified form that looks like a little clock. The iconified form is cute, but the graphical form is really more useful. We will assume that you use the graphical form.

Figure 2-1 shows a simplified performance meter. Here's a simplified graph:

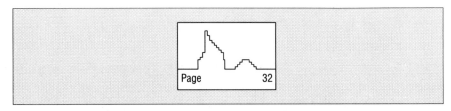

Figure 2-1. A performance meter

This meter shows paging activity. Over time, the curve gradually marches to the left. New paging activity appears at the right edge of the screen. This graph shows that there hasn't been any paging activity during the past few seconds (the right side of the graph is at zero). But there has been a lot of paging activity in the fairly recent past. The number 32 indicates the graph's scale. At its peak, this graph shows 32 paging operations per minute; however, the graph can dynamically rescale itself to accommodate a huge burst of activity.

To create a performance meter, use the *perfmeter* command. It is used like this:

```
% perfmeter options host &
```

where *options* are:

-s time   Sets the interval, in seconds, at which samples are taken to *time*; by default, *time* is 2.

-M start max min

Defines the scale used for the vertical axis of the performance graph. *start* is the initial scale. *max* indicates the maximum to which *perfmeter* can adjust the scale. *min* indicates the minimum. The defaults depend on which system parameter you're metering. All three values should be powers of 2.

-s param   Identifies the parameter you want to look at. A performance meter can show the following parameters:

cpu   CPU usage, in percent.

pkts   Ethernet packets per second.

page   Paging activity in pages per second.

swap   Jobs swapped per second.

intr   Number of device interrupts per second.

disk   Disk activity in transfer per second.

cntx   Number of context switches per second.

load   Average runnable process during the last minute.

coll   Ethernet collisions detected per second.

errs   Ethernet errors on received packets per second.

host is the host on which you want to collect statistics. It doesn't have to be a Sun workstation, provided that it is running the *rstatd* daemon. If you omit *host*, the meter will show statistics on your own system.

Although *perfmeters* can investigate many different parameters, they have some unfortunate limitations. The *swap* and *page* meters don't really show what you want. *swap* shows total swapping, both swap-ins and swap-outs. Likewise, *page* shows page-ins plus page-outs. But page-outs and swap-outs are far more important to overall performance than page-ins and swap-ins. You really can't get the paging and swapping statistics that are most important to you; nevertheless, *perfmeters* do give you a quick visual indication of your system's status.

2.9 Benchmarks

There is one crucial tool that only you can provide: a performance benchmark that tells you whether any particular change in the system's configuration improves or degrades performance. Designing appropriate benchmarks is as difficult as describing symptoms of bad performance. The appropriate benchmark for any situation depends on what problems your system has. Here are a few ideas:

• Any benchmark that tests system performance (compared to single-job performance) generally runs several copies of one or more jobs in the background. This is the only practical way to simulate a typical workload. A single job running by itself is not appropriate unless you run the system entirely in batch mode.

• To measure the overall I/O workload, write a C-language program that creates a large file. To minimize overhead, use the *write* system call rather than the standard I/O library and do as little other work as possible. The expression *elapsed-time/total-cpu-time* is a measure of the I/O workload. Compare the results when running with no load and with a light load to the results when running with a heavy load; this will help you to determine how the I/O subsystem is performing.

- For I/O performance to a single filesystem, a benchmark that copies one or more very large files may be appropriate. This test simulates one large, I/O-intensive application program. (It might be easier to use one of your site's applications as the benchmark.)

- For aggregate I/O performance to several filesystems (simulating several simultaneous independent jobs), create several processes that create and copy large files on different filesystems. Such a test simulates the effect of several processes simultaneously using different disks. Along these lines, an even better benchmark would initiate I/O requests randomly at a fixed random rate (for example, 30 requests/minute) and measure the average response time.* Doing this under UNIX is tricky because UNIX lacks asynchronous I/O, but it is by no means impossible.

- For virtual memory performance, a benchmark that runs several simultaneous compilations is usually appropriate.

- Running in combination the tests described above can help you to simulate kinds of workloads. To simulate the system's workload, you may want to pick a mixture of actual applications employed by the users at your site.

Here's a simple C-language program that creates a large file by repeatedly calling *write*. You can use it to measure single-file I/O throughput or you can add it to a more general script that tests the I/O system under load. There are a number of ways to improve it. You might want to read the file size and buffer size from the command line. You might want to build timing routines into the program, rather than rely on a */bin/time* to measure the filesystem's speed; nevertheless, this simple program will give you a good start:

```
#include <fcntl.h>
#define FAIL -1
#define BSIZE 8192   /*write buffer size; a multiple of page size*/
#define FSIZE 1000   /*number of times to write the buffer*/
main()
{
if (-1 == writeit(FSIZE)) printf("FILE OPERATION FAILED\n");
}

int   writeit(blocks)
int   blocks;
{
char buf[BSIZE];
int   fdes;
int   i;
int written;
```

---

*See Kenneth H. Bates, "I/O Subsystem Performance," *Digital Review* (September, 1990), pp. 56-68. While this article is on VAX/VMS, almost everything in it is applicable to UNIX.

```
if ( (fdes = open("./testfile.bm",O_WRONLY | O_CREAT,0777)) < 0 )
    return FAIL;
for (i=0; i< blocks; i++)
    {
    if (written = write(fdes,buf,BSIZE) != BSIZE) return FAIL;
    }
return 0;
}
```

The most important factor in designing a benchmark is that it be *repeatable*: you must know that you can run exactly the same test at any time in the future. The easiest way to create a repeatable benchmark is to write a shell script (UNIX terminology for a command file) that automatically starts test jobs and gathers system statistics. To do this, you can use any UNIX shell: the C shell (*csh*), the Bourne shell (*sh*), or the Korn shell (*ksh*) if it is available. Most UNIX programmers feel that the Bourne shell is best suited for writing scripts, but there is no reason you can't use the others.

Here's a Bourne shell script that runs a random assortment of jobs. All the jobs run concurrently in the background with the intent of simulating a high interactive load:

```
#!/bin/sh
# run a lot of jobs to force the load average up
cat [a-m]*.mS > /tmp/foo1
cat [m-z]*.mS > /tmp/foo2
# a big troff job
soelim *.mS | pic | tbl | eqn | troff -mS -a > /dev/null 2> \
        /dev/null &
# duplicate it with nroff
soelim *.mS | pic | tbl | eqn | nroff -mS > /dev/null 2> \
        /dev/null &
# a useless diff--should keep going for a while
diff /tmp/foo1 /tmp/foo2 > /dev/null &
# keep awk busy, just to use up some more memory
# and do something CPU-bound
awk 'BEGIN { for (i = 0; i < 1e6; i++){t[i]=i} }' - &
# just to be thorough, run the compiler
(cc -O bigfile.c; rm a.out) &
wait
```

The significance of this script has nothing to do with the particular commands that it runs. If you try to run it on your system, it will fail—it assumes that you have a special troff macro package and lots of properly named troff files around. I chose these commands because they take a reasonably long time, they're typical of the work I do, and they're CPU-intensive. Build your script from whatever seems reasonable. You should choose commands commonly used at your site. The more closely your benchmark simulates the system's actual workload, the more relevant its results will be. If your system's users are fond of *lex* and *yacc*, include a few invocations of these jobs. If your users run some proprietary numerical analysis code, find a good set of test data and do some numerical analysis. The important concept here is that you don't have to wait for the system to get bad before you can collect any data. With some cleverness, you can make the system as bad as you want on your own. And you can overload the system in exactly the same way at will. You have a controlled environment in which to test your changes.

For example, some simple tests may show that your system doesn't have enough memory. Run your test script and measure how much time it takes to complete. Then try making your changes: add memory, change your kernel configuration, do whatever you had planned to do. After making your changes, run your test script again and see whether the system has improved. If you don't have a repeatable test script, you may never find out whether any particular change has helped or hurt your system's performance.

3

Managing the Workload

Some Tricks for Users
Cleanup: Reducing the Workload
Scheduling Priority
Off-peak Job Submission
Shell Time Limits
CPU Capacity

Once you have looked at *ps*, your accounting records, and other data, you can start taking steps to improve your system's overall performance. No matter what problems your system is facing, it never hurts to reduce the workload: to get your users to be more efficient, to eliminate unnecessary daemons and other system processes, to give the highest priority to the most important jobs, and so on. Therefore, we'll start this chapter with some general hints about how users can improve their interactive response. These techniques can do a lot to make the system more pleasant to use. Next we proceed to general cleanup issues: how to reduce the amount of unnecessary work your system does.

At the end of this chapter, we'll discuss another kind of issue: system capacity. Tuning isn't just a matter of trimming away fat. Tuning may also mean configuring the system so that it can run more jobs: increasing the system's capacity, possibly at the expense of some other aspect of performance. Having the fastest UNIX system in the state is great but it won't help if you can't adequately support your users. Therefore, we will discuss how to tune the kernel so that its tables are large enough to accommodate your workload but not so large that they waste valuable memory.

3.1 Some Tricks for Users

There are a fair number of simple tricks that will improve a system's performance. Most of them don't matter much in the big scheme of things, but they do
help, particularly because users feel improvements in interactive performance and
keyboard response immediately. And some of these tricks (for example, using a
more efficient editor) represent genuine savings. If you can educate your
system's users to use these tricks, they will be a lot happier:

- Use the *dirs* command (built into *csh*) instead of the *pwd* command. *dirs* lists
  the directory stack, which is stored internally by the shell and is based on the
  directories you type as arguments to the *cd* or *pushd* command. *pwd* looks up
  the current directory and is therefore slower. The *dirs* command has one
  weakness: it cannot tell you if your current directory is really a link to some
  other directory or if your current directory has disappeared because its NFS
  server crashed.

- Avoid using *ps*, which is relatively slow. It's unclear how often users really
  need this information. *ps* is supposed to be faster in System V.4.

- Avoid long search paths. The *PATH* environment variable shouldn't be more
  than five or six directories long. Along the same lines, place the directories in
  which the most commonly used commands appear at the beginning of the
  path. Try to place large directories at the end of the path. Obeying this rule
  will minimize the startup time for commands. (Search path length should not
  be an issue for *csh* users.)

- Virtually all incarnations of the popular *emacs* editor are real hogs: they use
  a lot of memory and a lot of CPU time. If you can convince your users to use
  vi or some other editor,* you will gain a lot of ground. Most windowing systems, including SunOS, have some kind of built-in editor. These built-in editors tend to be underused; Sun's is quite useful. If you look through UUNET
  sources, you may find some public domain versions of *emacs* that have been
  written to minimize CPU load. If you feel like experimenting, try one of
  these.

- Minimize directory size. We'll discuss this further later.

---

*One of this book's reviewers commented: "Fat chance!" If you go this route, you have your work
cut out for you. *emacs* users (including the author) are a loyal bunch who would rather flame than
switch. And *emacs* is an incredibly versatile editor. But the rewards for getting users to change are
significant.

- Rather than use *find*, which is relatively slow, to look for files, run *ls -lR* at off-hours, saving its output in a publicly accessible file. Then ask users to *grep* through this file. Of course, if users already have some idea where their files are, it may be more efficient to use *find*, rather than *grep*ing through a listing of the entire filesystem.

- Rather than *grep*ing to search for strings, use *egrep*. Contrary to the standard UNIX manuals, *egrep* is almost always faster than either *grep* or *fgrep*. There are some public domain versions of *grep* that are even faster. These are available from UUNET.

Earlier, we promised some additional commentary on directory size. Directory lookups are relatively slow under UNIX, and their speed decreases radically as directories get large. Therefore, you and your system's users should keep their directories as small as possible. The *ls -l* command shows directory sizes for a BSD UNIX system:

```
% ls -l ~
total 110
drwxr-sr-x  2 mikel       512 Jun 20 14:16 Mail
drwxr-sr-x  3 mikel       512 Jul  2 21:07 fuser
drwxr-sr-x  2 mikel       512 May 31 10:11 gmacs
drwxr-sr-x  2 mikel      1024 Jun  7 08:43 lpimac
drwxr-sr-x  2 mikel       512 May 31 10:42 modem
drwx--S---  2 mikel       512 Jul  2 12:56 ora
drwxr-sr-x  6 mikel      1024 Jul  6 10:34 perf
drwxr-sr-x  2 mikel       512 Jul  2 12:15 power
drwxr-sr-x  2 mikel       512 Jun 20 14:17 rcs
drwxr-sr-x  2 mikel       512 Jul  2 17:03 sunview
drwxr-sr-x  2 mikel       512 Jul  3 20:50 time
drwxr-sr-x  2 mikel       512 Jun 19 19:00 uunet
```

Under BSD UNIX, directory sizes are always multiples of 512 bytes. Under System V, directories occupy 16 bytes per file, and all directories have at least two entries: . (dot) and .. (dot dot). In the example above, all of the directories are reasonably small. If you start seeing 2048-byte directory entries, it's time to start reorganizing. AT&T says you should worry when a directory is larger than forty 512-byte blocks. In our opinion, that's much too late. The 2048-byte directories aren't particularly large, but you shouldn't let the problem get out of hand.

However, reducing the size of a directory isn't as simple as it should be. Merely deleting a file from a directory doesn't change the directory's size. Any space that's allocated to the directory remains permanently allocated. To reduce the size of a directory, you need to delete (or move) the files you no longer need, copy the files you want into a new directory, then delete the old directory. For example:

```
% ls -l
drwxr-sr-x  2 mikel         2048 Jun 20 14:17 barfaz
                                          Too large for comfort
% rm barfaz/*.o *.tmp *.mail *.txt        Cleanup
% ls -l
drwxr-sr-x  2 mikel         2048 Jun 20 14:17 barfaz
                                          Size unchanged
% mv barfaz barfaz.tmp                    Move everything out
% mkdir barfaz                            Make a new directory
% mv barfaz.tmp/* barfaz                  Copy everything
% rm -r barfaz.tmp                        No more need for this
% ls -l
drwxr-sr-x  2 mikel          512 Jun 20 14:17 barfaz
                                          Directory reasonably small
```

System V.4 has some utilities to compress filesystems, which include shrinking directories to their minimum size. These utilities also rearrange files for optimal access. Of course, they won't delete the unneeded files that gave you a bloated directory in the first place. You must do your own cleanup or get the system's users to cooperate. To compress a filesystem, use the command:

```
# /usr/sbin/dcopy fs1 fs2
```

where *fs1* and *fs2* are the block special files for the filesystem you want to compress. Alternatively, you can run */usr/sbin/cmpress* yourself. The *cmpress* and *dcopy* utilities require you to have a cartridge tape drive and may not be available on all versions of System V.4. AT&T does not say what happens if your filesystem won't fit onto a single cartridge tape; one hopes these utilities can handle multiple volumes. Both commands are very dangerous. Always backup and dismount your filesystem before proceeding.

NOTE

I have seen one V.2 system that supported an early version of *dcopy*. While it would repack your filesystem properly, the situations under which you could use it were very restrictive. I have seen no other versions for either V.2 or V.3. Therefore, you probably don't have *dcopy* and, even if you do have it, you might not be able to use it. But check your manuals first.

3.2 Cleanup: Reducing the Workload

A UNIX system is always doing a lot of work whether or not you know it. Some simple cleanup, such as getting rid of unneeded daemons or running big jobs at low priority or at night, will go a long way toward solving even the most intractable problems. If your system's performance is bad, there's no reason to waste good cycles doing work that doesn't need to be done.

3.2.1 Daemons You Can Do Without

In this section we'll discuss the daemons that can be considered optional. Many of these daemons support network services through TCP/IP and NFS. As such, they are either standard or extremely common under BSD UNIX. Under System V, you will see them only if you are running optional TCP/IP or NFS software.

Here's a list of daemons you might be able to live without:

accounting   Not a daemon *per se*. The command *accton* enables system-wide accounting services. Accounting is not used on many UNIX systems. We've already told you why accounting is a good idea, but it's certainly possible to get by without it. For System V, you may find that the script *startup* is used to start accounting rather than the simple *accton* command. (All UNIX versions.)

biod   This daemon allows the system to access filesystems via NFS. You can start any number of copies of this daemon, but (once again) 4 is a "magic number." You don't need this daemon if the system doesn't mount any NFS filesystems. (BSD or System V with NFS.)

comsat   *comsat* is the program that prints the message "You have new mail" on your screen when mail arrives. Some users find this annoying and turn notification off with the command *biff n*. It is easy to get along without this feature. You can disable it without harm and may even gain a few friends. (BSD and System V with TCP/IP; started by *inetd*.)

lpd or *lpsched*   Printer daemons. These aren't needed if the system in question doesn't support printing (either locally or remotely). You may want to force users to submit all print requests on a single central system. In this case you need to run a printer daemon only on the system that does the spooling. (*lpd*: BSD; *lpsched*: System V.)

mountd   The *mountd* daemon listens for remote mount requests. It is needed only if your system is an NFS server. (BSD or System V with NFS.)

nfsd   This daemon services NFS requests from remote systems. You can start any number of copies of this daemon, but 4 is appropriate for most situations. The effects of changing this number are hard to predict and are often counterintuitive. For various reasons that are beyond the scope of this book, increasing the number of daemons can often degrade network performance. We recommend leaving this number at 4 unless the system is not an NFS server. Systems that are not NFS servers can disable *nfsd* entirely. (BSD or System V with NFS.)

nntpd   This daemon supports the USENET network news services. It is used on news server systems that receive news from the Internet and distribute it to other systems. You can disable this daemon if no one at your site uses network news, if you use UUCP to transfer all news, rather than the Internet, or if your system is not a *news server* (i.e., it doesn't interact with the network and is used only to read news). Network news has become extremely important to many confirmed UNIX users, so tread cautiously. (BSD and System V with TCP/IP; started by *inetd*.)

quotas   Started from */etc/rc*. The command *quotaon* enables disk quota checking. On many UNIX systems, quota checking is not used. If you can do without disk quotas, we recommend that you do. To disable quotas, find the lines that execute */etc/quotacheck* and */etc/quotaon*, and place a pound sign (#) before them. (BSD only.)

rlogind   The *rlogind* daemon services the *rlogin* and *rsh* commands. These commands are basic to networking. If you use any networking at all, you should run *rlogind*. If you are not connected to a local network, *rlogind* won't do you any good, so you can disable it. (BSD and System V with TCP/IP; usually started by *inetd*.)

routed   This daemon is responsible for routing network packets destined for other networks. If your system has a single Ethernet interface and if your local network has only one gateway to the outside world, you can disable *routed*. If you disable this daemon, make sure that */etc/rc.local* has a line such as this:

```
route add default gateway 1
```

where *gateway* is the name of any system on the local network that serves as a gateway to other networks. Omit the *routed* command if your network has no gateways (i.e., if it is isolated from any other networks).

If your local network has two or more gateways, you should leave *routed* running. (BSD and System V with TCP/IP.)

rwhod   This daemon provides information about users on other systems. If you disable it, the commands *rwho* and *ruptime* won't work. This daemon can require a fair amount of time, and *rwho* services aren't necessary for most purposes. In other words, *rwhod* is a lot of expense for relatively little gain. If you don't think you need *rwho*, disable *rwhod*. (BSD and System V with TCP/IP.)

sendmail   The *sendmail* daemon provides mail services, both internally (i.e., between users on the system) and externally (between this system and others). *sendmail* uses a lot of memory. If your system is short on memory, you may find that everything else stops when *sendmail* is active. On some systems it also runs at an oddly high priority and can hog the CPU. (BSD, System V.4, and many earlier System Vs.)

talkd   This daemon supports the *talk* command, which allows users to type messages to each other from their terminals. Personally, I have always found *talk* vastly inferior to a telephone conversation. This is another feature that you can easily live without. (BSD and System V with TCP/IP; started by *inetd*.)

timed   The time daemon attempts to synchronize system clocks across a network. If you are doing a lot of cross-network computing, synchronization is important. If one system has an incorrect time, a file's modification date may occasionally appear to be in the future. There are many *timed* implementations: some are more successful than others. If you understand that synchronization is important and you are willing to use some other means to manage it, or if you don't do significant cross-network work, you can get along without *timed*. (BSD and some System V with TCP/IP.)

ypbind   This daemon lets the system look up information in the NIS database. At least one system must be running *ypserv* before you can run *ypbind*. NIS greatly simplifies network administration, but it can burn a lot of CPU time, so you may want to consider doing without it. If you decide to forgo NIS, you may also have to do some work reconstructing standard administrative files. (BSD or System V with NIS.)

ypserv   This daemon makes a system act as an NIS server,* i.e., a system that can send information about the NIS database to other systems on the network. It must not be running if the system isn't a NIS server. (BSD or System V with NIS.)

3.2.2 Disabling Unnecessary Daemons

Most of the daemons mentioned in the preceding section are started by one of the */etc/rc* files: either */etc/rc* or */etc/rc.local* under BSD UNIX, or one of the files in */etc/rc.d* under System V. To disable any daemon, find the lines that start it and insert a pound sign (#) before them. For example, the lines below start *routed*:

```
if [ -f /etc/routed ]; then
        /etc/routed;            echo -n ' routed'   >/dev/console
fi
```

To eliminate *routed*, rewrite these lines to read as follows:

```
# if [ -f /etc/routed ]; then
#        /etc/routed;           echo -n ' routed'   >/dev/console
# fi
```

A few of the daemons we've mentioned are started by *inetd*, a superdaemon which is the glue that holds a lot of the networking software together. To disable these daemons, find the relevant line in */etc/inetd.conf* and insert a pound sign (#) before it. For example, to disable *comsat*, find the line that reads:

```
comsat dgram udp wait root /etc/comsat comsat
```

and insert a pound sign (#) before it. After making these changes to your */etc/rc* and */etc/inetd.conf*, reboot your system. You will be running without daemons. If you notice some performance improvement, great! You may not notice an improvement, since many daemons don't require much CPU time. You may notice some angry users in line at your office asking: "How come the system never tells me when I have mail any more?" or you may notice your computer behaving in some way that you didn't anticipate. If this is the case, turn the daemons back on. The system exists for the users, not vice versa.

---

*NIS stands for the *Network Information Service*. This service was formerly called the Yellow Pages. Sun Microsystems changed the name because Yellow Pages is a trademark in the United Kingdom. We will use the term NIS throughout.

3.2.3   Fighting with sendmail

sendmail is the sort of tool that gave UNIX its bad reputation. It is badly designed, its documentation is completely obtuse, and it is absolutely essential. It was written to solve a problem that no longer exists but happened to be general enough to solve problems that weren't originally anticipated. *sendmail* is the basis of the mail system. It is the program that makes sure your mail is delivered, whether it travels via UUCP, Ethernet, or Internet or simply to another user on the same system. It is really a multiplexer between different mail agents, different mail users, different mail transport mechanisms, and different mail networks.

sendmail can be a performance problem for two reasons. First, it requires a fair amount of memory to run; second, on some systems it runs at a very high priority. On a small workstation with little memory, it is not uncommon for almost everything to stop while *sendmail* is running. Even worse, you don't have a lot of control over when *sendmail* runs.

If you are managing a network of workstations, you can minimize or even eliminate these problems by concentrating mail services on a single system and running *sendmail* only on the mail server. If your network isn't already configured this way, consider it. By using NFS or RFS to export the mail directories (*/usr/spool/mail*) to other network hosts, you can create the appearance of local mail service. You may also need to modify your mail aliases database (*/usr/lib/aliases*, */etc/mail.aliases*, or */etc/aliases*, depending on your version). If your site uses mail heavily, it may be worthwhile to buy a small workstation and use it as a dedicated *sendmail* server.

NOTE

This strategy won't work if you use the *mh* mailer with the *smtp* option. In this case, you must have a *sendmail* daemon on the local system.

If you cannot concentrate your mail service onto one system, you may want to tune *sendmail* in other ways. A few types of tuning are possible, depending on your installation. Here are some possible solutions (some good and some bad) you may want to consider:

• Many UNIX systems try to call a *uucp* site whenever any user tries to send mail to that site. You are better off batching calls to each *uucp* site. Your mail turnaround will be slower, but you won't have to worry as much about *sendmail* starting at random times. Set up *cron* to poll your *uucp* sites periodically (as described in the Nutshell Handbook *Managing uucp and Usenet*). Then edit your *sendmail.cf* file so that its UUCP mailer specification looks something like this:

```
# UUCP Mailer specification

Muucp,P=/usr/bin/uux, F=msDFMhuU, S=13, R=23,
  A=uux - -r -a$f $h!rmail ($u)
# A=uux - -a$f $h!rmail ($u)          Original version of this line
```

The critical option here is *-r*. This tells *uux* that it should only queue *uucp* jobs, rather than initiating an actual transfer. Of course, this doesn't prevent other sites from calling your system and starting a transfer, but it will help.

- *sendmail* normally tries to deliver mail immediately, putting any undeliverable mail into a queue which it then processes periodically. The option *-odq* tells *sendmail* to queue all mail, inhibiting immediate delivery. It gives you more control over when *sendmail* does its work.

- *sendmail* is almost always invoked with the option *-qtime*, which tells it to process the queue every *time* interval. The *time* is normally *30m* (every 30 minutes). If *sendmail* is causing performance problems, you may not want to process the queue as often—perhaps only every three hours (*3h*) or even every eight hours (*8h*).

- You can prevent *sendmail* from sending mail when the load average is over some limit by using the *-oxlimit* option, where *limit* is the load average threshold. Users can still queue new mail, but it won't be delivered until the load average is tolerably low. This technique has a number of problems. First, it affects only mail handled via the SMTP network protocol. Local mail, UUCP mail, and some network mail with a high priority will still get out. Second, *sendmail* tries to process mail in parallel and increments the load average by one for each new process it starts. Therefore, it soon starts tripping over its own feet. If you try this solution, you will find that *sendmail* will deliver mail in short bursts, even under the best conditions. This may not be tolerable.

- Similarly, you can prevent *sendmail* from accepting incoming mail when the load average is over some limit by using the *-oXlimit* option, where *limit* is the load average threshold. This option only affects mail handled via the SMTP network protocol. Local mail and mail arriving via UUCP will still be handled. The threshold for receiving mail should usually be greater than the threshold for sending mail. This option has one serious problem: it can cause mail for your system to backup on the other systems with which you communicate. Maintaining good relations with other system administrators is important to doing an effective job, so try not to make them your enemies.

- *sendmail* has a *-oY* option which helps it to conserve memory. Invoking *sendmail* with *-oY* will do the trick. However, the standard UNIX documentation says that this option will reduce memory needs but can have other bad side effects on performance. *sendmail* will waste time repeatedly trying to contact hosts that are unreachable. All mail will eventually be delivered but if your mail partners are often unreachable, you may find that *-oY* is too slow.

- *sendmail* allows you to precompile the configuration file by giving the command *sendmail -bz*. Once you have run *sendmail -bz*, future invocations of *sendmail* will use a compiled database named *sendmail.fc* rather than the standard configuration file, *sendmail.cf*. The startup time using the precompiled database is significantly less. I originally thought that this option was useless because *sendmail* always ran as a daemon. But that isn't really true. Most mailers also invoke *sendmail* whenever you initiate a mail message. Therefore, you have to worry about two kinds of *sendmail* invocations: the daemonic *sendmail* that starts during initialization, for which precompilation is of no use, and the *sendmail* that your mail agent creates, for which precompilation is very relevant. If you choose this route, you must run *sendmail -bz* whenever you change the configuration file.

sendmail is usually invoked by a line in one of your */etc/rc* files. On BSD UNIX systems, this will be */etc/rc.local*; under System V, this will be */etc/rc3.d/S36sendmail*. Standard startup scripts invoke *sendmail* this way:

```
/usr/lib/sendmail -bd -q30m &
```

The standard options tell *sendmail* to run as a daemon (*-bd*). They don't make any statement about delivery policy. *sendmail* will attempt to deliver any queued mail every 30 minutes (*-q30m*; the time limit may differ, depending on your vendor). Add any additional options you want to this line. For example, to stop receiving mail when the load average is over 5, change the *sendmail* command to:

```
/usr/lib/sendmail -bd -q30m -ox5 &
```

To queue all mail and run the queue every three hours:

```
/usr/lib/sendmail -bd -q3h -odq &
```

Some users may complain if you only process the mail queue every three hours. You will have to weigh the importance of mail and your users' discomfort against your system's overall performance. Note: If the *-qtime* option isn't on the command line, *sendmail* will process the queue only once, when you invoke it.

One of this book's reviewers recommends a public domain program named *MMDF-II*. It is supposed to be much easier to manage and much less of a performance burden. I have no experience with this program, but it may help you to solve some problems.

3.3 Scheduling Priority

By controlling scheduling priority, you can force the CPU to spend most of its time working on some jobs, to the partial exclusion of others. You can use this feature to expedite work on jobs that are critical or to prevent the system from spending time on jobs that aren't important. Which approach to take depends on how your system is used. If you are supporting a large community of users, some of whom run large jobs, getting the users with big jobs to work at lower priority will make the system more pleasant for everyone. This solution is particularly effective if the users spend most of their time editing or preparing data and only occasionally kick off a large application program. Running everything but the editors at low priority will improve keyboard response without imposing much difficulty on the applications.

However, if you're supporting a system that's dedicated to some particular task and that supports other users by courtesy, it may be more important to expedite the jobs that are crucial to your mission, letting the other users suffer. There's also something to be said for running memory-intensive jobs at higher priority: get these out of the way so that the system can get back to normal. If your system has trouble with one or two memory-intensive jobs, it may be helpful to run them at higher priority. Everyone else will suffer, but you'll get these jobs out of the way faster. More pain for a short time is often preferable to less pain over a longer period. Of course, this solution is only appropriate if jobs that stress memory are relatively rare. If memory-intensive jobs are always running, increasing their priority will make everyone permanently miserable.

3.3.1 Setting Priorities with nice

The *nice* command modifies the scheduling priority of time-sharing processes (for BSD and pre-V.4 releases of System V, all processes). If you're not familiar with UNIX, you will find its definition of priority confusing—it's the opposite of what you would expect. A process with a high *nice* number runs at low priority, getting relatively little of the processor's attention; similarly, jobs with a low *nice* number run at high priority. This is why the *nice* number is usually called *niceness*: a job with a lot of niceness is very kind to the other users of your system (i.e., it runs at low priority), while a job with little niceness will hog the CPU. The term "niceness" is awkward, like the priority system itself. Unfortunately, it's the only term that is both accurate (*nice* numbers are used to compute priorities but are not the priorities themselves) and avoids horrible circumlocutions ("increasing the priority means lowering the priority ...").

Many supposedly experienced users claim that *nice* has virtually no effect. Don't listen to them. As a general rule, reducing the priority of an I/O-bound job won't change things very much. The system rewards jobs that spend most of their time waiting for I/O by increasing their priority. But reducing the priority of a CPU-bound process can have a significant effect. Compilations, batch typesetting programs (*troff*, TeX, etc.), applications that do a lot of math, and similar programs are good candidates for *nice*. On a moderately loaded system, I have found that *nice* typically makes a CPU-intensive job roughly 30 percent slower and consequently frees that much time for higher priority jobs. You can often significantly improve keyboard response by running CPU-intensive jobs at low priority.

NOTE

System V.4 has a much more complex priority system, including real-time priorities. Priorities are managed with the *priocntl* command. The older *nice* command is available for compatibility. We discuss the V.4 priority system in Appendix A, *Real-time Processes in System V.4*. Other UNIX implementations (including HP and Concurrent) support real-time scheduling. These implementations have their own tools for managing the scheduler.

The *nice* command sets a job's niceness, which is used to compute its priority. It may be one of the most nonuniform commands in the universe. There are many versions, each slightly different from the others:

- BSD UNIX *nice* that is built into the C shell.
- BSD *nice* that is not built into the C shell (and which can be used by other shells).
- System V *nice* that is built into the C shell.
- System V *nice* that is not built into the C shell (and which can be used by other shells).

Under BSD UNIX, you must also know about the *renice* command; this lets you change the priority of a job after it is running. Under System V, you can't modify a job's priority once it has started, so there is no equivalent.

We'll tackle the different variations of *nice* in order.

BSD C Shell nice

Under BSD UNIX, *nice* numbers run from -20 to 20. The -20 designation corresponds to the highest priority; 20 corresponds to the lowest. By default, UNIX assigns the *nice* number 0 to user-executed jobs. The lowest *nice* numbers (-20 to -17) are unofficially reserved for system processes. Assigning a user's job to these *nice* numbers can cause problems. Users can always request a higher *nice* number (i.e., a lower priority) for their jobs. Only the superuser can raise a job's priority.

To submit a job at a lower niceness, precede it with the modifier *nice*. For example, the command:

```
% nice awk -f proc.awk datafile > awk.out
```

runs an *awk* command at low priority. By default, *nice* will submit this job with a *nice* level of 4. To submit a job with an arbitrary *nice* number, use *nice* this way:

```
% nice +/-n command
```

where *n* is an integer between 0 and 20. The *+n* designation requests a positive *nice* number (low priority); *-n* request a negative *nice* number. Only a superuser may request a negative *nice* number.

BSD Standalone nice

The standalone version of *nice* differs from C shell *nice* in that it is a separate program, not a command built in to the C shell. You can therefore use the standalone version in any situation: within makefiles, when you are running the Bourne shell, etc. The principles are the same. *nice* numbers run from -20 to 20, with the default being zero. Only the syntax has been changed to confuse you. For the standalone version, *-n* requests a positive *nice* number (lower priority) and *--n* requests a negative *nice* number (higher priority—superuser only). Consider these commands:

```
$ nice -6 awk -f proc.awk datafile > awk.out
# nice --6 awk -f proc.awk datafile > awk.out
```

The first command runs *awk* with a high *nice* number (i.e., 6). The second command, which can only be issued by a superuser, runs *awk* with a low *nice* number (i.e., -6).

System V C Shell nice

System V takes a slightly different view of *nice* numbers. *nice* levels run from 0 to 39; the default is 20. The numbers are different but their meanings are the same: 39 corresponds to the lowest possible priority, and 0 is the highest. A few System V implementations support real-time submission via *nice*. Jobs submitted by root with extremely low *nice* numbers (-20 or below) allegedly get all of the CPU's time. Systems on which this works properly are very rare and usually advertise support for real-time processing. In any case, running jobs this way will destroy multiuser performance. This feature, if your system has it, is completely different from real-time priorities in V.4.

With these exceptions, the C shell version of *nice* is the same as its BSD cousin. To submit a job at a low priority, use the command:

```
% nice command
```

This increases the command's niceness by the default amount (4, the same as BSD UNIX); *command* will run at *nice* level 24. To run a job at an arbitrary priority, use:

```
% nice +/-n command
```

where *n* is an integer between 0 and 19. The *+n* entry requests a higher *nice* level (a decreased priority), while *-n* requests a lower *nice* level (a higher priority). Again, this is similar to BSD UNIX, with one important difference: *n* is now relative to the default *nice* level. That is, the command:

```
% nice +6 awk -f proc.awk datafile > awk.out
```

runs *awk* at *nice* level 26.

System V Standalone nice

Once again, the standalone version of *nice* is useful if you are writing makefiles or shell scripts or if you use the Bourne shell as your interactive shell. It is similar to the C shell version, with these differences:

- With no arguments, standalone *nice* increases the *nice* number by 10 instead of by 4; this is a significantly greater reduction in the program's priority.

- With the argument *-n*, *nice* increases the *nice* number by *n* (reducing priority).

- With the argument *--n*, *nice* decreases the *nice* number by *n* (increasing priority; superuser only).

Consider these commands:

```
$ nice -6 awk -f proc.awk datafile > awk.out
# nice --6 awk -f proc.awk datafile > awk.out
```

The first command runs *awk* at a higher *nice* level (i.e., 26, which corresponds to a lower priority). The second command, which can be given only by the superuser, runs *awk* at a lower *nice* level (i.e., 14).

3.3.2 Changing a Job's Priority Under BSD UNIX

Once a job is running, you can use the *renice* command to change the job's priority:

```
% /etc/renice priority -p pid
% /etc/renice priority -g pgrp
% /etc/renice priority -u uname
```

where *priority* is the new *nice* level for the job. It must be a signed integer between -20 and 20. *pid* is the ID number (as shown by *ps*) of the process you want to change. *pgrp* is the number of a process group, as shown by *ps -l*; this version of the command modifies the priority of all commands in a process group. *uname* may be a user's name, as shown in */etc/passwd*; this form of the command modifies the priority of all jobs submitted by the user. Again, only superuser can lower the *nice* number (raise a process's priority). Users can only raise the *nice* number (lower the priority) and can modify the priorities of only the jobs they started.

BSD UNIX systems automatically *nice* jobs after they have accumulated a certain amount of CPU time. This implicitly gives priority to jobs that don't run for a long time, sacrificing users who run long jobs in favor of users who run many short commands. The autonice time varies from system to system but is usually 20 minutes.

3.4 Off-peak Job Submission

Now that time sharing and interactive programming have become universal, many UNIX users have forgotten one of the best ways to get the most out of the system: running jobs at night or on the weekend. Interactive programmers tend to work from 9 to 5, which is roughly one-third of the day. If you can make use of the other hours (night and weekends), you can almost quadruple your system's throughput. Running jobs at night is less fun than running them interactively, but it is a lot less expensive than three new machines. If you can educate your users in the importance of off-peak hours, you will get a lot more work from your hardware.

There are a few mechanisms to take advantage of off-peak hours. The *at* command lets you submit jobs for execution at an arbitrary later date; it is standard on almost all UNIX systems. The *batch* command, which is available in System V.4 and SunOS 4.1, provides a simple (and simplistic) batch queueing system. Some more fully featured batch systems are available for UNIX systems. We'll mention these in passing but cannot afford the space for a full discussion here.

3.4.1   The at Command

The *at* facility submits a command (or a script) for execution at an arbitrary later time. It has the form:

```
% at options time scriptfile
```

This submits the *scriptfile* for execution at a later *time*. If you don't want to write a script, you can omit it and type your commands on the terminal, terminated by CTRL-D:

```
% at options time
Command 1
Command 2
...
CTRL-D
```

The *time* is most commonly a four-digit number representing a time on a 24-hour clock. For example, 0130 represents 1:30 a.m.; 1400 represents 2 p.m. You can also use abbreviations such as 1am, 130pm, and so on.

If you are using BSD UNIX, the *-c* option tells *at* to execute your script via the C shell; the *-s* option tells *at* to use the Bourne shell.

From time to time, users may need to delete jobs they have submitted incorrectly. Under BSD UNIX, use the *atq* command to find out job numbers for the jobs in the queue; use the *atrm* command to delete them. On System V, use the *at -l* command and option to list the queue and *at -r* to delete jobs. Here's an example of a job submission and deletion using System·V:

```
% at 1635
make biggestprogram
CTRL-D
warning: commands will be executed using /bin/sh
job 643494900.a at Wed May 23 16:35:00 1990
% at -l
643494900.a    Wed May 23 16:35:00 1990
% at -r 643494900.a
```

atq and *at -l* are more important than they seem. They give users a way to decide when to run their jobs. I suggest that users check *atq* before picking a time to run their job. If they don't, you may end up with a dozen huge jobs starting at midnight or 1 a.m. They will bring the system to its knees when there's no one around to help out. Here's an example of what can happen, using the BSD-style *at* commands:

```
% atq
Rank         Execution Date    Owner    Job#    Queue    Job Name
1st     Sep 21, 1990 01:00    mikel    4529     a       trashsys.sh
2nd     Sep 21, 1990 01:00    johnt    4531     a       flame.sh
3rd     Sep 21, 1990 01:00    davek    4532     a       stdin
4th     Sep 21, 1990 01:00    joek     4533     a       troffit
5th     Sep 21, 1990 02:00    bobr     4534     a       stdin
```

Four of the five users happened to pick 1 a.m. as their submission time. Therefore, four big jobs will start in the middle of the night. Will your system survive? Will any of these be done in the morning? These are good questions. If you don't think this scenario is likely, think again. You'll find that a lot of users will submit their jobs to run at 1 a.m., at midnight, or at some other integral number. Nobody is going to start a job at 3:48 a.m. If you notice this situation on your system, use *atrm* (System V: *at -r*) to delete some of the jobs and get the users to reschedule. But you can avoid this problem entirely if you train users to look at the queue before submitting an *at* job.

at takes little administrative effort, if any; however, it does require some attention to education. At most sites, the system administrator or manager is *de facto* responsible for educating the users about UNIX, its tools, and how to do their job most efficiently. No matter what else you do, you will be a successful administrator if you can educate your users effectively.

3.4.2   System V.4 Batch Queues

At many UNIX sites, batch submission systems are considered a thing of the past. This is unfortunate. Batch execution is an effective way to get a lot of work done, particularly in a production-oriented environment. A batch queue is one of the best ways to ensure that a computer remains active during off hours. The *at* command leads to "bursty" execution: you will see a lot of activity at midnight, 1 a.m., 2 a.m., and other popular submission times, trailing off as the jobs complete. A batch queue will keep the system running on an even keel as long as there is work left to do.

System V.4 and SunOS have added a very simple batch queue facility. This facility is really just a variation of the *at* command, except that you can't specify when you want to run the job. The system has a single batch queue, which executes jobs in the order in which they are entered into the queue. Submit a job to the queue with the command:

```
% batch
Command 1
Command 2
CTRL-D
```

If you have written your job as a shell script, you can submit it as:

```
% batch script-name
```

To delete jobs from the queue, use *atq* and *atrm* (SunOS) or *at -l* and *at -r* (V.4).

The queue facility is so simple that it's pathetic: it doesn't support multiple queues, queue priorities, and other features that you really need if you want batch submission. But it will do one important thing. If you can convince your users to use batch queues for their big jobs, they will guarantee that, at most, one large program (whether it is the compiler, an engineering application, or whatever) is running at a time. That may be all you need to restore order to a troubled system.

3.4.3 More Complex Queueing Systems

NQS (*N*etwork *Q*ueueing *S*ystem), an optional feature with some large UNIX systems, is a much more advanced queueing system than the native *batch* command. However, it does the same thing: it prevents congestion by deferring jobs until the system has time to run them.

NQS is a very complicated facility that requires a book in itself. It is being pushed by supercomputer manufacturers (particularly Convex and Cray) who are, by the nature of their business, particularly interested in system performance. Unfortunately, it reeks of what most UNIX users hate: it has hundreds of obscure options and a complex system of priority and permission. It is exactly what you thought you left behind when you were moved from a central data processing facility to a departmental computer or workstation. And that's intentional to some extent. NQS is very useful if you want to put a supercomputer to work 24 hours a day. It's less attractive and probably irrelevant if you are running a network of workstations.

Another queueing system with some adherents in the UNIX community is *mdqs*; I believe it is popular at military installations.

The Task Broker, developed by HP/Apollo, can also implement queueing policies. Unlike NQS, it fits neatly into a network of workstations but probably isn't as effective at managing a large compute-server.

We can't discuss any of these systems thoroughly here. Refer to your system's documentation for more information. Note that queueing systems may not be able to handle programs that use menu systems, graphics, or any modern user interface techniques.

3.5 Shell Time Limits

Have you ever seen a user who runs unreasonably large jobs in the middle of the day, gets everyone mad, and refuses to reform? No? You liar! There are some of these on every shared system. Under BSD UNIX, the C shell (*csh*) supports limits on the amount of CPU time that a job can consume. Unfortunately, it is very easy to get around these limits—but you should know that they exist.

The *limit* command below sets an upper bound on total CPU time:

```
% limit -h cputime time
```

If the *-h* option is not present, UNIX sets the soft limit. When a soft time limit expires, the offending process is sent the signal *SIGXCPU*. This normally kills the program, but the program is allowed to "catch" the signal and attempt to increase its soft limit before dying. If *-h* is present, UNIX sets a hard limit on CPU time. When a process exceeds a hard limit, it is killed without getting a chance to reset the limit. A soft limit can never be greater than a hard limit. The *unlimit* command removes limits.

Use the following notations to express a CPU time limit:

*hours*h	Limit in hours.
*minutes*m	Limit in minutes.
seconds	Limit in seconds (default; no scale factor).
minutes:*seconds*	Limit in minutes and seconds.

For example, the next C shell command limits a job to 200 minutes of CPU time per process:

```
% limit cputime 200m
```

NOTE

If the job spawns more than one process, the limit applies separately to each process; it does not apply to the job as a whole. Each process can consume up to 200 minutes. To place system-wide limits, you may add appropriate *limit* commands to the *.cshrc* initialization files of each user. It is easy for users to circumvent you by changing their initialization file, but at least you can put an obstacle (albeit a small one) in their way.

System V (prior to V.4) and XENIX cannot impose limits on CPU time.

3.6 CPU Capacity

It's a mistake to think that tuning only involves making a system run faster. Tuning also means making sure that your system has enough capacity to handle its workload. As your system gets more users or as you install features like X or NFS, your system has to do more work. It must be able to handle more simultaneous processes, a larger number of files will be open at once, and so on. The UNIX kernel has a number of statically allocated tables that determine the maximum number of processes that can run at once, the maximum number of files that can be open, and so on. From time to time, you may need to adjust these parameters so your system will be able to handle its workload gracefully.

The next few sections discuss the kernel tables and how changing them affects your system's behavior. Memory performance isn't the topic at hand (we'll discuss it in the next chapter), but you should be aware that memory performance and kernel table size interact with each other. As a general rule, increasing these parameters increases the amount of memory the kernel needs. The amount of memory these tables require isn't huge, but it isn't negligible, either. Furthermore, the kernel searches some of these tables linearly, so increasing the table size makes the search slower. Therefore, expanding the kernel tables may lead to slightly worse performance, particularly on a system whose memory is already marginal. The tradeoff should be small, but you should be aware of it. If you need to expand the tables, don't hesitate to do so, but don't make them unnecessarily large. I've seen many administrators double any parameter that seems too small. In many cases, that's appropriate—but this isn't one of them.

3.6.1   What the Basic Kernel Tables Are

Enough abstractions! We need to spend some time talking about the most important tables and what they are. The important tables are common to System V and BSD implementations. Of course, the names have been changed to protect the innocent. To further add to your confusion, System V.4 dynamically manages some of the important tables, so V.4 users don't need to worry about some configuration parameters. First we'll discuss the tables themselves:

Process table   The size of the process table sets the total number of processes that the system can run at any time. This isn't the number of processes per user—it is the absolute total number of processes and, therefore, must account for all users, daemon processes, processes that serve remote users, etc. If the process table overflows, the system will simply refuse to start a new process. On a programming level, the *fork* system call will fail with the error number *EAGAIN*; it's up to the program that calls *fork* to report the error. If it's a user process, you will get an angry visitor. But if the system is trying to start a daemon process when the table overflows, you may never find out about it; you may just notice that the system behaves strangely.

Text table   The size of the text table limits the number of text segments that can be active at one time. Basically, this means the number of different executables that the system can run at once. On most versions of UNIX, different invocations of the same program can share the same text segment. When this table is full, the system will refuse to start a process that requires a new executable. It will print a message on the console.

Region table   Some implementations of System V have a region table instead of a text table. Each UNIX process has at least three regions: text, data, and stack. The text regions can be shared, but the data and stack regions are private. If the table is full, the system will refuse to start a new process and will print a message on the console. The region table is usually roughly three times the size of the process table.

Inode table   The *inode table* is really a cache of active inode entries. An *inode* is a data structure that contains important information about a file. An inode is used for each open pipe, each file or link (symbolic or hard), each current directory of each user, the mount point of each filesystem, and each active I/O device (special file). Performance will suffer when the table is full, but nothing bad will happen. When the inode table is full, you will get a warning message on the console.

System V has complicated the inode table situation. V.3 has two tables controlled by the parameters *NINODE* and *NS5INODE*; these are usually the same size. V.4 has separate inode tables for Berkeley-style (UFS) and System V-style (S5) filesystems.

File table   The size of the file table limits the total number of files that can be open at once, system-wide. There's a close relationship between this table and the inode table, but it's not one-to-one. When the file table is full, the system prints a warning on the console, and the *open* system call will fail with the error number *ENFILE*.

Callout table   The size of the callout table limits the number of timers that can be active at once. Timers are used by all device drivers to determine whether or not an I/O device is responding. When the callout table overflows, the message "Timeout table overflow" is printed on the console and the system crashes.

Character list (clist) table

The size of the *clist* table limits the number of character list structures that are used to buffer terminal I/O. When these buffers overflow, the system starts losing characters that are typed on terminals. You will certainly start getting complaints from users. A BSD system typically needs at least 15 *clist* buffers per terminal. AT&T recommends 5 to 10 *clists* per terminal for System V.

Quota table   If the quota configuration option is included, the quota table defines the number of quota structures. This table should have at least one entry per user per filesystem with quotas enabled. I/O performance suffers when the table overflows but there are no other ill effects. Quotas are supported only for BSD filesystems and UFS filesystems under System V.4.

3.6.2 How These Parameters are Defined

Under BSD UNIX, the sizes of most important kernel parameters are computed from a configuration variable called *maxusers*, which is an estimate of the number of users the system will have to manage. The easiest way to tune these table sizes is to change *maxusers* in your configuration file and let the system do the rest. We'll tell you how to compute an appropriate value below. You can also modify the parameters themselves, if you wish. They are defined in the configuration file *param.c*. Before building a new kernel, edit *param.c* and change these definitions. For System V, these parameters are just constants, defined in a number of system-dependent configuration files. Use your system's configuration utilities to change their values.

The next table shows the name of each configuration constant for BSD and System V versions. It also shows the standard definition of each parameter under BSD UNIX. BSD users, be aware that your vendor may have changed the definition of any parameter. Furthermore, most UNIX versions (and, in particular, SunOS) use *#ifdef* statements to vary the definitions according to whether or not certain options are built into the kernel. Be sure that you modify the right definition.

Table 3-1: Configuration Parameters for Kernel Tables

Table	V.2 Name	V.3 and V.4 Name	BSD Variable	BSD Default Setting
Process	*PROCS*	*NPROC*	*nproc*	20+8*maxusers
Text	*TEXTS*		*ntext*	36+maxusers
Region	*REGIONS*	*NREGION* (V.3)		
Inode	*INODES*	*NINODE*	*ninode*	nproc+80+13*maxusers
BSD Inode		*UFSINODE* (V.4)		
File	*FILES*	*NFILE* (V.3)	*nfile*	16*(nproc+16+maxusers)/10+64
Callout	*CALLS*	*NCALL*	*ncallout*	16+nproc
Character list	*CLISTS*	*NCLIST*	*nclist*	60+12*maxusers
Quota table		*NDQUOT* (V.4)	*ndquot*	ninode+(maxusers*nmount)/4

3.6.3   Some Other Important Definitions

In addition to the table definitions, the following kernel parameters are worth noting:

Processes per user   The total number of processes that any given user is allowed. Note that windowing systems encourage a user to start more processes than simple ASCII terminals. It is easy to create six or seven windows, each of which usually counts as two processes (a terminal emulator and a shell), plus whatever processes are running within the window.

Files per process   The total number of files that a process is allowed to have open at one time.

Mounted filesystems   The total number of filesystems that can be mounted at any time. This includes all remote (RFS or NFS) filesystems. If you use NFS or RFS heavily, you may want to increase this parameter. Using the NFS *automounter* (a facility that mounts remote directories as they are used) will tend to increase further the number of mounted filesystems even further.

These parameters don't affect the kernel's static memory requirement; therefore, reducing them won't free memory. But they shouldn't be extraordinarily large, either. Making these parameters overly large will tend to slow down the system.

For BSD systems, these parameters are defined in the header file *sys/param.h*. To change any parameter, change the header file and build a new kernel. For System V, these parameters are distributed through a number of system-dependent files; use your configuration utilities to change their values. This table shows the names assigned to these parameters. The typical value assumes a moderately large BSD UNIX installation.

Table 3-2: Other Parameters Determining System Capacity

Variable	V.2 Name	V.3 and V.4 Name	BSD Name	Typical Value
Processes per user	*MAXPROC*	*MAXUP*	*MAXUPRC*	25
Files per process		*NOFILES* (V.3)	*NOFILE*	256
Mounted filesystems	*MOUNTS*	*NMOUNT* (V.3)	*NMOUNT*	40

3.6.4 When to Change These Parameters

The common wisdom on performance tuning has been to increase the table sizes whenever you add more memory, so you will be able to support more users efficiently. However, that's not always appropriate. If you don't plan to add more users, there's no good reason make any changes. If you need to support more users, you may want to expand the kernel tables even if you aren't adding more memory. Plugging in a few more terminals and letting the new users bang away at them may get you into trouble.

For BSD UNIX, the easiest way to change these variables is to change the definition of *maxusers* in your configuration file. Here's a simple way to compute an appropriate value:

- Start with 2 to account for basic system daemons.

- Add one for every user, including yourself, that will be simultaneously active.

- Add 1 for every NFS client that boots from your system.

- Add one-half for every NFS client to which you export filesystems, and round up.

Most System V implementations don't provide an equivalent to *maxusers*.* You have to think about what the parameter means, estimate a reasonable value (taking into account network usage), and add a suitably large safety factor. Chapter 8, *Kernel Configuration*, shows typical values for most System V configuration parameters.

3.6.5 The X Window System and Table Size

If your site uses the X window system heavily, you should consider increasing the size of the process table. The process table is particularly important if many of the users are using the X window system via an X terminal or some other kind of remote display. X hurts in two ways. First, it requires processes of its own. Second, it encourages users to open a lot of windows, each of which requires at least two processes and often more (typically a terminal emulator, a shell, and an application). If you have many X users, you should therefore increase both the process table size (the total number of processes) and the per-user process limit. For BSD systems, increase the value of *maxusers* and alter the definition of *MAXUPRC* in the *param.h* header file. You should also increase *maxusers* to account for network filesystem usage. For System V, increase both *NPROC* and *MAXUP*. But don't get carried away. X is memory-intensive and is painfully slow when the system starts swapping, so you don't want to make your kernel too large.

3.6.6 Measuring Table Usage (BSD)

How do you find out whether your tables are too small? The consequences are usually obvious, ranging from irate users in your office, to messages on the console, to a crashed system. Fortunately, there is one method (short of waiting for disaster) that shows you whether your kernel configuration is sufficient. On BSD

---

*At least one System V.3 implementation (Stardent's) provides a *maxusers* equivalent.

UNIX and SunOS, the *pstat -T* command shows you the state of the file, inode, and process tables:

```
% pstat -T
297/963 files
350/644 inodes
115/340 processes
 38/ 92 texts active,   92 used
...Additional information about the paging area...
```

This report was taken from a large, heavily used supercomputer. The file table has 963 entries, of which 297 are in use; there are 644 entries in the inode table, of which 350 are in use; there are 340 entries in the process table, of which 115 are in use; there are 92 entries in the text segment table, of which 38 are currently active. When this report was taken, all of the tables had ample room to handle the current load. However, don't look at one *pstat* report and decide you can reduce your table sizes. While the situation looks good now, it might be completely different in four or five hours. For example, if this report was taken at 8 a.m., we would be concerned. A system running at one-third of its capacity before the day has begun may not make it through noon. Of course, an idle computer isn't doing nothing. It is running many daemons, *gettys* (which will disappear as users log in), and other programs. Before you decide whether the system's kernel tables are large enough, run *pstat -T* at off hours, at peak hours, when the system is running well, when the system is heavily loaded, and so on. Remember that the kernel tables should be large enough to handle your worst-case load with a little room to spare.

Here's a quick shell script that automates the process:

```
# !/bin/sh
# Show maximum table usage; invoke as % scriptname interval
pstat=/usr/etc/pstat                    # set path correctly for
                                        # your system
while true
do
  $pstat -T | sed -e 's/\//\ /g'  # change / to space; easier
                                        # for awk
  sleep $1                              # rest for an interval
done |  awk '                           # awk reports maximum table usage
/files/{ if ($1 > files) {             # test for maximum usage and
              files = $1                # report it when it happens
              print "max files ", files, "out of ", $2, "or", \
                 100*files/$2,"percent"}
        }
/inodes/{ if ($1 > inodes) {
              inodes = $1
              print "max inodes", inodes, "out of ", $2, "or", \
                 100*inodes/$2,"percent" }
        }
/processes/{ if ($1 > processes) {
```

```
                   processes = $1
                   print "max procs ",processes, "out of ", $2, "or", \
                      100*processes/$2,"percent" }
             }
/texts/{ if ($1 > texts) {
                   texts = $1
                   print "max active texts ", texts, "out of ", $2, "or", \
                      100*texts/$2,"percent" }
          }' -
```

This script runs *pstat* at regular intervals, specified by the first argument. It then uses *awk* to report the maximum usage for each table, both as an absolute number and as a percentage of the table size. It's easy to imagine many improvements: for example, taking a fixed number of samples at a specified interval and making one report when the samples are all finished. Furthermore, I have observed a lot of minor differences between *pstat* reports on different BSD systems, so you may have to customize this script for your site. But this script will get you started. Letting this program run for a day or so should tell you how large the crucial tables have to be.

Unfortunately, there's no way to discover whether the character list and callout tables are close to capacity.

3.6.7 Measuring Table Usage (System V)

Under System V, the *-v* option to *sar* provides similar information. Here's a typical report:

```
% sar -v
ora ora 3.2 2 i386     05/21/90

00:00:01 proc-sz ov inod-sz ov file-sz ov lock-sz
01:00:03  62/170   0 163/500  0 132/500  0   0/100
02:00:02  67/170   0 171/500  0 135/500  0   0/100
03:00:01  58/170   0 155/500  0 121/500  0   0/100
...
23:00:01  59/170   0 160/500  0 133/500  0   0/100
```

The columns in this report show:

proc-sz   The size of the process table.

inod-sz   The size of the inode table.

file-sz   The size of the open file table.

lock-sz   The size of the file-locking region table.

ov   Overflow: the number of times the table to the left has exceeded its capacity. The overflow fields should always be zero on a healthy system.

The first line of this report shows the table statistics as of three seconds past 1 a.m. At this time, the process table had 170 slots, of which 62 were in use; the inode table had 500 slots, of which 163 were in use; and so on. None of these tables suffered an overflow during the 24-hour period that this report covers: all of the ov fields are zero.

By scanning a day's activity (or even better, reports for a few consecutive days), you can quickly see when peak activity occurred and how much breathing room you had at these peak times. If an overflow field (the ov column) is ever nonzero, the table to the left is too small; you need to rebuild your kernel.

3.6.8 Time Slice (System V)

Here's one last CPU-related kernel parameter. It doesn't fit with any of the system capacity parameters, but it provides an important element of control over your system's dynamic behavior. Many System V implementations let you adjust the *time slice*, which is the maximum amount of time that a process can run without being rescheduled. This parameter has been called *TSLICE*, in some V.2 implementations, *MAXSLICE* in 386/ix and many other V.3 implementations, and *MAXQUANTUM* in at least one V.3 implementation that I've seen (Stardent's). Some implementations (Stardent's, at least) have a system call that lets programs running as root adjust their own time slice.

How does the time slice work? The scheduler processes run for up to *time-slice* clock ticks, where the length of a tick is 1/100 of a second for virtually all System V implementations. During its time slice, a process can go to sleep of its own accord or wait for some I/O operation to complete. When this happens, the scheduler chooses another process to run and rewards the sleeping process by increasing its priority. Processes that are CPU-bound (i.e., it doesn't sleep or do very much I/O) usually use up their entire time slice without stopping. When this happens, the scheduler selects another process to run (conceivably the same one, if the system isn't very busy) and lowers the CPU-bound process's priority.

Adjusting the time slice can have a significant effect on your system's behavior if you run a lot of CPU-bound processes. Increasing the time slice will lower the scheduling overhead and make the system slightly more efficient; the system does a little more real work and spends less time worrying about scheduling. In exchange, you get slightly poorer interactive performance: it is harder for interactive processes to get hold of the CPU. If the system doesn't run many CPU-bound processes, changing the time slice won't have much of an effect. In this situation, few processes are running to the end of their time slice, so changing it won't alter the system's behavior.

On most systems, the time slice is about 1 second. Reasonable values range from 30 milliseconds (three clock ticks) to a few seconds, although you can usually adjust the time slice over a much wider range. Of course, with a very large time slice, interactive performance is likely to be very uneven. Single-user systems tolerate long time slices much better than shared systems, if for no other reason that that you're more likely to accept uneven performance if you're the one causing it.

Because real-time processes have been added, V.4 has a much more flexible and complex mechanism for setting the time slice. The time slice can be changed on a per-priority (and even per-process) basis. See Appendix A, *Real-time Processes in System V.4*, for a discussion of the V.4 scheduler.

BSD systems don't let you control the time slice. If there are any exceptions to this rule, they have to do with manufacturer-specific features.

4

Memory Performance

Paging and Swapping
How to Tell if Your System is Paging
Conserving Memory
Tuning the Paging Algorithm
Managing the Swap Area
Computing Memory Requirements

The memory subsystem becomes the limiting factor for system performance when the programs that are actively running (including the UNIX kernel) require more physical memory than is available. Past this point the operating system begins copying pages of memory to and from disk. After copying one or more pages from physical memory to disk, the system gets to reuse that physical memory for some other purpose. This is called *paging*. Once paging has started, overall performance drops sharply until the system's memory requirements are again within its capacity. Up to this point (i.e., before the system is out of memory), memory is not a system performance issue. In other words, memory performance is binary. Either the system has enough memory for its current needs and performance is good or the system doesn't have enough memory and performance is poor.

Memory performance problems are simple: at any given instant, either you have enough memory or you don't. However, this summary doesn't do justice to the complexity of memory management nor does it help you to deal with problems as they arise. To provide the background to understand these problems, we need to discuss virtual memory activity in more detail.

After a general introduction to virtual memory activity, we will discuss what you can do to find out whether or not you are paging, what you can do to conserve memory, some kernel changes that might improve the behavior of the paging algorithm, how to manage your swap area on the disk, and how to predict a system's overall memory needs.

4.1 Paging and Swapping

Modern operating systems use two mechanisms to make sure they can meet the system's memory requirements: *paging* and *swapping*. Swapping moves entire processes to disk in order to reclaim memory. The next time the system runs the process, it has to copy the process's entire memory image from the disk's swap area back into memory. All UNIX systems implement some kind of swapping. Paging moves individual pages of processes to disk and reclaims their memory. Most of the process can remain in memory. The paging algorithm keeps track of when each page was last used and tries to keep pages that were used recently in physical memory. By doing so, it may be able to move part of a process out of memory without hurting its performance at all. Most UNIX systems (BSD, System V.3, System V.4) practice paging in addition to swapping, which requires significantly less I/O traffic and gives finer control over the system's memory. XENIX and some System V.2 implementations only perform swapping, although some V.2 systems provide paging as an option. On systems that perform paging and swapping, swapping occurs in two situations:

- Swapping is often a part of normal housekeeping. Jobs that sleep for more than 20 seconds are considered "idle" and may be swapped out at any time, just to keep them from cluttering the system's memory. On BSD systems, *ps* typically shows many idle and swapped-out jobs.

- Swapping is also an emergency technique used to combat extreme memory shortages. This is called *desperation swapping*.

When do swapping and paging become problems? It depends on exactly what processes or pages the system is moving to disk. When paging begins, the system is moving pieces of active processes to disk in order to prevent the available memory from dropping below some threshold. Paging doesn't present a problem as long as the UNIX kernel does a good job of picking infrequently used pages to move to disk. An entire program doesn't need to be in memory whenever it runs; only the parts of the program that are in use need to be present. Since most programs spend 80 percent of their time executing 20 percent of their code (a surprisingly accurate rule of thumb), paging can often take place without damaging a program's performance at all. However, performance always degrades when paging begins. The degradation is small at first and may even be unnoticeable, but performance will drop sharply if the system's memory requirements don't fall back into line.

Desperation swapping indicates that the system has a more severe memory shortage, which is probably hurting other aspects of system performance. When swapping, the system moves entire processes to disk. This is relatively slow and requires a lot of disk overhead. To reduce the overhead, and to minimize the probability that a process that has just been swapped-out will need to be swapped-in in the immediate future, the swapping algorithm tries to avoid active processes. Even under desperation swapping, active processes are the last to go. But what processes are likely to be inactive most of the time? The processes you depend on most: shells, editors, almost everything that responds directly to the keyboard. These are commonly victims of swapping. Therefore, when desperation swapping begins, interactive performance goes to pieces. You may pause for a few seconds to think about a command and, in those seconds, your shell will be swapped out. When you type the next keystroke, your shell must make the long trip from disk back to memory (a trip made longer because the disk subsystem is probably under heavy load) before it can even echo the characters you have typed.

Paging and swapping prevent the system from crashing for lack of memory, but they can't solve the basic problem: they can't make more memory appear out of nowhere. Further, the situation degrades if users continue to submit new jobs at the same rate. The load average increases because the system can't process jobs as quickly, and I/O performance drops because the disks are busy handling paging requests. Memory overload quickly becomes I/O and CPU overload. You can live with moderate paging, but desperation swapping is often intolerable. We will show you how to configure your system so that swapping is extremely rare—but, in return, more paging will be done.

4.2 How to Tell if Your System is Paging

A confusing miscellany of tools report paging and swapping activity. For BSD UNIX and XENIX, *vmstat* (in several different flavors) gives the information you need. For System V, look at the reports from *sar*. Whichever tools you use, you will get information about:

- *page-ins*, or pages moved from disk to memory.
- *page-outs*, or pages moved from memory to disk.

- *swap-ins*, or processes moved from disk to memory.
- *swap-outs*, or processes moved from memory to disk.

If your system performs "demand paging," there is a complication you have to be aware of. All UNIX systems except for XENIX and some System V.2 implementations support demand paging. Demand paging means that UNIX uses the paging mechanism to get a new process running. Remember that a process can run without being entirely in memory; the kernel sets up its memory maps appropriately and lets the paging mechanism move pages back and forth between disk and memory as they are needed. Demand paging takes this a step further. Rather than copy the entire program into memory and execute it, the kernel only sets up its memory maps. It then jumps to the program's starting address, which isn't in memory. This causes a page fault, which in turn causes the paging mechanism to bring the first page of the executable from disk. The program is brought into memory one page at a time, on an "as-needed" basis.

Therefore, page-in activity is happening all the time: this is how processes get started. It is completely normal and has nothing to do with memory shortage. Likewise, the process of starting a process, whether or not you have demand paging, is indistinguishable from a swap-in. Therefore, swap-in activity doesn't give you any useful information. To find out whether or not your system is suffering a memory shortage, you have to look at page-out and swap-out activity.

Opinions differ on how many page-outs you should consider excessive. To a large extent this depends on how your system reacts under load and what kind of performance you consider acceptable. Occasional page-out activity is normal; paging is a great mechanism for handling occasional peaks in memory demand. If your system is paging most of the time, your performance is suffering whether or not you have noticed it. There's a more practical way to look at this problem, though: what is your system doing when performance is noticeably bad? If you see paging activity every time someone complains about performance, you've found your problem. Don't even worry about how much paging is acceptable — worry about whether or not the complaints are serious enough to merit immediate action.

For swapping, look at the swap-out activity, if your system reports it. Both swap-out and swap-in activity are common. But if you see substantial bursts of swap-out activity while your system is paging, you can bet that desperation swapping is taking place. Desperation swapping indicates that your system is experiencing severe memory shortages and that you have memory problems you should investigate.

4.2.1 Using vmstat

Under BSD UNIX or XENIX, *vmstat* provides the most accurate way to determine whether or not page-outs are occurring. There are three ways to invoke *vmstat*:

% **vmstat**	*One report, showing averages*
% **vmstat** *per*	*Produce an infinite series of reports,*
	at intervals of per seconds
% **vmstat** *per num*	*Produce num reports,*
	at intervals of per seconds

No matter how you invoke *vmstat*, the first report *vmstat* displays is an attempt to show averages since the system was booted. These aren't really meaningful and probably aren't reliable. Always discard the first line of data you get. This means that the *vmstat* command with no arguments is next to useless. The only report it gives provides data you can't trust.

The other ways to invoke *vmstat* provide a series of reports, taken at regular intervals. Five seconds is a good sampling interval. These reports provide a wealth of information about the virtual memory system:

```
% vmstat 5 20
 procs     memory              page            faults                cpu
 r b w    avm    fre re a   p po fr de sr  d0 d1 d2  in  sy   cs us sy id
 0 0 0 39168 11904 0   0    5 1  2  0  0   5  0  1   37 113  40 7 13 80
 ...
 0 0 0 45792  11904   0   0 0  0  0  0  0   0  0  0    5  29   3 0  1 99
```

The most interesting fields in this report are:

r   The number of runnable processes during the interval. It does not include processes that are waiting for I/O or "sleeping" of their own accord.

b   The number of processes that are blocked waiting for high-speed I/O or some other external event. If your system consistently has a large number of blocked processes, you may have disk throughput problems. Processes waiting for terminal I/O aren't counted.

w   The number of runnable processes that have been swapped out. If this field is nonzero, swapping is occurring: your system is suffering from a serious memory shortage.

avm   The total amount of active virtual memory. I have never seen any use for this statistic. SunOS 4.0 and 4.1 do not compute it and always put 0 into this field.

fre   The number of pages currently on the free list; the amount of physical memory, in kilobytes, that is not currently allocated to a process or the I/O buffer cache.

pi The number of 1-KB pages per second that have been paged in. This field is often nonzero. It is particularly significant because it includes page-ins that result from starting a new process.

po The number of 1-KB pages per second that have been paged out since the last report. If the number of page-outs is consistently zero, you have no memory problems. If the number of page-outs is significantly greater than zero for several intervals, system performance is suffering. UNIX always reports page-outs in terms of 1-KB pages, regardless of the system's actual page size.

de The "anticipated short-term memory shortfall." I have never seen a report in which this field was nonzero. If it is nonzero, you have an extremely severe memory shortage. The system is certainly performing desperation swapping.

d0, d1, d2 The number of disk operations per second on each disk drive.

sy There are two columns labeled **sy**. The rightmost column reports the percentage of total CPU time spent in the system state.

us The percentage of total CPU time spent in the user state.

id The percentage of total CPU time that the CPU is idle.

By far, the most important columns are **po** (page-outs) and **s** (the number of swapped-out processes). Looking at these tells you at a glance whether your system is paging and swapping. If you want a finer picture of how memory is reacting, watch the **fre** column. You will see paging begin when the free memory crosses a threshold given by the configuration parameter *LOTSFREE*. When the system crosses another threshold, *DESFREE*, desperation swapping begins. Both these parameters are defined in *vmparam.h* and are discussed later in this chapter.

The other statistics (percent idle time, number of runnable and blocked processes, and so on) aren't as important but will help you to decide whether or not your system is healthy. Under a reasonably heavy load, you should see roughly 70 percent "user" time, 30 percent "system" time, and only 1 or 2 percent idle time. The exact ratio of user time to system time depends entirely on the programs you are running, though, and is extremely variable. Under light loads, the system will spend a lot of its time idle. However, if the load average is high and the system is spending a lot of idle time, you should look for problems—most likely in the I/O subsystem.

4.2.2 Some Examples

Now that we've seen the report, let's look at some examples taken from real systems. These examples will show you what to expect under different loads. The system in question was a supercomputer with 64 MB of memory. Because the system was so large, *LOTSFREE* was set fairly high: somewhere over 2 MB. A more typical value for a workstation or a small system would be 256 KB or 512 KB. Consequently, this supercomputer starts paging when there's still a lot of free memory left. Otherwise, the results are similar to what you might see on a typical workstation. We took the report below when the system was moderately loaded (load average roughly 2.5) and running acceptably well:

procs			memory				page			faults				cpu				
r	b	w	avm	fre	re	at	pi	po	...	d0	d1	d2	in	sy	cs	us	sy	id
1	3	0	126080	2360	0	0	184	0	...	34	0	2	73	254	84	20	35	46
4	0	0	117576	2080	0	0	72	0	...	4	0	2	63	287	95	64	35	1
5	0	0	104760	2064	0	0	80	0	...	11	0	2	64	235	113	56	38	6
1	2	0	93160	2048	0	0	48	0	...	5	0	0	57	246	124	60	40	0
1	1	0	84600	2560	0	0	8	0	...	5	0	0	51	193	91	67	31	2
1	2	0	88744	2528	0	0	0	0	...	9	0	2	63	128	63	67	33	1
2	1	0	80320	2424	0	0	0	0	...	2	0	0	51	140	72	65	34	1
0	2	0	79856	2192	0	0	120	0	...	21	0	0	61	138	78	44	33	22

Page-ins are occurring almost constantly, indicating that users are starting a lot of new jobs. Consequently, almost all of the paging activity is on the root filesystem (*d0*), where the standard system executable files are located. No page-outs take place during this period, indicating that virtual memory usage is not an issue. The system spends a fair amount of time servicing system calls. The CPU spends some of its time idle. Together with the number of blocked processes, this suggests that there are some disk performance problems. However, given these statistics, we would consider this system healthy. There are no glaring problems that require immediate attention.

Here is a report from a more heavily loaded system:

procs			memory				page			faults				cpu				
r	b	w	avm	fre	re	at	pi	po	...	d0	d1	d2	in	sy	cs	us	sy	id
3	0	0	99200	5440	0	0	0	0	...	4	0	1	5	20	8	93	7	0
4	0	0	105568	5088	0	0	64	0	...	10	0	1	23	30	35	91	9	0
2	3	0	118176	3040	6	0	128	416	...	3	7	2	43	28	57	81	19	0
4	1	0	128128	2144	11	0	0	160	...	2	1	0	12	19	13	97	3	0
4	1	0	123808	2112	4	0	0	96	...	1	1	0	7	18	8	99	1	0
4	1	0	107520	2080	3	0	0	32	...	1	1	0	4	15	5	99	1	0
3	2	0	103296	1952	15	0	256	224	...	5	16	1	23	16	29	91	9	0
2	3	0	104000	1472	15	0	448	384	...	3	20	1	33	16	42	94	6	0
4	1	0	104512	1792	8	0	288	192	...	4	6	1	23	15	32	92	8	0
2	3	0	105184	1952	4	0	96	128	...	0	2	1	14	15	17	98	2	0
3	2	0	106688	1952	7	0	256	224	...	4	4	12	29	21	39	91	9	0
4	2	0	104672	6240	4	0	384	32	...	3	1	3	32	75	51	82	18	0

```
4 1 1 123232 5248  1  0 256    0 ...  8  1  0 34 159   51 76 24  0
2 3 0 105184 1952  4  0  96 128 ...   0  2  1 14  15   17 98  2  0
```

When we took this snapshot, the load average was roughly 5. The command *ps -au* reveals that several memory-intensive programs were running (several compilations); we'll give that report shortly. Page-outs begin as the size of the free list approaches 2 MB and continue until the free list is again over 2 MB. The users are still getting most of the CPU's time (no idle time, generally low system time), and the number of blocked processes remains small. Disk activity is fairly evenly distributed. This system is obviously under a very heavy load, but at first glance it appears to be surviving fairly well.

However, one aspect of this report is very troubling. The second to the last line shows one swapped-out job (the **w** column is 1). Because the sampling interval is fairly long relative to the speed of the CPU, it is very rare to see swapped-out jobs at all. Could this mean that desperation swapping is taking place? Yes. Note what else happens at roughly the same time. The free list suddenly jumps from about 2 MB to over 6 MB, and we see a jump in the amount of system-state time. It's a good guess that this means a large job has been swapped-out to solve a severe memory shortage. I would guess that some swapping is also going on roughly in the middle of the report, where another jump in system time occurs, but this isn't as clear.

The first few lines from *ps -au* show the workload responsible for this situation:

```
% ps -au | more
USER        PID %CPU %MEM    SZ    RSS TT STAT TIME COMMAND
bart       7266 27.8 14.6 10464   8800 p2 D    0:04 fcom ...
research   6680 22.7 22.0 40000  13248 p3 R    2:39 ccom ...
arnolds    7259 22.7  3.1  2784   1824 p5 R    0:10 ccom ...
howard     7217 22.6 17.4 13152  10464 p9 R    0:23 fcom ...
myself     7267 17.7  2.2  2272   1280 p8 R    0:00 ps -au ...
myself     7268  4.4  0.8  1344    416 p8 S    0:00 more ...
bart       7265  0.7  1.0   544    512 p2 S    0:00 rfc ...
bart       5346  0.4  2.3  1536   1312 p2 S    0:52 make...
```

This report shows at least four compiler invocations (*fcom* and *ccom* are parts of the FORTRAN and C compilers, invoked as *cc* and *f77*). The total amount of virtual memory required for the data and stack segments for these four processes (i.e., the sum of their **SZ** fields) is roughly 64 MB, which is the memory capacity of this particular system. It is no wonder, then, that the system has started paging, and it wouldn't be at all surprising if the system has started swapping.

If this kind of memory activity is the exception rather than the rule, you might not want to take any action. If repeated invocations of *vmstat* at different times reveal that this report is typical, you should take some action to reduce paging activity: add memory, reduce the number of filesystem buffers, or restrict memory traffic. Ways of implementing these options are described later.

4.2.3 Watching vmstat Automatically

It is a genuine pain to watch *vmstat* intently, waiting to see paging activity. Here's a script that watches the page-out field for you. It takes an infinite series of *vmstat* reports, and checks the **po** field from each. If there are more than *limit* consecutive reports for which **po** is nonzero, the script starts letting the data get through to standard output. Otherwise, it is silent. You can run this script in the background, trusting it to inform you when any serious paging activity is taking place.

```
interval=5          # interval between vmstat reports
limit=3             # warn after 3 nonzero po's
vmstat $interval | awk "
NR==2      { print \$0 }
NR <= 3    { next }  # throw out initial trash
NF != 22   { next }  # field overflow--discard (should warn)
/avm/      { next }  # discard intermediate headers
           # count consecutive nonzero page-outs; notify by printing
           # the vmstat line if more than $limit (consecutive)
           # are nonzero
           { if (\$9 > 0) { npo++ }            # page-out nonzero
             if (npo > $limit) { print \$0 }   # notify user
             if (\$9 == 0) {npo = 0}           # reset
           }"
```

This tool could be augmented in many ways. If you use *nawk*, you could modify it to label each report with the time. On some systems, you may need to take "field overflow" into account: the possibility that one field from *vmstat*'s output will get so large that it will overflow into another. Note that this script, or any script of this type, has a big drawback. *awk* is a big program that takes a lot of memory to run. Therefore, running this script loads your memory system significantly and may contribute to the problems you are trying to observe.

4.2.4 Sun vmstat

Now that you've heard the theme, let's look at the variations. SunOS 4.0 has added a -*S* option to *vmstat* that will report swapping statistics directly. If you run *vmstsat* -*S*, you will see the number of swap-ins and swap-outs. Swap-outs should always be zero unless your system is seriously short of memory. They start to happen if the amount of memory available drops below *DESFREE* (the desperation swapping threshold). Here's a report from a Sun 3/60 that is extremely short of memory:

```
% vmstat -S 5
 procs   memory         page            faults        cpu
 r b w avm fre si so  pi po ...  s0 s1 s2  in  sy  cs us sy id
 3 0 0   0 192 11 27   6  3 ...   2  0  0   7  24  10  2  3 95
```

```
 0  9 0    0 192   2   6 136 80 ... 32   0   0 234 125   83 36 42 22
 1  7 0    0 152   0   0 144 96 ... 28   0   0 210 115   92 41 40 19
010  0     0 192   0   1 152 80 ... 30   0   0 180 108  106 44 40 16
 1  8 1    0 224   2   1 152 64 ... 32   0   0 208 105  129 51 36 14
212  0     0 192   4   1 160 72 ... 29   0   0 236  77  172 40 36 24
 0  9 0    0 176   1   1 152 48 ... 29   0   0 365 120  158 42 41 16
 2  5 0    0 200   0   1 144 80 ... 29   0   0 219  81  121 63 33  4
```

Ignoring the first line (which reports unreliable averages), we see that this system is constantly paging. We also see continuous swapping. Furthermore, although as many as 14 jobs are runnable at once, the number of blocked jobs is large, and the CPU is spending a lot of idle time. This system is in serious trouble.

By the way, this report demonstrates why we were so suspicious about a single paging event on our heavily loaded supercomputer. Although the Sun workstation is clearly swapping its brains out, *vmstat* only reports one swapped-out process, slightly below the middle of the report. This happens to coincide with a jump in the free list, from 192 KB to 224 KB. On the supercomputer, *vmstat* couldn't isolate swapping activity. Therefore, when the w column showed a swapped-out process, we started to play detective. If your system can't report swapping activity explicitly, you must learn to look for its symptoms.

4.2.5 XENIX vmstat

XENIX provides a *vmstat* command, but its output is a lot different. Here's some output from a XENIX system:

```
% vmstat 5
       procs              paging              system           cpu
   r  b  w  si  so  ch  cm ffr swr sww ...  pf   in   sy  cs  us su id
   1 24  0   0   0   2   0   0   0   0 ...  32   56   62  18   0 10 90
   1 24  0   0   0   0   0   0   0   0 ...  30   53   56  26   0  8 92
   1 24  0   0   0   0   0   0   0   0 ...  21   65   37  20   0 10 90
   1 24  0   0   0   0   0   0   0   0 ...  11  120   24   8   0  5 95
  13 34  0   0   0  28   0   0   0   0 ... 195  254  263  55   8 41 51
  13 34  0   0   0  10   0   0   0   0 ... 188   31  266  30  77 23  0
  12 35  0   0   0   1   0   0   0   0 ...  83   60  212  22  84 16  0
   9 38  0   0   0   0   0   0   0   0 ...  61   42  226  13  86 14  0
   7 40  0   0   0   0   0   0   0   0 ...  52   84  207  35  86 13  1
```

While we were taking this report, we started a large number of jobs to try and swamp the system. It's pretty obvious when we did this: the number of running processes (the leftmost columns) jumps suddenly in the fifth line. We were only partially successful. We noticed some disk I/O problems but failed to force the system into paging.

Here is an explanation of the most important fields from the report:

r, w, b   The number of processes currently runnable, blocked, and swapped out. These fields are similar to their equivalents in BSD's *vmstat* except that processes waiting for terminal input are considered blocked. For example, the beginning of this report shows 24 blocked processes. An analysis of *ps* (which we won't repeat here) would show that some of these processes are waiting for terminal input. When we start a large number of processes, the number of runnable processes and the number of blocked processes increases. The increase in blocked processes reflects two factors: some of the new processes are waiting for input, but some are waiting to access the disk.

si   The number of processes that were swapped in during the last interval.

so   The number of processes that were swapped out during the last interval. Under XENIX, this figure will be zero unless the system does not have enough memory to satisfy its needs and performance is suffering.

swr   The number of pages read from the swap area.

sww   The number of pages written to the swap area. **sww** is zero during normal operation (i.e., when enough memory is available to run all the processes). If it is nonzero, performance is suffering.

XENIX doesn't perform paging, so there are no columns for page-in or page-out activity. The crucial columns to watch are **so** and **sww**. If these columns are consistently nonzero, your system is spending a lot of time swapping. You don't have enough memory.

4.2.6 Memory Statistics (System V.3)

If you are running some version of System V other than XENIX, you must use *sar* to gather virtual memory statistics. The command *sar -r* shows how much free memory is available. Here is a sample:

```
ora ora 3.2 2 i386    05/21/90

00:00:01 freemem freeswp
02:00:02      89   77392
04:00:01      91   77392
06:00:00     101   77392
```

```
08:00:00      101     77392
08:40:00       83     77392
09:20:01       75     77392
```

The **freemem** column reports how much free memory is available, in pages. System V UNIX starts paging when the free memory drops below the configuration constant *GPGSLO*. Paging then continues until the number of free blocks passes *GPGSHI*. These are called the memory "low-water" and "high-water" marks, respectively. On 386/ix systems, *GPGSLO* and *GPGSHI* default to 25 and 40 blocks. This system is close to paging but isn't yet in trouble. Later in this chapter, we'll discuss how to adjust these configuration parameters.

To look directly at swapping statistics, look at *sar -w*. Here is a report taken from a 386/ix system that is reasonably heavily used but far from having memory problems:

```
% sar -w
ora ora 3.2 2 i386     05/21/90

02:00:01 swpin/s bswin/s swpot/s bswot/s pswch/s
03:00:01   0.00    0.0    0.00    0.0      34
04:00:01   0.00    0.0    0.00    0.0      31
05:00:02   0.00    0.0    0.00    0.0      31
06:00:00   0.00    0.0    0.00    0.0      20
07:00:00   0.01    0.1    0.00    0.0      19
08:00:00   0.01    0.1    0.00    0.0      19
Average    0.01    0.1    0.00    0.0      32
```

The columns in this report show:

swpin/s   The average number of swapping transfers into memory per second during the interval. This includes demand paging activity. Demand paging and swap-in activity are normal. They are not signs of memory problems.

bswin/s   The average number of 512-byte blocks transferred into memory per second.

swpot/s   The average number of swap-outs per second during the interval. This should be zero.

bswot/s   The average number of 512-byte blocks swapped out of memory per second. This should be zero.

pswch/s   The number of process switches per second during the interval.

To see paging activity, look at *sar -p*. Systems V.3 and V.4 have different versions of this report. We show the V.3 version:

```
% sar -p
ora ora 3.2 2 i386     05/21/90
```

00:00:01	vflt/s	pflt/s	pgfil/s	rclm/s
01:00:03	2.60	2.94	0.20	0.00
02:00:02	2.53	2.72	0.24	0.00
03:00:01	3.00	3.42	0.21	0.00
04:00:01	2.45	2.75	0.17	0.00
05:00:02	2.01	2.34	0.16	0.00
06:00:00	0.58	0.73	0.04	0.00

The columns in this report show:

vflt/s The number of address translation faults per second. Address translation faults occur when a process references a valid page that isn't in memory. Translation faults occur when a process references a page that has been paged-out during demand paging and in other situations. The kernel has many ways of resolving address translation faults, depending on the exact situation. For 386/ix systems, AT&T suggests that an address fault rate greater than 15 per second indicates a memory shortage. This criterion is a rather indirect way to look at paging, but it is appropriate. It is saying that if processes reference paged-out memory very often, the system is short of memory. This is exactly what you need to know. After all, you don't really care if the swapping daemon is forcing only inactive pages to disk; swapping out pages that aren't used often won't hurt performance. Swapping out pages that will only be swapped back in will hurt performance.

pflt/s The number of page faults per second. Page faults occur when a process references an invalid page. They are normally a consequence of "copy on write" activity and don't have anything to do with system tuning.

pgfil/s The number of address translation faults that were satisfied by a page-in (essentially, the number of page-ins per second).

rclm/s The average number of "page reclaims" per second. This is the number of pages that have been "reclaimed" and added to the free list by page-out activity. It should be zero.

By using *sar -w* and *sar -p*, users of System V.3 can get a fairly good idea of how the memory system is holding up. If *sar -p* shows that page reclaims are zero and that the address translation fault rate is satisfactorily low and if *sar -w* shows that swap-outs are zero, you have nothing to worry about. If the system is doing a significant amount of swapping or paging, you have memory problems. Either add memory, configure your kernel to use less memory, or start thinking about ways to conserve memory. We'll discuss the latter two strategies later.

4.2.7 Memory Statistics (System V.4)

System V.4 has greatly improved memory management. With these improvements come several new *sar* reports and a few changes in the old reports. The *sar* -*r* command, which told you how much memory was free at any time, has remained unchanged, as has the basic paging algorithm. The *sar* -*g* command, which is new, provides exactly what you need to understand your system's paging behavior:

```
% sar -g
ora ora 4.0 2 i386     05/21/90

00:00:01 pgout/s ppgout/s pgfree/s pgscan/s %s5ipf
01:00:03   0.00     0.0     0.42     1.2     2.00
02:00:02   1.11     3.4     4.39     5.6     0.00
```

The columns in this report are:

pgout/s   The average number of page-out requests per second during the interval. In other words, this is the number of times the memory management subsystem decided it was short of memory and needed to free memory. Ideally, this should be zero. In the second sample period shown above, the system has started paging.

ppgout/s   The average number of pages per second that were paged out. More than one page may be paged out in a single operation, so this field is generally greater than **pgout/s**.

pgfree/s   The average number of pages per second that were added to the free list by the "page-stealing" daemon. In other words, this is the average number of pages the system has forcibly freed. If this is significantly nonzero (AT&T suggests greater than 5), the page-stealing daemon is spending a lot of time trying to reclaim memory. This may indicate that you are short of memory.

pgscan/s   The average number of pages the page-stealing daemon had to scan in order to find more memory. Again, AT&T suggests that values greater than 5 indicate your system is short of memory.

%s5ipf/s   The percentage of inodes from old-style (System V) filesystems that were taken off the free list. It should be less than 10 percent. If it is greater, reconfigure the kernel with more inodes in its old-style (System V) filesystems.

As you've probably noticed, we're wary of pronouncements like "You should worry if such-and-such is greater than 5." The actual threshold depends on your system and, even more, on how much of its time the system spends over that threshold. Furthermore, gathering data from many reports will give you a much better picture than any single report can. If *sar* -*g* looks suspicious, compare its results with *sar -p*. The report differs slightly from the V.3 report we discussed above, but **vflt/s** is still there. Again, AT&T suggests that this should be under 15. Then see whether or not swapping activity (*-w*) is also significant, see whether or not the system is heavily loaded (*-u* and *-q*), see how much memory is free (*-r*), and see whether or not the page daemon is taking a lot of CPU time (by looking at *ps -el*).

4.2.8   A System V Example

System V provides a lot of different data about memory performance, but it's hard to tie it all together. Here's an example, taken from a 386/ix system, that shows how these reports work together. We started the command *sar -rwp 20 20* to take 20 samples of memory usage at 20-second intervals. The reports show free memory, swapping statistics, and paging statistics. After we started the sample, we started a number of big jobs. Here are the results:

```
% more sar-rwp.out

bronson bronson 3.2 2 i386      09/22/90

09:41:18 freemem freeswp
         swpin/s bswin/s swpot/s bswot/s pswch/s
         vflt/s  pflt/s  pgfil/s  rclm/s
09:41:58     192   27800
            0.00     0.0    0.00     0.0       3
            0.00    0.00    0.00    0.00
09:42:08     158   27800
            0.10     0.8    0.00     0.0      23
           13.10    6.40    6.50    0.00
09:42:18      32   27552
            1.70    13.6    3.50    28.0      33
           15.60    1.60    8.20   12.80
09:42:28      26   27264
            6.27    50.1    6.27    50.1      41
           22.59    8.56    4.68   23.18
09:42:38      39   27328
            3.22    25.7    0.70     5.6      34
           17.49   18.29    6.83    5.23
...
09:43:08      60   26944
            2.50    20.0    0.80     6.4      20
           11.30   12.70    2.90    2.20
09:43:18     142   27064
            1.60    12.8    0.00     0.0       8
            3.00    1.80    0.70    0.00
...
```

sar's habit of interleaving the reports is ungainly, but it does keep the interesting statistics together. When we first started sampling, there were 192 pages of free memory and no swapping or paging activity: free memory was well above the low-water mark. After we started several big jobs, the amount of memory decreased. At its low point there were only 26 pages of memory in the free list. As free memory dropped and dipped below the low-water mark, we saw both swapping and paging start. The **swpot/s** was as high as 6.27 (6.27 swaps per second), while the **rclm/s** field jumped to 23.18 (23 pages added to the free list by paging). The number of address translation faults (**vflt/s**) was also high, showing that programs are referencing a lot of paged-out memory. **pswch/s** also grew, showing that the system was switching between several different processes. This statistic isn't really interesting, although it is a measure of the system's load.

Swapping and paging continued for several intervals, during which the system's response was noticeably slow. As the big jobs terminated, the number of free pages grew. As free memory increased, swapping and paging decreased and, by the end of the series of reports, had practically ceased.

As we've said previously, the question isn't: "Can you observe your system doing this?" You can force any system to swap or page. And almost all systems periodically suffer from brief intervals of memory shortage. The important question is: "Is this report typical of my system's behavior?" If it is, you are significantly short of memory.

4.3 Conserving Memory

If you are swapping or paging regularly, you need to get more memory. Buying more memory is the easy way out, and it's often the only solution. But if your shortage is small enough and you are willing to make the effort, you can effectively get more memory by using what you have more efficiently. Good memory conservation practices can let you squeeze by with your current configuration for a while longer. The price of memory has been dropping steadily, so the longer you wait, the less you'll have to spend.

There are a number of ways to conserve memory, some of which are implemented by default. Make sure that your programs are all using shared text segments. Appropriate use of shared libraries, software that can run with less memory. It's also worth noting that the X window system requires a lot of memory. While you can't reduce X's memory needs, you should be aware that it might be causing problems.

Once you've looked at the applications you are running, you should look at the kernel itself. By reducing the amount of memory devoted to kernel buffers, you can often reclaim a lot of memory. By making the kernel's tables smaller, you can also reclaim some memory, though not as much.

4.3.1 Shared Text Segments

By default, the UNIX linker (*ld*) creates programs that can share text segments. This means that several invocations of the same program can use the same pages of physical memory for the program's text segment (the program's executable). To allow shared text, the linker must make the text segment read-only and must make the text segment's size a multiple of the system's page size.

Because shared text is the default, you should not need to invoke it explicitly. However, if you have some old UNIX software and makefiles, you may have some programs that explicitly request a nonshared text segment. Such programs will be linked with the *-N* option. If you have such programs, regenerate them with the *-n* option, which explicitly requests shared text segments. This reduces virtual memory requirements when several users invoke the program simultaneously.

The *sticky bit* was a hack added to PDP-11 versions of UNIX. A lot of UNIX material recommends setting the sticky bit on commonly used executables. It causes the executable to remain in the swap area. It reduced startup time because the kernel didn't need to copy the executable into the swap area before it could get the program running. To avoid wasting too much swap space, you would only set the sticky bit for commonly used programs that were always making the trip from */bin* (or wherever) to the swap partition.

Demand paging and shared text tend to make the sticky bit obsolete. However, there are many versions of UNIX on which the sticky bit is still relevant, for these reasons:

*   Data in the swap area is not fragmented, while the actual executable may be fragmented. This means the kernel can use faster code to load the executable from swap space; it knows that the entire executable will be in one place. Demand paging (bringing the executable into memory only as it is needed) minimizes the need for the sticky bit. Knowing the program isn't fragmented isn't important if you're only loading the program one page at a time. However, if your system does not support demand paging, you will find the sticky bit useful. XENIX and many V.2 implementations don't support demand paging.

- Some systems, even though they support demand paging, still copy the executable into the swap area. If your system copies the executable into the swap area, you will find the sticky bit useful.

- Shared text also makes the sticky bit obsolete. Shared text allows different invocations of the same program to share the same text segment in memory. Therefore, the kernel doesn't need to load the program from disk at all, provided that some invocation of the program is running. Most systems that support demand paging also support shared text.

How do you know if you need the sticky bit? The information you really want is never documented well and varies from manufacturer to manufacturer. The best way to tell is to experiment. Pick any large program. Start it and let it terminate. Then try starting it again. If the program takes noticeably less time to start the second time, you probably don't need the sticky bit. And if you don't need the sticky bit, you shouldn't set it at all. Setting it will just waste swap space.

4.3.2 Shared Libraries

The standard BSD UNIX linker (*ld*) handles library references by extracting routines from a library and inserting the routines in their entirety into the executable file. Some new versions of UNIX (in particular, recent SunOS and System V releases) support shared libraries. With shared libraries, library routines are always mapped into the system's virtual memory. When a program references a library routine, the linker generates a jump into the shared library. As a result the executable file itself is usually smaller because the library code is not a part of the executable. Considered by itself, the program requires the same amount of virtual memory or possibly slightly more: the library function is still a part of the program's address space and must be in memory in order to run. However, the system as a whole requires less memory because all programs that reference the same function share the same copy of the function.

Shared libraries therefore use the system's memory and disk more efficiently. But before deciding to use shared libraries for any program, you should consider these two issues:

- Some implementations of shared libraries are significantly slower than standard, nonshared libraries. The performance penalty can be as much as 25 percent while you are executing the library code. The SunOS and System V implementations of shared libraries do not entail a performance penalty. If you are running some other implementation, build the program both ways (with or without shared libraries) and run some benchmarks.

- Under some circumstances, shared libraries can lead to considerably larger executables. While the text segment is shared, the data segment is not. Furthermore, the executable is burdened with the data region for the entire library, not just the functions it calls. This penalty may be greater than the savings. AT&T therefore notes that you shouldn't use shared libraries if you are only calling one or two functions from the library. My experiments (on SunOS and 386/ix) have shown that shared libraries are uniformly smaller in both text and data areas, even in programs that make minimal use of library functions. You can perform your own experiments by building the program both ways and using *size* to find out how large the data and text segments are.

Unfortunately, we can't tell you how to use shared libraries effectively in a book like this. Every system that supports shared libraries has a completely different implementation. For compatibility reasons, some systems support two different implementations. Consult your vendor's documentation to find out whether or not shared libraries are supported, when they are used by default, and how to use them if they are not the default.

4.3.3 Programming Techniques

If *ps* shows that a few locally developed programs are running and consuming a lot of memory whenever performance is bad, you should encourage the developers responsible for these programs to write them in a way that is more memory efficient. For example, a program that manipulates large arrays may be modified to use an "out-of-core" matrix solver to minimize memory usage. On a system with marginal memory capacity, a program with an "in-core" solver may be very fast when it's the only program running but will drag the entire system down under a more typical workload. Likewise, a program may be modified to maximize "locality of reference" (i.e., to concentrate memory references in a particular area, rather than scatter memory references throughout the entire address space). Locality of reference doesn't reduce your program's memory requirements, but it does improve memory performance in two ways. First, it allows the program to take advantage of your system's data cache (caches are effective only when programs access the same block of data repeatedly). Second, locality of reference also allows UNIX's paging algorithms to work more effectively. When memory references occur randomly throughout the program's address space, it is very difficult for UNIX to predict which pages will be needed in the immediate future. "Out-of-core" matrix solvers and techniques for maximizing locality of reference are beyond the scope of this book but are well known among numerical analysts.

It is also a good idea to make sure that locally developed programs are diligent about freeing the memory they have allocated when they no longer need it. UNIX programs never release memory until they terminate. A program's size always stays at its maximum, even if you are diligent about freeing memory. However, a program can reuse memory that it has freed—it just can't give the memory back to the system until it terminates. Therefore, a program's peak memory requirements may be smaller if you free memory as soon as it isn't needed. Memory usage is most efficient if you always allocate and free memory chunks of the same size—for example, if you always allocate and free 128-byte buffers. This prevents your program's local memory from fragmenting, making it easy for the system to reuse the memory its has already allocated to you.

NOTE

> There is another side to this coin: calling *malloc* (the memory allocation function) too frequently also hurts performance. The proper tradeoff between allocating and freeing memory too frequently and minimizing total memory usage depends entirely on the application.

Many systems (in fact, most) have a penalty for nonaligned memory references. In other words: for the best performance, the address of a 32-bit quantity should be a multiple of 4 and addresses of 16-bit quantities should be multiples of 2. Some systems require addresses of 64-bit quantities to be multiples of 8. In some cases, the penalty can be extremely large. Making sure that data is aligned properly will never hurt your performance and may help it significantly.

4.3.4 Setting Memory Limits

One way to conserve memory is to prevent the system from running programs that require a lot of memory. This may be counterproductive in the long run, but it is worth considering. BSD UNIX provides some ways to limit memory usage. The C shell (*csh*) supports limits on the size of the data and stack segments for programs that are executed by the shell. It also supports a pseudo-limit on the resident set size of a program, which is what you really want to control. Prior to V.4, System V supported only a limit on file size. The C shell for V.4 supports the full Berkeley limit mechanism.

The following *csh* commands set upper bounds on the stack size, data segment size, and working set size for a process:

```
% limit -h stacksize size
% limit -h datasize size
% limit -h memoryuse size
```

If the *-h* option is present, UNIX sets the *hard limit*. If this option is not present, UNIX sets the *soft limit*. Programs that exceed the soft limit are allowed to try and raise their limit, and then acquire more of whatever resource they want. However, a program may never raise its soft limit above its hard limit. And only a program running as root (superuser) can increase its hard limit. Therefore, the hard limit sets an absolute upper bound to resource usage. More specifically, the hard and soft limits work as follows:

stacksize   If the program's stack segment exceeds the soft limit, the program is sent the segmentation violation signal (*SIGSEGV*). A program can catch this signal and try to increase its stack limit. If it does not catch the signal, it will terminate.

datasize   If the program's data segment exceeds the soft limit, attempts to allocate more memory will fail. The program can continue executing, but it won't be able to get more memory until it increases its soft limit or frees some of the memory it already has.

memoryuse   If the process' resident set (the portion of the program physically in memory) exceeds the soft limit, the system preferentially steals pages from the process when it is short of memory. The process does not receive any notification.

Any of these *limit* commands can be placed in the *.cshrc* initialization file. If you want to make such limitations into a system-wide policy, add *limit* commands to the default initialization files that you give to all new users. You can also customize the kernel to enforce the segment size limits on a global basis, but this probably isn't desirable. There may be valid reasons for discouraging large jobs or requiring special permission to run them, but I don't see any good reason to build a system that can't run large jobs.

Of course, users need to get their work done. If the applications your users run typically exceed the limits you impose, your limits may prevent effective usage of the machine, rather than encourage it. In this situation, your only viable options may be expanding the system's memory or enduring mediocre performance.

4.3.5 The Buffer Cache

The *buffer cache* is a pool of buffers that provides intermediate storage for data moving to or from the system's disk drives. The buffer cache allows the system to optimize disk accesses in two ways: it allows the I/O subsystem to make large, ordered transfers that minimize seek time on the disk, and it allows programs to avoid reading or writing a disk if the data they want happens to be in the buffer cache already.

Until recently, all UNIX systems used a buffer cache. System V.4 and SunOS 4.0 have adopted a different filesystem management strategy, which avoids the buffer cache. The kernel handles buffering by playing tricks with memory management: it maps the file into the kernel's address space and reads (or writes) data directly into the file, which is now a part of main memory. At some later time the modified portions of the file are written back to disk. In a way, all of memory acts as the buffer cache. The amount of memory used for buffering disk operations varies according to the system's needs. Therefore, users of SunOS or System V.4 can ignore the buffer cache—but not quite entirely. We'll give you a hint or two later in this section.

If, however, you are running any version of UNIX other than V.4 or SunOS 4, you must contend with the buffer cache. It is the system's biggest memory consumer aside from the kernel itself. On systems with a lot of memory, the buffer cache may be substantially larger than the UNIX kernel. And it is allocated statically: when the system is booting, it reserves a large chunk of memory for the cache and keeps it forever. Therefore, if you can reduce the size of the cache, you can increase the amount of memory available for running processes. But you will pay a penalty. Disk operations will be less efficient. The converse is also true. When you make the cache larger, disk operations become more efficient but virtual memory performance degrades.

In this section we'll discuss how to manage the cache to improve memory performance. There's a parallel discussion of the cache in Chapter 5, *Disk Performance Issues*, that looks at the other side of the coin: optimizing disk performance at the expense of memory.

Sizing the Buffer Cache

Before adjusting the buffer cache, you should find out how large it presently is. We'll go in order of increasing difficulty. If you are running XENIX, finding the size of the buffer cache is easy. Poke through the file */usr/adm/messages* (a log of all your system's console messages) until you see the messages that appear with your system boots. These messages will tell you precisely how much memory is allocated to the buffer cache, how much is available for the user, how much is consumed by the kernel, and so on. Here's a sample from a XENIX system:

```
...
type=W0 unit=0 cyls=1024 hds=9 secs=17
Autoboot from rootdev 1/40, pipedev 1/40, swapdev 1/41
L4L5L6MNOPmem: total=9216k, reserved=4k, kernel=1224k, user=7988k
kernel: drivers=4k, 10 screens=68k, 600 i/o bufs=600k, msg bufs=8k
nswap=6000, swplo=0, Hz=50, maximum user process size=9788K
QRSTUVWXYZ
Sun Apr 15 17:29:39
...
```

The boot message says plainly that there are 600 I/O buffers, totaling 600K of physical memory. We wish that all UNIX systems were this verbose.

Unfortunately, they aren't. If you are running 386/ix or System V.3, you have to look in your configuration files to find the cache's size. Look at the file *stune* in your system's configuration directory (in the directory */etc/conf/cf.d*). It probably has lines like these:

```
NBUF            500
S52KNBUF        500
```

The first line shows the number of 1-KB buffers; the second shows the number of 2-KB buffers (only used for a 2-KB block filesystem, which is an option with Interactive's 386/ix implementation). This system therefore has 500 1-KB buffers and 500 2-KB buffers, for a total of 1.5 MB reserved for the buffer cache. In reality, buffers are associated with buffer headers which occupy a bit more storage. Fortunately, buffer headers are relatively small and can be ignored for our purposes.

If *NBUF* is missing, your system is using the default buffer setting, which you can find in the *mtune* file. If *S52KNBUF* is missing and you have not installed the 2-KB block size option, ignore it. If you have installed this package, look up *S52KNBUF* in the *mtune* file. The relevant lines look like this:

```
NBUF            500     200     2000
S52KNBUF        100     100     500
```

The numbers show, in order, the default value for the parameter, the minimum legal value, and the maximum legal value. The default setting for this system is 500 1-KB buffers plus 100 2-KB buffers, for a total of 700 KB reserved for the buffer cache. On a BSD system you have to be a little more tricky. The *BUF-PAGES* parameter, if set, tells you how many pages of memory to allocate to the cache. It isn't usually set, which means that the kernel calculates the cache size upon initialization, depending on the memory that's available. The buffer cache takes 5 percent of the first 2 MB of available memory plus 10 percent of any remaining available memory. Let's assume that the kernel's text and data segments occupy 1 MB (you can check this assumption by giving the command *size /vmunix* and adding the text and data segment sizes). Further, let's assume that your system has 8 MB of memory. Then you have 7 MB of available memory. By default, the buffer cache occupies 200 KB (10 percent of the first 2 MB) plus 250 KB (5 percent of the remaining 5 MB), for a total of 450 KB.

Tuning the Buffer Cache

Finding the best compromise between disk performance and memory performance is one of the most difficult aspects of performance tuning. It is also one of the most important. How large should the cache be? The answer depends entirely on how you use your system. Restricting the cache's size frees physical memory for use by the system, but I/O performance will suffer. Increasing the cache's size decreases the memory available but improves I/O performance. No single answer can take into account all situations.

We can, however, make a few general recommendations:

- If your system runs a lot of programs that use the filesystem heavily—i.e., if your users spend a lot of time working with very large files—then disk performance may well be more important than memory performance.

- However, no matter how large the cache is, its size is only finite. If you are accessing files that are much larger than the cache, the cache isn't helping you very much, and you might as well optimize memory performance and use a smaller cache. After all, all that data is going somewhere, isn't it? Making the cache large enough to be a real help might leave you with almost no usable memory. Furthermore, if you read these files only once, caching isn't helping you much anyway. Again, try getting by with a smaller cache.

- If your system is CPU-bound—that is, if it is used for programs that do a lot of computation but relatively little I/O—it might be reasonable to make the buffer cache as little as 5 percent of your available memory (total memory minus kernel executable size).

- If you use the X window system heavily, memory is at a premium. Make the buffer cache as small as you can get away with.

- In general, I would resolve the conflict between memory performance and disk performance in favor of memory. When your system starts paging or swapping, it is not only running out of memory, it is also using up disk bandwidth. Therefore, preventing memory shortages also helps I/O performance.

To change the cache's size, you have to build a new kernel using your system's configuration process. We discuss configuration for the most popular UNIX versions in Chapter 8, *Kernel Configuration*. Unfortunately, you can't change the cache's size dynamically. Once you have configured the cache to a certain size, you are stuck with it until you generate a new kernel.

If you are running System V, you can use *sar -b* to find out the effect of any changes you make. We will discuss this option when we talk about disk I/O. If you are using some variant of BSD UNIX, you will have to use your own benchmarks and your sense of how the system behaves to determine whether or not the benefits of reducing the cache are greater than the costs.

Buffer Headers in System V.4

As we've said, you don't need to worry about the buffer cache for System V.4 and SunOS. However, V.4 places a system-wide limit on the amount of memory that can be occupied by filesystem buffers. This is the configuration parameter *BUFHWM*, which is defined in the file */etc/master.d/kernel*. Because this memory is managed dynamically, *BUFHWM* can be large without sacrificing performance. Some V.4 implementors have recommended values as large as one-quarter of your physical memory.

System V.4 also lets you use the *NBUF* parameter to set the number of buffer headers that can be allocated at one time. Buffers are allocated in groups of size *NBUF*, and once allocated, they are never freed. Therefore, the number of buffers in the system stays fixed at the maximum number of buffers you need, rounded up to the next multiple of *NBUF*. Reducing *NBUF* increases the overhead of allocating buffers. If you allocate fewer at a time, you have to spend more time allocating them. But increasing *NBUF* increases the amount of wasted memory. It is a good idea to keep *NBUF* fairly small; 100 is appropriate, or possibly even 50 or 25. By choosing a small value, you aren't restricting the number of buffer headers that are available. You are only limiting the number that can be allocated at one time.

4.3.6 BSD Network Buffers

The network software for BSD UNIX, and all network implementations that are derived from BSD UNIX, uses a separate pool of buffers called *mbufs*. There isn't much you can do about *mbufs*, but you should know about their existence.

Network buffers are allocated dynamically but never freed. Therefore, the amount of memory that they are taking increases from the time you boot the system until the time it hits its peak network load. On BSD and SunOS systems, the command *netstat -m* will show how much memory is allocated to *mbufs* at any time.

As we've said, you have to be a fatalist about network buffers. There are some configuration constants that control *mbufs*, but these are really black magic. We strongly recommend that you leave these alone. We won't discuss them in this book. There are a few minimal things you can do:

- The only way to reclaim *mbufs* memory is to reboot your system periodically. This isn't a very good method, though it might be a good idea if your system is subject to rare bursts of extremely heavy network traffic. In most circumstances, though, we suspect that network traffic is more or less constant. Your system's *mbufs* usage will hit a plateau fairly early and not grow very much afterwards. Therefore, rebooting your system is usually a futile exercise. You may save memory, but only for the first few minutes.

- Much more important: You should be aware that configuring your system, or any system, in a way that increases network traffic will also increase the number of *mbufs* that are required. Therefore, if you buy a file server for a network of workstations, you shouldn't skimp on memory. If you rearrange your network in a way that substantially changes its traffic patterns, you may also want to buy more memory for the heavily loaded systems.

4.3.7 STREAMS Buffers

If you are using System V.3, XENIX, or SunOS 4.0, the STREAMS facility has a large supply of preallocated buffers. While this set of buffers isn't as large as the buffer cache, it can also be significant. It is divided into nine size classes: 4-byte buffers, 16-byte buffers, 64-byte buffers, up to 4096-byte buffers. The number of buffers in each class is controlled by the parameter NBLKn, where n is the buffer's size. A 2-KB or 4-KB buffer can chew up a lot of memory fairly quickly, so you might be able to save a lot of memory by reducing the number of large buffers. However, there is a performance tradeoff. If you don't have enough buffers, applications that use the network will run much slower because they will have to wait until a buffer is free before they can transmit data.

Where does this leave us? Here are some considerations:

- The X window system uses buffers very heavily. However, looking at *netstat -m* (which shows you how many buffers are in use from each class) on many different systems suggests that X relies more on small buffers (128 bytes or less) than on large buffers.

- Terminal drivers also use the STREAMS facility. Therefore, if you support many terminals, you should consider increasing the number of small buffers.

- The largest possible Ethernet packet is roughly 1.5 KB long, so you should also have some 2048-byte buffers available. Ethernet packets of the maximum length are relatively rare, though their frequency depends on exactly what your system is doing—in particular, how you access remote systems. If you use *rlogin* to get at remote systems, most Ethernet packets will be relatively short. If you do your work locally but use NFS or utilities like *rcp* heavily, you can expect to generate many large packets.

- If you look at *netstat -m* periodically, you will also see that 4-KB buffers are rarely, if ever, needed, so you can probably set *NBLK4096* to zero or some small value without any adverse consequences. This happens to be the default for 386/ix, but most systems with X installed have increased its value. Note that you may need 4-KB buffers even though Ethernet packets are always smaller than 2 KB. A single block of data may occupy one or more 4-KB buffers before being broken into Ethernet packets. Reducing the number of large buffers tends to starve large network transfers, which are the basis for remote file access. If you watch *netstat* and listen to the rumblings from your users, you will know when you've gone too far.

System V.4 and SunOS 4.1 allocate STREAMS buffers dynamically, so their requirements are not an issue for memory performance—at least as far as tuning is concerned. Of course, if you use the network heavily, you are using network buffers, and that memory has to come from somewhere. If you don't have enough memory, the system will spend additional time allocating and deallocating buffers, programs that access the network will have to wait for buffers to become available, and so on. Dynamic allocation allows the system to use its memory more efficiently but doesn't really reduce a system's memory requirements.

4.3.8 Kernel Tables

Once you've squeezed the buffer cache as much as you dare, you can attack the other kernel tables (the process table, inode table, file table, etc.). However, you won't reclaim a lot of memory this way; these tables aren't extremely large to begin with. You may buy back 4 or 5 KB, but that's it. There are no 100-KB victories to be found here.

We have already discussed the consequences of fiddling with the kernel tables in Chapter 3, *Managing the Workload*. The tradeoff is simple: small is beautiful, provided it's not too small. You save memory and also increase the kernel's efficiency. However, too small equals broken. The system will crash or be flaky in other ways. For Berkeley users, *pstat -T* will help you determine whether or not your tables are sufficiently large. System V users need to look at *sar -v*, which provides similar information. For discussions of *pstat -T* and *sar -v*, see Section 3.6.6, "Measuring Table Usage (BSD)," and Section 3.6.7, "Measuring Table Usage (System V)."

4.4 Tuning the Paging Algorithm

We mentioned earlier that desperation swapping can destroy interactive performance and that many system administrators like to prevent it at all cost. Here's how swapping and paging are related. Regular swapping can occur at any time. The system normally swaps out programs that have been idle more than 20 seconds. Paging begins when the system crosses some threshold, as it tries to keep enough free memory around to satisfy its needs. If the system can reclaim enough memory to get itself safely above the threshold, paging stops. If the system falls below another critical threshold, it will resort to desperation swapping: swapping processes that are active in order to reclaim memory.

The best way to prevent swapping is to raise the point at which paging begins. This will give the paging algorithms more time to find memory before a memory shortage becomes critical. Under Berkeley UNIX, paging begins when the amount of free memory falls below the level set by *LOTSFREE. LOTSFREE* can be, at most, one-eighth of your system's physical memory. The default value depends on your system but is probably something like 256 KB. Increasing *LOTSFREE* means that your system will start paging earlier, but is much less likely to cross the minimum threshold at which swapping begins.

Another configuration parameter, *DESFREE*, sets the point at which desperation swapping begins to take place. Swapping begins when the free memory drops below *DESFREE*. It can be at most one-sixteenth of your system's memory and should always be less than *LOTSFREE*. A good value is one-quarter of *LOTSFREE*. Alternatively, setting *DESFREE* to zero disables desperation swapping entirely. This can have strange and bad side effects if you really need to swap (i.e., if you have a drastic long-term memory shortage) but is acceptable provided your system has enough memory for all but the worst-case situations.

My recommendation—increasing *LOTSFREE* to avoid severe memory problems—is very counterintuitive. After all, why make paging start earlier if you are really trying to prevent paging? Remember, though, that limited paging is tolerable, but the paging and swapping that result from an extreme shortage isn't. I am arguing that you should endure a bit more paging in order to prevent the bad paging that will really make you suffer. At the same time, I have to admit that there are many situations in which my recommendation won't work and many performance experts who would try the opposite. Here's the rationale. There are several worst-case paging situations, of which the most common is called *thrashing*. Thrashing occurs when the pager forces the active pages of process A out of memory in order to run process B; then when it is A's turn to run, it forces the active pages of B out in order to run A; and so on. If you are thrashing, increasing *LOTSFREE* won't help. Decreasing *LOTSFREE* just might lower the paging threshhold enough so that you can run both processes at the same time without any paging.

In my opinion, the chance that you'll be able to solve the problem by lowering *LOTSFREE* is slim. You might be able to lessen the carnage, but that's at best a minor victory. And remember: The lower you set *LOTSFREE*, the less protection you have against desperation swapping. If your system is thrashing (the quickest way to tell is to run *ps* and look for two or more CPU-bound processes with huge memory requirements), there are really only two practical solutions: prevent the two programs from running at the same time or buy enough memory so you can run the two at the same time. You're not likely to solve this problem by playing with the virtual memory parameters.

A third parameter, *MINFREE*, is the absolute minimum of memory that can be free. When free memory drops below this amount, the system refuses to allocate any more memory until the paging or swapping daemons have found more. Don't touch *MINFREE*. Increasing it will hurt performance while reducing it leads to unreliability.

You can see how well paging and swapping are working by comparing the amount of free memory (the column labeled **fre**, reported by *vmstat*) with the values of *LOTSFREE* and *DESFREE*. If the amount of memory available is usually less than *DESFREE*, your system is suffering from a serious memory shortage and is spending a lot of time paging.

You may also want to tweak the *HANDSPREAD* parameter. This controls the point at which pages become subject to a page-out. For every page of physical memory, the kernel keeps a flag that is set whenever the page is referenced. The kernel then envisions a clock with two hands that are constantly sweeping through memory. These hands are separated by *HANDSPREAD* bytes. Whenever the first hand touches a page, the kernel clears the page's referenced flag. Whenever a process touches a page, the kernel sets the page's referenced flag. If the flag is still clear by the time the other hand passes by, it hasn't been accessed recently, and may be paged-out. Increasing *HANDSPREAD* puts more distance between the clock's hands. A process has more time to reference a page of memory before that page becomes a candidate for a page-out. If your system runs a lot of large applications that touch memory randomly, increasing *HANDSPREAD* might improve the performance of these applications. This change probably won't be good for small programs or programs that access memory sequentially.

Under System V, many parameters adjust the system's paging behavior. There are many system-to-system differences:

- Many System V implementations do not support paging. These include XENIX and many V.2 ports.

- Even if the system supports paging, the parameters you can get your hands on vary from system to system. For example, 386/ix lets you adjust a relatively small subset of these parameters. But it does let you adjust *AGEINTERVAL*, which I haven't seen on other V.3 implementations.

- Parameter names have changed from V.2 to V.3. The older names are similar but nevertheless different. We'll use the V.3 names.

- V.4 incorporates a completely different virtual memory system, based on SunOS 4.0. There are relatively few tunable parameters. However, such parameters as remain have been given names analogous to V.3.

We'll describe the most important aspects of the V.3 virtual memory system. From this scaffolding, you should be able to work backward to V.2 systems, forward to V.4 systems, or sideways to variant V.3 implementations.

While the paging algorithm of System V.2 and V.3 differs significantly from the BSD algorithm, its gross behavior is similar. The paging daemon starts when the amount of free memory drops below some limit, set by the variable *VHANDL*. During startup, *VHANDL* is set to the maximum of *GPGSHI* and *memory/VHANDFRAC*; you can't set it explicitly. The paging daemon runs every *VHANDR* seconds, at which point it looks around and notes any pages that might be available for a page-out. Paging starts when the amount of free memory drops below a "low-water mark," which is set by the variable *GPGSLO*. Once started, paging and swapping stop when the free memory rises above the "high-water mark," *GPGSHI*. Another parameter, *AGEINTERVAL*, exempts a process from page-outs until it has run for at least *AGEINTERVAL* clock ticks. The rationale for *AGEINTERVAL* is that it is better to let a program that has just been swapped in run for a while, rather than risk paging the program out almost immediately. This is particularly important for jobs that run very quickly: it's better for interactive performance to let them run to completion. If the system becomes extremely short of memory, desperation swapping starts.

Here are some suggestions about what to do with this nest of parameters. As we've said, which parameters are settable on any particular system depends on that system.

- Increasing *GPGSLO* makes the system start paging earlier. This has a complicated effect on performance. My tendency would be to increase *GPGSLO* on systems if performance is suffering, in hopes that letting paging start earlier will prevent the more drastic performance loss that comes from severe shortages. However, as I said for BSD systems, there is another side to this story: some authorities recommend decreasing *GPGSLO* in hopes that your system will just barely squeak by on the available memory without paging. Careful experimentation may be the only way to tell how best to set this parameter. A good starting value is one-sixteenth of your system's total memory. If several users share your system, the 386/ix defaults are probably too low.

- Increasing *VHANDR* decreases the frequence at which the paging daemon runs, once paging has started. This decreases the overhead required for paging. On many systems, it also controls the amount of time a page can remain in memory without being touched before it is subject to a pageout (roughly 2*VHANDR*). Increasing *VHANDR* is only a good idea if your system isn't generally short of memory. If your system chronically suffers bad memory shortage, you may want to decrease *VHANDR*. Making the paging daemon more active will help the system to deal with these shortages.

- Increasing *AGEINTERVAL* increases the number of processes that will be exempt from paging. This can improve interactive performance for quick commands like *ls*, *mv*, and other programs that don't require a lot of processing. It can also reduce the paging overhead. However, the more programs you exempt from paging, the more difficult it will be for the system to reclaim memory. If the system is chronically short of memory, decrease *AGEINTERVAL*. I have seen recommendations that *AGEINTERVAL* should be one-half to one-third of the average CPU time of any process. However, a gross generalization like this doesn't make any sense to me: an appropriate value depends entirely on what your system spends its time doing.

- I don't see any good reason to change *VHANDFRAC*. The paging daemon (*vhand*) runs when the amount of free memory is less than *memory/VHANDFRAC* or *GPGSHI*, whichever is larger. I can't see any reason to start the daemon any earlier than necessary, and your ability to start the daemon later is limited by *GPGSHI*. A good starting value for *GPGSHI* is one-tenth of your system's total memory. If several users share your system, the 386/ix defaults are probably too low. But I'm humble. If I am missing some occult lore, let us know and we'll add the information to the next edition.

Some System V implementations provide some version of "prepaging," which means paging-in a group of contiguous pages with one operation. Prepaging makes disk access more efficient, particularly when a process is first starting: rather than reading a single block into memory, the system can transfer several blocks with one operation. However, support for prepaging varies from system to system. Some implementations allow you to set the number of pages that are read from the disk at one time.

The parameters *NAUTOUP* and *BDFLUSHR* (*FSFLUSHR* for V.4) are often considered part of the paging mechanism. They are discussed in the section covering System V disk updates, 5.5.1, "Disk Updates (System V)."

4.5 Managing the Swap Area

Under Berkeley UNIX, there is little you can do to control the size of your swapping area. For any disk type, the swapping area (if one is used) is partition *b*; the size of this partition is set in */etc/disktab*. In theory you can change the size of the partition by modifying this file and reinitializing the disk drive. In practice, this won't work. The disk management utilities get partition size information from *disktab*, but the starting locations are either stored on the disk itself, where all of the information really should be kept, or hard-wired into the device driver. You obviously can't change the size of a partition without also changing starting addresses, unless you only want to make things smaller and don't care about reclaiming the space you've saved. Therefore, *disktab* doesn't contain all the information that it should. Changing it can ruin your disk.* With these limitations, BSD UNIX only gives you two ways of managing your swap area:

- Buy more disk drives and add swapping partitions on these drives.
- Enable swapping on disks where you aren't currently swapping.

The latter alternative probably involves an extensive reorganization of your filesystem. If you are already using all of a disk drive, the only way to dedicate one area of a disk to a swap area is to give up some storage that you are probably using for something else. In other words, to create a swap partition, you must make some other partition smaller. Because BSD partition sizes aren't inflexible, adding a swap partition is an all-or-nothing affair.

---

*By now, most commercial BSD filesystem implementations have fixed this problem, including Concurrent, MIPS, and Sun. It has also been fixed in the "tahoe" release of 4.3 BSD. However, these solutions all differ. Consult the manufacturers documentation to find out how to partition a disk drive.

Assuming you have enough free space, you can reorganize your disks with a spare partition. For the sake of argument, let's assume that the spare partition is */dev/disk2b* (partition *b* of disk 2). Then you take the following steps to start swapping:

* Back up all the filesystems on the disk and use *newfs* to initialize new filesystems on the partitions you will be using for user storage. The partition */dev/disk2b* should not have a filesystem on it. In the next chapter, we'll discuss BSD disk organization.

* Build a new kernel that can use */dev/disk2b* for swapping. The kernel's configuration file should have the line:

  ```
  config vmunix swap on disk0b and disk2b
  ```

  or some variation. *disk0b* is almost always a swapping partition on BSD systems, though there's no reason it has to be. We discuss kernel configuration in Chapter 8, *Kernel Configuration*.

* Modify */etc/fstab* to reflect the disk's new organization. Among other things, this file must include an entry for the new swapping partition. Depending on whether or not your system supports NFS, the entry will look like one of the lines below:

  ```
  /dev/disk2b swap swap rw 0 0 # systems that support NFS
  /dev/disk2b:swap:sw:0:0 # systems that don't support NFS
  ```

* Check */etc/rc* to make sure the appropriate *swapon* commands are present. The command */etc/swapon -a* enables swapping on all swap partitions listed in */etc/fstab*. The command */etc/swapon /dev/disk2b* enables swapping on *disk2b* only.

System V implementations give you more flexibility with swap area management. System V generally lets you set the size of each partition, including dedicated aswap partitions, when you install the disk drive. The exact procedure for specifying partition size depends largely on the system's vendor.

If you decide to add a swapping area on your second (or third or fourth) disk drive, you must execute the *swap* command to begin using it. As superuser, you can give this command from the terminal, but it really should be added to one of your system's startup files in *letc/rc2.d*. To add a swapping area, use *swap* as follows:

```
# swap -a dev low len
```

where:

dev   The special file for your swapping partition.

low   The starting address of the swapping area within the swapping partition.

len   The size of the swapping partition, in 512-byte disk blocks.

How do you know what values to place here? If you are running 386/ix, changing a disk configuration automatically updates the *letc/partitions* file. Assume that you are adding a swapping area on disk 1. You will see the following entry in *letc/partitions*:

```
swap1:
        partition = 2, start = 459, size = 29988,
        tag = SWAP, perm = NOMOUNT, perm = REMAP, perm = VALID
```

The special filename for the swapping partition has the form /dev/dsk/c*mn*s*p*, where *m* is the number of the disk's controller, *n* is the disk drive number, and *p* is the partition number. c*m* must be omitted for disks attached to controller zero. In this case, the special filename is */dev/dsk/1s2*; our disk is on the first controller (number 0), it is disk 1, and the swap partition is partition 2.

The starting address for the swapping area is always 0. The swapping area should occupy the entire partition, so it should begin at the first block of the partition. (The **start** field in the *partitions* file reports the starting address of the partition itself, which isn't relevant here. You may wonder why you have to specify a starting address at all—wouldn't you always want to use the entire partition? This is a relic of older days, when swapping was done in unused areas at the end of user partitions. This is still possible, but not recommended.) The length of the swapping partition may be as large as the size reported in the *partitions* file. Many administrators like to play it safe by subtracting 4 from the size reported in *partitions*, thus leaving a buffer between the swapping partition and the next partition. For the swap area described here, add the command:

```
swap /dev/dsk/1s2 0 29984
```

to one of the *letc/rc2.d* files.

If you are running System V.4, use the *storage_devices* option to the *sysadm* administration utility to find out the address and size of each partition. Then use this information to write an appropriate *swap* command.

4.5.1 Filesystem Paging

A number of UNIX implementations including SunOS 4.1, System V.4, HP-UNIX, and Concurrent support *filesystem paging*, which allows completely flexible swap area management. Filesystem swapping does away with separate swapping partitions. The kernel uses regular files rather than dedicated disk partitions for swapping and paging. You can expand or shrink these files at any time as your needs change; you can locate these files anywhere you want within the filesystem. And BSD systems no longer need to have their swap devices configured into the kernel. All of these developments make swap management much more convenient.

Of course, every new convenience has a tradeoff. Filesystem paging is slightly less efficient than using a dedicated swap partition. In the best case, filesystem paging can equal the speed of a dedicated swap partition, but this assumes special high-performance filesystems that haven't generally been adopted by UNIX vendors. Fortunately, the worst case isn't very bad. And it's not too difficult to make sure that the worst case never occurs. Disk fragmentation is the big enemy of filesystem swapping: paging performance is better if the file is one contiguous area on the disk than if the file is scattered all over. Although neither standard UNIX filesystem can promise to avoid fragmentation, fragmentation will be minimal if you create swapping files on relatively new, relatively empty filesystems. In other words, don't create a swapping file on a filesystem that's 99 percent full and has been in use for two years. If need be, delete as many junk files as possible, backup the filesystem, use *mkfs* or *newfs* (BSD only) to reinitialize the filesystem, restore the filesystem from your dump tape, and create your swapping files before anyone has had a chance to disturb the filesystem.

If you have a system that supports filesystem swapping, rejoice. But remember one thing: filesystem swapping is *not* a way to save disk space. It is tempting to say, "Great, now I can reclaim my 100-MB swapping partition. I won't buy a new disk after all." Nothing could be further from the truth. If you needed 100 MB before, you need 100 MB now. You just have more freedom to place this 100 MB in areas that are more convenient. Many trends seem to require more swapping space, rather than less: programs and memory systems are both becoming larger as time goes on.

Under SunOS, creating and using a swapping file is particularly simple. The command *mkfile* creates a swapping file; the command *swapon* enables swapping and paging on the file. These are used as follows:

```
# mkfile size filename
# /usr/etc/swapon filename
```

where *size* is the size of the swapping file. By default, *size* is in bytes. However, you can follow `size` with m to indicate megabytes or k to indicate kilobytes.

For example, *mkfile 32m sw1* requests a 32-MB swap file named *sw1*. Do not use the *-n* option to *mkfile*, which creates a file but does not allocate its data blocks. The system will panic (i.e., crash) when it tries to use the file for swapping.

Under V.4, the *swap* command can add paging files in addition to disk partitions. To create a paging file, give the command:

```
# swap filename
```

You don't need to provide the starting address (always zero, or the beginning of the file) or the swapping file's size. Use any mechanism you wish to create an appropriately large swapping file.

4.5.2 Swap Area Size

There are no good rules of thumb for computing the total amount of swap area your system needs. An old rule of thumb is to give yourself a total swap area that is four times your system's physical memory capacity. However, there are plenty of reasons not to believe this rule.* In many situations this will not be enough and you will have to increase the swapping area further. Interactive's algorithms for computing the default swap area size take into account the number of small, medium, and large applications the system will be running at one time and whether or not the system is working as an NFS or RFS file server. If you decide to create your own swap area, you should take the same factors into account. The larger the programs you run (in terms of both their executable size and the amount of memory they allocate), the more different programs you run simultaneously, and the more extensively you use NFS and RFS, the larger you should make your swap area. It isn't wise to save disk space by skimping on your swapping area.

If you are running BSD UNIX, *pstat -s* shows you how much of your swap space is in use:

```
% pstat -s
swap partition space:
7232k used (832k text), 120152k free, 2592k wasted, 0k missing
avail: 14*8192k 1*2048k 2*1024k 1*512k 2*256k 1*128k 2*64k 88*1k
```

The format of this report varies from system to system. This report shows that 7232 KB of the total swapping area is currently in use; 120152 KB are free. From this report, you can conclude that the system is only lightly loaded and is currently in no danger of running out of swap space. The next line shows how

---

*Of the many rules of thumb offered in this book, this one certainly is the worst. One IBM technical bulletin astutely states that rules of thumb come from people who (a) live out of town and (b) have no production experience. (*MVS Performance Management*, GG22-9351-00.)

the swapping area is fragmented: there are 14 contiguous segments of 8 MB, one segment of two MB, two segments of 1 MB, etc. This information is interesting but not particularly useful. Swap fragmentation isn't good, but there's nothing you can do about it. Here's a *pstat* report from SunOS:

```
% /usr/etc/pstat -s
4312k allocated + 2560k reserved = 6872k used, 23040k available
```

This system also has a sufficiently large swap area. Almost 7 MB are in use, and 23 MB are still unused. The total swap area is roughly 30 MB.

System V users can use the command *swap -l* to find how much swap area is in use at any time. Here's a report:

```
% /etc/swap -1
path                    dev  swaplo blocks    free
/dev/dsk/0s2            0,2       0  29984   29496
```

In this case, there is one swapping partition (*/dev/dsk/0s2*) with a total swapping area of 29984 512-byte blocks (roughly 14 MB). At the moment, virtually all of the swap area is free, or not in use.

You can also use *sar -r* to get a long-term picture of swap usage. Here's some sample output:

```
% sar -r
ora ora 3.2 2 i386     05/21/90

00:00:01 freemem freeswp
01:00:03     887   29496
02:00:02     899   29496
...
```

At 1 a.m., this system had 887 1-KB pages of free memory and 29496 blocks of swap space free. An hour later, the free memory had increased slightly and the swap area usage was unchanged. This system is nowhere near close to running out of swap space. That is as it should be. If half or more of the swap area is regularly in use, we would worry that the swap area is too full for comfort. Disks may not seem cheap, but they are much cheaper than memory. Skimping on swap space is only asking for trouble.

If BSD UNIX runs out of swap space (i.e., if physical memory and the swapping areas are both full), it starts to kill processes until it reclaims enough free space to keep running. In deciding which processes to kill, UNIX tries to minimize the users' pain by killing as few processes as possible (i.e., it tries to kill processes with large virtual memory requirements) and avoiding jobs that have been running a long time (i.e., it tries to minimize the amount of work that is wasted).

4.5.3 Swap Area Distribution

For the best performance, paging and swapping activity should be evenly distributed across the system. In this section, we will discuss how to measure and balance swapping activity.

For the best performance, place swap partitions or swap files on as many different disks as possible. However, if your system mixes high-speed disks and low-speed disks, use the fastest disks for all your swapping. There is no good reason to place swap areas on slow disks or disks that are accessed through slow controllers or buses. There is also no good reason to place more than one swapping area or swapping file on any disk.

Avoid configurations in which the controller, rather than the disk, limits performance. Most modern disk drives and controllers can support multiple simultaneous operations efficiently, but some can't. The most conservative strategy is to limit yourself to one swapping area for each independent channel of each high-speed disk controller. If your controller supports several disk drives in a daisy chain, you may be able to use several drives in the same chain effectively, provided that the disk controller and your system's device driver can manage *overlapped seeks* (i.e., if one controller can manage several concurrent operations on different disks). However, some older technologies and many device drivers don't support overlapped seeks. The most conservative strategy is to stick to one swapping area per daisy chain.

NOTE

SunOS allows you to use remote (NFS) files as swapping areas. We do not recommend this unless you are configuring the swap area for a diskless workstation, in which case you have no choice. For the best performance network-wide, swapping areas should always be on a local disk. It has been alleged that swapping over the network to an SMD or IPI-2 disk drive is faster than swapping on a local SCSI disk drive, particularly if the SCSI drive is relatively slow. I find this hard to believe, though it may be true for individual swapping operations. However, you have to take into account the performance of the network as a whole. Swapping across a network places a heavy burden on everyone who uses the network and should be avoided unless it is necessary.

BSD UNIX systems use *vmstat* to show the number of disk operations per second on each of four disk drives. In the default display, the disk drives are listed as *d0*, *d1*, *d2*, and *d3*. The correspondence between these drives and the actual disk drives installed on your system is complex:

- *d0* is always your system's root disk drive.

- The next drives in this list are the drives that have dedicated swapping partitions, in the order in which they are listed in the kernel configuration file.

- The remaining drives are listed in the order in which they are checked by *fsck*; this is determined by */etc/fstab*.

The default display only shows drives *d0*, *d1*, *d2*, and *d3*. On most systems, *d0* will be the most heavily used. The root drive also holds the most commonly used executables, so most "page-in" activity will be on the root disk. You can alleviate this somewhat by placing any local executables (i.e., any third party or locally developed software) on other disk drives.

The 386/ix implementation of System V does not have any workable mechanism for showing disk activity. The *sar -d* command should be able to produce this information, but it requires special features that are unique to the disk controllers for AT&T's 3B series. "Off-the-shelf" disk controllers that can support *sar -d* don't exist, at least in the 80386 world. Other System V implementations may support this option.

No matter what tool you use, your goal is to spread disk activity as evenly as possible among your disk drives. Your root disk drive will be the most heavily used, but you can alleviate this problem somewhat by moving commonly used programs to other filesystems. All other things being equal, your root disk drive should be the fastest drive available because it will be heavily used.

4.6 Computing Memory Requirements

So far, we have discussed how to manage the memory requirements of an existing system; we've assumed that you have little control over the system's configuration.

Before deciding on a configuration for a new system or upgrading an existing system, it is a good idea to compute the system's expected memory requirements.

First, you should know the amount of memory that's available to user processes. UNIX systems always report this figure when they boot. Either reboot your system and watch its startup messages or look through the log file *lusr/adm/messages* until you see a report like the one below:

```
Mar 31 14:38:00 myhost vmunix: real mem = 67108864
Mar 31 14:38:00 myhost vmunix: avail mem = 57483264
```

This report shows that roughly 54 MB of memory are available for running user processes. Of course, the format of this report varies from implementation to implementation. However, if you look long enough you will find the information you need.

Next you must compute the amount of memory needed for users, daemons, etc. First, decide on a typical workload by estimating how many processes will be running during the peak hours of the day. To develop this estimate, use *ps* to get an idea of what's running at any given time or read the daily command summary from your accounting reports. Your final estimate should certainly take into account any performance agreements you have established. You don't want to configure a system that will be unable to meet the performance goals you have already committed yourself to.

For example, assume you have a system with 16 users. You estimate that half of the users will be actively using the system at any given time. The others will be in meetings, on the telephone, reading technical journals, or something else. Each of the users will have one editor (let's assume the *emacs* editor) and one C shell (*csh*) at any time. You also notice that *ps* tells you that there is usually one compilation in progress at any time (*ccom* or *fcom* is often the name to look for). You also have agreed that the users can run four invocations of application A during working hours, and you know that this program usually takes about an hour to complete. Therefore, you want to allow room for running one invocation of application A at any time. You also expect to see one invocation of application B at any time. The users will be running other utilities (*mail*, *troff*, etc.), but you hope these are ignorable. You should take account for the system's daemon processes (*nfsd*, *biod*, *lpd*, etc.). Fortunately, most daemons aren't very active and therefore spend a lot of time swapped out. This is your typical job mix. Let's see how much memory is required to run these programs.

4.6.1 Estimating Memory for BSD Systems

Under BSD UNIX, the command *ps -avx* will help you estimate your system's memory requirements. This version of *ps* produces a report that emphasizes virtual memory statistics. This report will help you determine a typical job mix and the typical memory requirements of every job in the mix. This command produces a report that is similar to the standard *ps* reports but includes the following additional fields:

SIZE   The total amount of virtual memory allocated to the program's data and stack segments, in kilobytes. This excludes memory allocated to the program's text segment (the executable), which must be considered separately.

RSS   Resident set; the total amount of physical memory currently allocated to the program's data and stack segments, in kilobytes. Again, this excludes memory allocated to the program's text segment (the executable).

LIM   The limit applied, if any, to the program's resident size.

TSIZ   Text size; the total amount of virtual memory allocated to the program's text segment, in kilobytes. If you use shared text for all programs at your site (the default), the **TSIZ** fields for all programs running the same executable should be identical.

TRS   Text resident set; the total amount of physical memory currently allocated to the program's text segment, in kilobytes. If you use "shared text" for all programs at your site, the **TRS** fields for all programs running the same executable should be identical.

COMMAND   The name of the command that is being run.

The resident set sizes are the most critical to computing the memory needs of any process. With demand paging, parts of a program are brought into memory only as they are used. With most programs, large portions of the text segment are only used rarely. A surprising amount of any program is devoted to error handling, rarely used features, and other code that rarely gets executed. Therefore **TRS** is always smaller than **TEXT** and is often much smaller. Likewise, **RSS** is always smaller than **SIZE**.

Estimating the text size is relatively simple. Because programs share their text segment, all identical programs should show the same text resident size (**TRS**).* Use this figure. Note that it may not be the same every time you measure it. The size of the text resident set depends on the amount of code that has been exercised since the program was first invoked and increases over time until no invocations are running. The longer a program runs, the greater the chance it will trip across some rarely used code.

---

*It is probably worth while to make sure that the programs in question share their text segments. To do so, use the *file* command (e.g., *file /usr/local/myprog*). This command will state that a program is a "pure" or "demand paged" if it shares its text segment.

Computing the expected resident set size for a program's data area is more complicated. For many programs, the resident data size will differ for each invocation, depending on the data on which the program is working. There are two ways to approximate the expected size of the resident set for a program's nontext memory:

- If you have a good understanding of what the program does and how it does it and if you have access to the program's source code, you can calculate how much memory you expect the process to allocate. This requires computing the storage required for each array, understanding how and when the program allocates dynamic memory, etc. It also requires that you know in some detail how the program is typically used.

- You can estimate the expected resident set size for any program by averaging the RSS fields for the process, as shown in the *ps* report.

If you use *ps* to estimate the resident set size, you should be aware of how this size varies depending on the data. For programs that dynamically build large data structures, you should give greater weight to invocations that have a large resident set. For programs like editors, you can concentrate on the invocations that seem more typical. For example, if there are ten invocations of *emacs*, of which most have roughly 500K in their resident set, you can ignore invocations that have an abnormally large working set. Perhaps a user is editing a very large group of files. By the same token, you should also ignore invocations that have an abnormally small working set, and omit invocations that have a zero working set (these have been swapped out). Furthermore, you should use *ps* to measure working set size only when the system isn't paging. By definition, paging artificially shrinks the working set and will make your estimates turn out too small.

For example, here are some lines covering *csh* invocations. For convenience, we've supplied the *ps* header. If you gave this command, *grep* would strip the header away. We have also omitted a few columns that aren't needed for this kind of analysis.

```
% ps -vax | grep csh
27541 p3 I   0:07 53 99  114 1984  304 59424  448 432  0.1  0.6 csh
24756 q6 I   0:02 99 99   53 2000  192 59424  448 432  0.0  0.4 csh
25141 q7 S   0:02  2 54   75 2016  176 59424  448 432  0.6  0.4 csh
12738 pa I   0:09 99 99  157 2016  152 59424  448 432  0.0  0.4 csh
21369 p9 I   0:04 99 99  106 1976   56 59424  448 432  0.0  0.2 csh
 9665 q3 I   0:00 99 99    3 1968    0 59424  448 432  0.0  0.0 csh
```

It's pretty clear that you need 432 KB to run the *csh* executable (but all invocations of the shell share the same executable) and that on the average you need roughly 150 KB per process for the shell's data and stack. Here are some similar data for the *emacs* editor:

```
% ps -vax | grep emacs
17643 p0 S  0:36  1 99  53 2688 1960 121952 14961496  8.8  1.9 emacs
14468 q7 S  2:11 16 99  54  760  712 121952 14961496  0.7  0.8 emacs
11001 p7 T  0:17 99 99  48  600  520 121952 14961496  0.0  0.7 emacs
20421 q7 TW 0:01 99 99  49  624    0 121952 14961496  0.0  0.0 emacs
```

In this case, you need 1496 KB for the executable. Individual invocations generally require about 700 KB for the data and stack segments. It is safe to ignore the process with a huge working set, as well as the processes that are swapped out (zero working set). Now let's look at some typical lines for the C compiler. These lines combine reports that were taken from different computers, so their text sizes differ:

```
 7355 p1 R < 0:31 0 37  54 11768 10184 59576 8840 6264 90.4 27.2 ccom
16748 p2 R   0:46 0 99  27 12000 10720 59584 8864 8032 35.7 31.1 ccom
23968 pc R   0:16 0 83 346  7584  6000 59424 9264 6688 17.5 19.6 ccom
23989 p4 P   0:03 0 30 306 10808  9312 5942410872 6744 12.2 18.7 ccom
```

For the compiler, it looks like we need roughly 10 MB for the data area (per process) and roughly 7 MB for the text. The compiler's memory usage depends on the degree of optimization requested. Higher optimization levels usually require more memory.

NOTE

When computing compilation memory requirements, remember that the compiler is a group of programs. The standard UNIX C and FORTRAN compilers are named *cc* and *f77*, but the actual work is done by programs you never see, named *ccom* and *fcom*. The compiler also invokes the preprocessor (*cpp*), the assembler (*as*), and the loader (*ld*), as appropriate. You can usually ignore *cpp*, *as*, and *ld* because they are smaller programs that run sequentially with *ccom*. In some situations, *ld*'s memory needs can become a problem.

Go through a similar process to determine the memory requirements for applications A and B. Look at *ps -vax* while these programs are running and determine the average resident size for the text and data portions of these programs. Let's assume that you have done this work already and know that A requires 10 MB for data and 1 MB for the program's text and B requires 2 MB for data and 1 MB for text.

Now that we know the typical job mix and the typical memory requirements for each job in this mix, we can compute total memory requirements. The amount of memory needed to run any single process is the sum of its text size plus its resident set size (**TRS+RSS**). Assuming that all invocations of a process share the same text segment, the amount of memory required to run *n* invocations is *n****RSS+TRS**. If programs don't share their text segments, then you need *n**(**RSS+TRS**) to run *n* invocations. The algorithm below summarizes this computation:

```
For each shared_text_program_I_want_to_run
   {
   this_program_needs := RSS * invocations + TRS
   shared_total := shared_total + this_program_needs
   }
For each non_shared_text_program_I_want_to_run
   {
   this_program_needs := ( RSS + TRS ) * invocations
   non_shared_total := non_shared_total + this_program_needs
   }
total := shared_total + non_shared_total
```

In the following table, we perform this calculation for the programs we have discussed in our example. The rightmost column shows the total memory requirements for each program. The bottom of this column shows the total system-wide memory requirements:

Program	# of Invocations (*n*)	Data Size (*d*)	Text Size (*t*)	Memory Needs (*n**d+*t*)
Compiler	1	10000 KB	7000 KB	17000 KB
Application A	1	10000 KB	1000 KB	11000 KB
Application B	1	2000 KB	1000 KB	3000 KB
Editor (*emacs*)	8	700 KB	1500 KB	7100 KB
Shell (*csh*)	8	200 KB	500 KB	2100 KB
TOTAL SYSTEM				**40200 KB**

Previously, we determined that roughly 54 MB are available for user processes. Such a system should be able to handle a 40-MB job mix comfortably. The remaining 14 MB should be plenty for running other utilities, system daemons, and other tasks. It also leaves a fair amount of excess capacity, allowing the system to handle above-average loads gracefully and giving you room to add additional users before memory gets cramped. We would not expect to see this system swapping under normal use (as we've defined it) or even under moderately heavy use.

4.6.2 Special Considerations for SunOS

SunOS 4.0 and following have changed the *ps -vax* report slightly. They do not report the text resident set size (**TRS**); instead, they give some other statistics that aren't particularly useful.

Unfortunately, this leaves you in a hole. You can use the *size* command to find out how large a program's text segment is. But there isn't any good way to find out how much of a program's text is actually in memory. The size of the text segment's resident set is at most as large as the text segment and may be a lot smaller. To complicate this, most standard programs use "dynamic linking," or shared libraries.

Sun provides no way to get the information you really want. Therefore, our only recommendation is to use the *size* command and use the size of the text segment as an overly large approximation to the size of the text resident set. Here's an example of the *size* command:

```
% size /bin/cc /lib/ccom
text      data    bss     dec      hex
65536     16384   304     82224    14130    /bin/cc
245760    65536   69144   380440   5ce18    /lib/ccom
```

The size of the text segment for the C compiler's user interface (*cc*) is 64 KB. However, the program that does the compilation, */lib/ccom*, is much larger: 240 KB.

4.6.3 Estimating Memory for System V

Now let's assume that you're running System V. You have a handicap to work against: *ps* won't really supply the information you need. However, it is still possible to estimate memory requirements using *ps -el*. In this case, you want to:

- Use *file* to determine whether or not the process is shared text. Shared text files are either "pure" or "demand paged." Some System V versions of *file* don't give you this information. However, V.3 and V.4 make programs "shared text" by default, so you should assume that programs share their text segments unless you can prove otherwise.

- If the process is not shared text, its size (in 1-KB pages) is given by the **SZ** field in *ps*. Multiply this number by the number of invocations you expect. The result is the total memory required for all invocations of the program.

- If the process shares its text segment, the **SZ** field only gives its data and stack size. Multiply this number by the number of invocations you expect; this is the total data and stack memory required for all invocations. To find the text size, use the command *size*. For example:

```
% size /usr/local/bin/myprog
20996 + 6080 + 3000 = 30076
```

The first number is the program's text size. Add this number to the total data and stack area; the result is the total memory required (text, data, and stack) for all invocations of the program.

For example, let's compute the amount of memory required to run four invocations of *myprog* simultaneously. Here's the data you need:

```
% file /usr/local/bin/myprog
/usr/local/bin/myprog:    80386 pure executable
% ps -el
  F S UID  PID  PPID  C PRI NI  ADDR  SZ  WCHAN TTY   TIME CMD
...
  1 S 204  3903    67 0  30 20   8aa 364 14ec4  10   0:14 myprog
...
% size /usr/local/bin/myprog
20996 + 6080 + 3000 = 30076
```

file says this program is a pure executable, so we need to account for the text and data/stack segments separately. For each invocation, we need to allow 364 KB for the data and stack segments. For all invocations, we need to allow for 20 KB for the executable. Therefore, the program's total requirement is 364*4+20 KB, or 1476 KB. To estimate the total system requirement, perform a similar computation for all the programs your system will be running. Don't forget to account for daemons and other system processes.

4.6.4 Summary

We've just been through a lot of computation and may be guilty of focusing on the trees rather than the forest. There's a quick moral to this story: your memory requirements depend heavily on how many users your system has and what they are doing. Large scientific applications like structural analysis, computational chemistry, simulations, and signal processing often have large executables (500,000 line programs are common) and can easily require many megabytes of in-core data. Given the right application, it is easy to imagine a computer with 64 MB of memory or more that can only support one user. General editing and program development don't stress the memory system as much (particularly if your system's compiler isn't a memory hog). In a general editing environment, the same computer may support 20 or 30 users comfortably.

If memory requirements like this still seem large, remember that Sun Microsystems' single-user workstations now have a minimum memory configuration of 8 MB. Most of us can remember when 128 KB was a huge amount of memory that you would only find on a large multiuser system: a 128-KB memory upgrade required an entire rack of equipment. We all know that the world no longer works this way: 128 KB isn't even one state-of-the-art chip. But a lot of system managers act as though buying more memory were still something horrendously expensive and painful. It isn't. Perhaps the biggest advance in computer hardware in the last decade has been the ability to assemble huge memory systems for relatively little money. Take advantage of it. Don't run systems that are starved for memory.

5

Disk Performance Issues

I/O Subsystem Configuration
Partitions and Filesystems
Planning and Creating Filesystems
Balancing I/O Workload
Filesystem Buffers
In-memory Filesystems
Striped Filesystems
Conserving Disk Space

Disk performance is the single most important aspect of I/O performance. It affects many other aspects of system performance. Good disk performance enhances virtual memory performance, reduces the elapsed time required to run jobs that perform a lot of I/O, reduces the time needed to run a program, etc.

In the best of all possible worlds, you would like to optimize three factors:

Per-process disk throughput

> The speed at which any single process can read or write to a disk. Per-process performance is relatively easy to determine: measure the time it takes to copy a large file, or, even better, write a short program that creates a large file with minimal overhead.

Aggregate (total system) disk throughput

> The total speed at which all processes together can transfer data to and from the disks. Aggregate throughput is difficult to measure effectively. The best way to get a handle on aggregate throughput is to write a script that simulates many different jobs accessing different filesystems simultaneously.

Disk storage efficiency

> The efficiency with which you use disk storage. Disks, particularly large disks, tend to be a good portion of a system's total cost, so you want to use them effectively.

The first two goals are often compatible. A system that gives good per-process performance will probably give good aggregate performance; I must emphasize the word *probably*. Per-process throughput and total system throughput are two distinct quantities. A single process usually accesses a single file, reading it sequentially. To optimize per-process throughput, you want to maximize the speed at which you transfer many sequential bytes from one filesystem. To optimize global throughput, the system as a whole must be able to handle many concurrent and asynchronous file operations efficiently, accessing many different parts of different disks. The system as a whole is neither sequential nor synchronous. Optimizing scattered accesses to many disks is not the same problem as optimizing sequential access to a single filesystem.

Given that single-process performance and aggregate performance are not necessarily the same, which do you care about? That depends on how the system is used. If the system exists to run programs that sequentially access large data files, single-process performance may be more important than total throughput. In this environment you care more about running the big programs than about optimizing *ls* or *vi*. If the system supports many users doing program development work, running standard UNIX utilities, or any other work that does not stress single-file I/O, it is more important to optimize total throughput. If your system is used for both kinds of work, you can optimize some filesystems for single-process performance and optimize other filesystems for aggregate performance.

The third goal, storage efficiency, is often incompatible with disk throughput. Most techniques for increasing throughput decrease your ability to use the disk effectively. For example, increasing a filesystem's block size will improve the filesystem's throughput but can also waste a large portion of disk space. One approach to this problem is to isolate performance-critical files in a single filesystem (or group of filesystems), suffer the storage inefficiencies there, and optimize the rest of the filesystems for storage efficiency. This solution works surprisingly well. Performance-critical files are almost always large, and storage efficiency is less critical for large files (per-file wasted space is small compared to the file's size).

5.1 I/O Subsystem Configuration

Some simple configuration considerations will help you obtain better I/O performance regardless of your system's usage patterns. The factors to consider are the arrangement of your disks and disk controllers, and the arrangement of disk controllers on your system's I/O buses.

The best policy is to spread the disk workload as evenly as possible. If you have a large system with multiple I/O subsystems, split your disk drives evenly among the two subsystems. Most disk controllers allow you to daisy chain several disk drives from the same controller channel. For the absolute best performance, give each disk drive its own controller, provided that you can afford the cost. This is particularly important if your system has many users who all need to make large sequential transfers. If your needs aren't so stringent, you can live with daisy-chained disks, provided that your disk controllers and your system's disk drivers support multiple simultaneous operations (formally called *overlapping seeks*). If your system can handle multiple simultaneous operations, the performance penalty for using multiple disk drives should be small; although only one drive may be able to transfer data at a time, disk drives typically spend most of their time looking for data and relatively little time transferring it. It is a good bet that SMD-E or ESDI disk controllers and drivers can manage multiple simultaneous transfers. While SCSI controllers can manage multiple simultaneous transfers, historically, SCSI disk drivers have not been as sophisticated.

Some controllers support two or more independent channels, each of which can be daisy chained. Don't hesitate to use both channels, but attach only one drive to each channel. There may be some penalty for using both channels on a multi-channel controller, but this shouldn't be significant if the controller is well-designed.

The most expensive solution to disk throughput problems is to buy faster disks. SCSI disks are often used on small computers, such as 80386 systems and small workstations. Historically, the SCSI interfaces used on these systems have been relatively slow. The newest SCSI interfaces, however, particularly those using the NCR C700 chip set, provide extremely good performance. A high-speed variant of the ESDI interface can communicate over the SCSI bus; it also allows larger disks and faster transfer rates.

If I/O performance is critical, you should be using a VMEbus-based I/O subsystem. The VMEbus has become fairly standard on moderate or large computers (i.e., anything larger than a small workstation)* and is essential if you want to support more than two or three disk drives. The VMEbus theoretically allows aggregate transfer rates as high as 40 MB/second. In practice, the speed of the VMEbus is limited by the speed of your system's memory and the speed of the memory used in your disk controllers; therefore, beware of "creeping specsmanship." A more typical limit to VMEbus speed would be 10 to 20 MB/second. A controller may be able to deliver 40 MB/second (we have seen parallel disk controllers advertising transfer rates in that range) but that's useless unless your CPU or I/O processor is equally fast.

Once you have settled on the VMEbus, you have three different disk interfaces from which to choose. There are many VMEbus controllers for SCSI disks and other SCSI bus peripherals. The most recent provide exceptional performance, particularly for multidisk arrays. Many high-performance systems with VMEbus I/O use disks with an SMD-E interface. The SMD-E interface allows raw transfer rates of up to roughly 3 MB/second. More recently, a new disk interface called IPI-2 has become available, supporting raw transfer rates up to 6 MB/second. IPI-2 disks and disk controllers for the VMEbus are very fast, but not cheap. If your system's manufacturer supports the IPI-2 interface and you have particularly high I/O needs, you should consider this solution seriously. However, investigate carefully before you buy. We have heard reports that on some systems the IPI-2 interface is no faster than the SMD interface. No doubt these problems will be fixed by the time you read this book, but a little caution never hurts.

Notice we haven't said anything yet about seek times, transfer rates, and the other low-level disk information that shows up on a lot of spec sheets. This information is important, and it's pretty obvious that faster is better; but it is more important to get the shape of your I/O subsystem right. For example, let's assume that you have an older 80286 system with a relatively slow SCSI controller with one SCSI disk. You want to buy another disk and you want the best performance possible. Many users, deceived by brochures and statistics, run out and buy the fastest disk on the market that has a SCSI interface. If your system is heavily used, the new fast disk probably won't do you much good. We'd be willing to bet that, in a daisy-chained two-disk configuration, the SCSI controller has more of an impact on your total performance than your disk drive. You would be better off

---

*You may see Multibus on older systems but by now this bus architecture is obsolete. A new version of Multibus, Multibus II, has performance characteristics that are roughly similar to VMEbus. Ultrahigh-speed buses with transfer rates in excess of 100 MB/second are under development but systems using these buses aren't commercially available.

buying a slower, cheaper disk and investing in a better SCSI controller. If you can't buy the new controller, you might as well save money on the disk, too.

Here's another variation on the same theme. You have a large computer with a VMEbus I/O system. You have two IPI-2 disks, each with its own controller, because I/O performance is critical to your mission. You need to buy a third disk. What will happen to your I/O throughput? Unfortunately, your I/O throughput will probably go down. It certainly won't increase much. Three IPI-2 disks can easily move data faster than the VMEbus can carry it, so you won't be able to take advantage of your new disk's speed. The additional bus activity will increase the time required for bus arbitration. If you want to increase your total I/O throughput, add another VMEbus I/O subsystem.

If you think we've beaten this horse to death, go on to the next section. But there's one more example. Now assume that you have a relatively slow VMEbus I/O subsystem with a maximum throughput of, say, 3 MB/second. This isn't surprising; a lot of manufacturers don't put as much effort into I/O as they should, particularly when they first release a new product. Assume you have a single SMD disk drive with a throughput of 2.4 MB/second. Now the manufacturer announces a newer, shinier VMEbus I/O subsystem that is capable of 10 to 15 MB/second. Should you buy it?

The answer depends on what you want to accomplish. If you want better I/O performance now, forget it. Your old I/O system can handle all the data that your disk drive can push. Buying the new subsystem won't make your disk any faster. But if you are willing to buy more disks (or plan to in the near future), the new subsystem may be a good investment. As soon as you add a second disk, the I/O subsystem will become the performance bottleneck.

These considerations may seem obvious, but they are very often overlooked. Specifications are important, but what's more important is the way the pieces are hooked together. Although this shouldn't be news to anyone, you would be surprised how many otherwise competent users leave their common sense at the door when they start talking to salesmen. If you understand how your system is configured and how you intend to use it, you will be much less likely to buy equipment you don't need or that won't solve your problem.

5.1.1 Disk Specifications

Now, finally, a word about disk specifications. When you start looking at disk drives, you will see several different performance-related specifications. The most important specifications are the disk's seek time, raw transfer rate, and rotational speed (RPM). Why? They show you how fast the disk can move data (raw transfer rate) and how fast the disk can find data (seek time and RPM). Neither datum by itself tells the entire story.

Seek Times

The *seek time* is the time required to move the disk drive's heads from one track of data to another. This obviously depends on how far the heads have to move: moving from one track to the next takes much less time than moving across the entire disk. Not as obviously, there is no simple relationship that lets you compute how long any seek will take, given the number of tracks you want to move. Seek time is highly nonlinear: the heads have to accelerate, decelerate, and then stabilize in their new position. To reduce confusion, disk manufacturers typically specify a minimum seek time (one track to the next), an average seek time, and a maximum seek time.

In many applications, perhaps in most, the seek time is the most important indicator of a disk's performance—even more important than the raw throughput. Here's why: on a typical system, many different processes are accessing the disk at the same time. They are accessing different files and usually reading small amounts of data (one disk block, or 512 bytes) at one time. Therefore, the disk's heads are jumping back and forth between different tracks all the time. The disk spends relatively little time moving real data; it spends a lot of time setting up transfers. The ratio of time spent seeking to time spent transferring data is usually at least 10 to 1, and often much higher. Therefore, if you reduce the seek time, you will see a big performance improvement. The disk drive will be able to handle more I/O operations in a given interval, vastly improving its aggregate throughput. In a multiuser environment that stresses total aggregate throughput, it is important to choose disks with low seek time.

Rotational Speed

Once the disk drive has moved the heads into place, it has to wait until the data you want has moved underneath the head. This requires at most one turn of the disk itself—on the average, the disk will have to spin one-half turn. Therefore, the disk's rotational speed also determines the disk's latency, or the amount of time it takes to set up a data transfer.

Rotational speed is important, but in practice you can usually ignore it. Almost all modern disk drives have the same rotational speed: 3600 RPM. There are a few exceptions, but they don't deviate much from 3600 RPM. I haven't seen a disk drive more than 10 percent faster or 1 percent slower.

Raw Transfer Rate

A disk's raw transfer rate is the speed at which it moves data. A program never receives useful data this fast; the raw transfer rate just measures the speed at which bits come from the disk drive; it doesn't account for formatting data that your program never sees, wasted space on the disk, and other factors. Nevertheless, the raw transfer rate is a good indicator of disk speed, particularly in applications stressing *single-process throughput*: a single process making large sequential transfers to or from a single file.

Remember, however, that if your site stresses aggregate throughput (many processes reading or writing many different files in small chunks), seek time gives a better indication of how your disk will perform. For a small transfer, the amount of time required to locate the data (seek time plus rotational latency) is much longer than the time required to read or write the data.

Disk Capacity

We haven't yet mentioned disk capacity: how much information the disk drive actually holds. Disk manufacturers specify their disks' "unformatted capacity." Formatting a disk and creating UNIX filesystems on it uses up a lot of space. Some of this space is wasted and some is damaged and, hence, unusable.* Some of it is reserved to handle defects that might show up in the future, and some of it stores data structures that are used for management. In bad cases, we've seen formatting "shrink" a disk by one-third. Unfortunately, you don't have any control over formatting. Your system's manufacturer has decided how to format disks, and you are stuck with what he or she gave you.

How does capacity interact with performance? In theory, the two should be completely independent. However, the more data you have on one disk, the more likely it is that many users will want to access the disk simultaneously; therefore, disks with larger capacities should have lower seek times.

If you are going to invest in a really large disk drive (1-GB drives are now available from several vendors), you may as well spend the extra money and get one with good performance characteristics.

---

*Even the best disks have many defects—part of formatting is setting up the disk so that you never use its defective parts.

5.2 Partitions and Filesystems

In order to work with disk drives, you need to know how a UNIX disk is organized. No matter what version of UNIX you are using, a disk drive is split into several *partitions*. A disk partition holds one filesystem, which consists of a directory (called the filesystem's root, but don't confuse this with the root directory for the system as a whole) and its subdirectories. A filesystem's root directory can be "mounted" (or positioned) at any point within the global UNIX filesystem. For example, the */usr* filesystem occupies one disk partition. The root directory of the */usr* filesystem is usually mounted on the directory */usr* (hence the name), which is part of the root filesystem. Alternatively, a disk partition can hold a dedicated swapping area.

5.2.1 Filesystem Types

Under UNIX, you will see two different kinds of filesystems, corresponding roughly to the two major UNIX versions:

- The old filesystem, which is also called the Version 7 filesystem, the original filesystem, or the System V filesystem. We'll call this the System V filesystem, although this name is the least precise; the old filesystem predated both System V and BSD UNIX. (AT&T grants the name some legitimacy by calling this the System V filesystem in Release V.4). At any rate, the old filesystem is now most commonly associated with System V.

- The so-called Berkeley Fast Filesystem, which first appeared with Release 4.2 of BSD UNIX. This is also called the BSD filesystem or the UFS filesystem.

You will see the System V filesystem on most System V implementations and Version 4.1 of BSD UNIX. You will see the fast filesystem on BSD 4.2 and 4.3 and on some implementations of System V. Both XENIX and 386/ix use the System V filesystem but the BSD filesystem has been grafted onto some System V implementations. HP-UX is one System V implementation that provides the BSD filesystem, and there are others. System V.4 provides both filesystem types, adding to the confusion. In addition, V.4 uses a third type of filesystem (BFS) to boot the system. We'll ignore the BFS because it has no effect on performance once the system is running.

The BSD filesystem has several advantages over the System V filesystem:

- The BSD filesystem gives better overall throughput because it can tolerate a larger block size without excessive fragmentation. Therefore, the disk drives can make larger transfers.

- The BSD filesystem is more reliable in case of a crash.

- The BSD filesystem supports symbolic links and disk quotas. Symbolic links are a tremendous convenience in many applications. Quotas are an effective, if draconian, way to allocate disk storage fairly.

If you don't know which filesystem your system has, look at the manual page for the *fsck* command. If it has the *-s* or *-S* option, your UNIX implementation has the old System V filesystem. These options reorganize the free list to minimize fragmentation and they aren't implemented for the fast filesystem.

If you are running System V.4, you will find that the BSD (UFS, using AT&T's nomenclature) is almost always faster than the System V (S5) filesystem. Are there any exceptions to this rule? It's hard to say because so few V.4 implementations are currently available. Some V.3 vendors have put a lot of effort into improving filesystem performance. When these vendors bring out their V.4 implementations, it will be interesting to compare results from the two filesystems. But unless you have some specific reason to believe that the System V filesystem is faster on your system, we recommend that you make the switch. Use the BSD (UFS) filesystem wherever you possibly can.

Some vendors, particularly those who live or die according to their disk performance, have replaced the standard UNIX filesystems with filesystems of their own development. These vendors include Concurrent, Convex, Cray, Silicon Graphics, and Stardent. They have implemented *extent-based filesystems*, which reserve a contiguous sequence of disk blocks when a file is created. They are immune to fragmentation and provide better performance than either the BSD or System V filesystem, particularly for large files. All implementations differ to some degree. If your system supports an extent-based filesystem, check your documentation to find out how to use it.

5.2.2 Disk Organization (BSD)

BSD UNIX splits disk drives into as many as eight partitions. As we've complained elsewhere, BSD UNIX doesn't let you control partition sizes. The partition sizes themselves are in the */etc/disktab* file, but the starting address for each partition is hard-wired into the disk driver. In the past, the most intrepid UNIX administrators have patched the kernel to change the starting addresses, but their bravery exceeded their wisdom. Do you really want a kernel that works with your particular disks and no others? Do you really want to give up the ability to move a disk drive from one UNIX system to another? If you're sane, the answer to both questions has to be "no." By now, most vendors (beginning with Concurrent, and including Sun and MIPS) have taken the initiative to fix this problem. Unfortunately, there is no standard for disk labeling. Each vendor has developed a unique set of utilities for working with disk partitions.

If your system lets you control disk partitioning, here's something to keep in mind: UNIX thinks of a disk drive as a number of concentric cylinders. For example, track 10 across all of the disk's platters constitutes one cylinder. A *partition* is a group of cylinders. Physically, a partition is a donut-shaped chunk of disk that cuts across all of the platters. For any kind of reasonable performance, all partitions must begin and end on a cylinder boundary. A partition may occupy cylinders 13 through 129, but it cannot begin in the middle of cylinder 13. If you don't obey this rule, the disk will be horrendously slow. It is hard to imagine a disk management utility that would let you start a partition in midcylinder—most would round the partition to the nearest whole cylinder—but stranger things have happened.

Now prepare yourself for another surprise. On a standard BSD system, in which you can't adjust the partition sizes, disk partitions are usually chosen so that they overlap. This is useful because it lets you choose between several different ways of using the disk. But it is your responsibility to ensure that the partitions you're using on any disk don't overlap. If you happen to use overlapping partitions, chaos ensues. Figure 5-1 shows one way of partitioning a large disk.

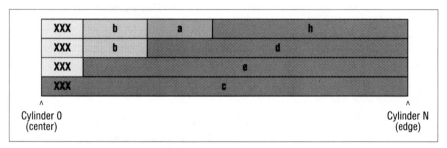

Figure 5-1. Typical BSD disk partitioning

The X's mark a portion of this disk that is inaccessible. It contains the bad block list and other record-keeping information that can only be touched by disk management utilities. The diagram says that you can look at this disk in four ways:

1. A *b* partition, an *a* partition, and an *h* partition, in which case you can build three filesystems on the disk.

2. A *b* partition and a *d* partition, in which case you can build two filesystems.

3. A single large *e* partition, in which case you can build one filesystem that occupies the disk's entire usable area.

4. A single large *c* partition, which includes the entire disk, including the inaccessible parts. Using the disk in this way will destroy the critical information on the first few cylinders—do this and, in most cases, you might as well throw the disk drive in the trash. You don't dare build a filesystem on the *c* partition.

Figure 5-2 shows another disk-partitioning scheme used for the ubiquitous (though dated) Fujitsu Eagle.

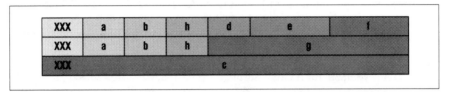

Figure 5-2. Disk partitioning—Fujitsu Eagle

This scheme divides the disk into an excessive number of smaller partitions. No matter which layout you choose, partitions *a*, *b*, and *h* are available. You can choose whether you want three more small partitions (*d*, *e*, and *f*) or a single large partition (*g*). Again, *c* refers to the entire disk, including some areas that are reserved for the disk management utilities.

Regardless of which disk you are using or how your system partitions it, BSD UNIX follows these conventions:

- Partition *a* on disk 0 is always the root filesystem. On other disks, *a* can be anything you want.

- Partition *b* on disk 0 is always a swapping area. Additional swapping areas are usually placed on the *b* partitions of other disks. However, there is nothing sacred about the letter "b": you can put a filesystem in partition *b* if you want to, and you can put your swap areas elsewhere.

- Partition *c* refers to the entire disk. For many manufacturers, this includes areas that you aren't allowed to touch. These restricted areas contain the disk's bad block list and other nonreplaceable information. NEVER try to use partition *c* without checking with your manufacturer. (SunOS is a notable exception to this rule. It keeps the administrative information outside of the *c* partition so you can build a filesystem on partition *c*.)

- In UNIX lore, partition *d* is sometimes considered a "spare root." In my own experience, systems with a spare root filesystem are fairly rare. However, it isn't a bad idea. If you set up a spare root filesystem on some disk other than the root disk and the root disk fails catastrophically, you will have a much easier time putting the system back into order.

- Partition *g* on disk 0 is often the */usr* partition.

- Partition *e* on disk 0 is often the */tmp* partition (if you decide to keep a separate partition for */tmp*).

- Partition *h* on disk 0 is often used for the user's home directories. SunOS is now calling this the */home* filesystem. On older BSD systems, home directories belonged to the */usr* filesystem.

Of course, these are only conventions. Moving the root and swap partitions requires building a new kernel and is of questionable value. But you can reassign the other partitions in any way you please. If you have several disks, there is no reason to keep */usr* and your home directories on the root disk drive. Moving them elsewhere will probably help balance your disk workload.

5.2.3 Disk Organization (System V)

The System V filesystem also divides each disk into many partitions. There aren't as many conventions about how to use these partitions, so the rationale behind any filesystem layout is somewhat easier to understand. However, you should be aware of one confusion. People who run System V on 80386-based systems use the word "partition" in two ways: one borrowed from DOS; the other the familiar UNIX partition. A disk is first divided into one to four DOS-style partitions which may be split between DOS and UNIX. The UNIX partition (or partitions) may then be split into up several UNIX-style partitions in which you can build UNIX filesystems. The confusion will be minimal if you stick to your system's tools for installing and initializing disk drives. These tools will recommend default partition sizes and will let you specify your own partition sizes if you want. Under 386/ix, the file */etc/partitions* records what happened when you partitioned your disks. If you need to find out the size, starting address, or ending address of any partition, look in this file.

5.3   Planning and Creating Filesystems

Having said all of this, how should you use your disks? When laying out filesystems, you must take several conflicting demands into account. Here are some goals to strive for:

- Distribute the workload as evenly as possible among different I/O systems and disk drives. This lets you take full advantage of the system's I/O bandwidth.

- Keep similar types of files in the same filesystem. This makes it easier to choose appropriate configuration options for the filesystem.

- Keep projects or groups within the same filesystem. This makes life easier for users (it is easier to find the files that are part of a large project if the filesystem is organized logically) but may make it harder to distribute the workload evenly.

- Give each filesystem a block size appropriate for the files it will contain. A larger filesystem block size yields better single-process speed but wastes space. Filesystem block size is discussed in more detail in Section 5.3.2, "Filesystem Block Size."

- Use as few filesystems per disk as possible. On the root disk, you will usually have three partitions and a swap area (a root partition, a /usr partition, and a partition for home directories). You may want to create separate partitions for /tmp and /usr/spool. On other disk drives, create one or at most two partitions.

- Use filesystem paging if your system supports it. Filesystem paging is discussed in Section 4.5, "Managing the Swap Area."

- If you are running System V and your system doesn't support filesystem paging, put swap areas into separate partitions. System V used to put swap areas in unused space at the end of a disk partitions. This left room for many interesting problems: if you were the slightest bit careless, your swap area could collide with a filesystem, creating chaos. System V still lets you put dedicated swap space in the same partition as a filesystem, but there's no good reason to do so.

One of these recommendations—minimizing the number of partitions on any disk—is fairly controversial. A more common recommendation is to create a larger number of smaller filesystems. The standard partitioning scheme for the Fujitsu Eagle (shown previously in Figure 5-2) reflects this philosophy. The argument for breaking a disk into several small partitions goes like this: If you can force a group of frequently accessed files to be close to each other on the disk, you can minimize the time spent seeking (i.e., the time that it takes for the disk to move its heads to the right place). You can force heavily used files to be close together by putting them in a separate small partition.

There's a good bit of truth to this. This is one reason why most modern UNIX systems make the root filesystem as small as possible, place /usr in a separate and relatively small filesystem, and use a third filesystem for home directories and all user storage. Continuing with this logic, it is a good practice to give /tmp and /usr/spool their own filesystems—as much in the interest of administrative sanity as performance. Filesystems can only grow so much, whereas an active /tmp or /usr/spool can easily take over another filesystem like kudzu.

However, I have several reservations about taking the disk locality argument further. First, it doesn't apply to single-process throughput to one sequentially accessed file. If fragmentation is minimal, the data you want will be physically close on the disk, and minimizing fragmentation is easier on a large, relatively empty filesystem than on a small crowded one. Furthermore, you don't frequently access large files (for which single-process performance is critical). When you are working with a big file, it will dominate the system's behavior. But unless you read the same 20-MB file every minute (unlikely), the total number of times you access any block will be relatively small. In a histogram showing the number of accesses to any cylinder (the System V utility *sadp*, which we will discuss later, can produce this plot), the effect of large files is likely to be negligible. The disk locality argument is then telling you to ignore the most important aspect of your filesystem.

Furthermore, isolating commonly used files in a small filesystem will only work if there's little other activity on the disk. In practice, you will build other filesystems on the rest of the disk. The more these are used, the smaller the advantage of clustering heavily accessed files in one place. You could easily end up with two activity peaks at the center and periphery of the disk, a situation in which your performance would be worse than a typical random-access pattern.

Finally, aside from special cases such as /bin and /tmp, it is hard to come up with a scheme for grouping commonly used files that is also easy to understand. You don't want to burden your users with an arbitrary and complicated filesystem organization. In short, we think you are better off creating a few large filesystems and trusting your disk driver to minimize seek times.

To be fair, there is one other advantage to small filesystems that I haven't mentioned. When you are doing backups, it is very convenient to use one tape per filesystem. Multivolume save sets are a pain. Using standard tape technology (1/4-inch cartridge or 1/2-inch magtape), you have to divide a disk into small partitions if you want to get an entire filesystem onto a single volume. However, there is a better way to avoid multivolume save sets. Get one of the new 8-mm helical scan cartridge tape drives. These can place over 2 GB on a single tape that is physically smaller than an audio cassette. Unless you have gigantic disk drives, you should never need multivolume save sets. In the long run, the helical scan drive will save you money, too: the tapes are much cheaper than either 1/4-inch cartridges or 1/2-inch magtapes, and you don't need as many of them.

5.3.1 Filesystem Tools

Now that we've told you the principles behind organizing an I/O system and the goals you should try to achieve in your filesystem layout, we'll get down to concrete. The UNIX filesystem provides several tools for creating filesystems (i.e., initializing the data structures needed so that a formatted disk can be used as a filesystem) and for modifying these structures during operation. The basic tools are:

mkfs   The basic tool for creating a filesystem. Both BSD and System V provide a *mkfs* command, although the two commands differ significantly.

newfs   A more convenient front-end to *mkfs*. Using *mkfs* requires a lot of low-level information about the disk. Rather than providing this information explicitly, it is easier to use *newfs* (which calls *mkfs* with an appropriate set of arguments). (BSD only.)

tunefs   A program that can modify certain filesystem parameters. Unlike *mkfs* and *newfs*, *tunefs* does not destroy the filesystem. You can run it without performing a backup. (BSD and V.4 only.)

The most important parameters for filesystem tuning are filesystem block size, rotational delay, number of inodes (maximum number of files), and minimum free space. The latter parameter only applies to BSD ("fast") filesystems.

5.3.2 Filesystem Block Size

A block is a unit of data that the filesystem will always atomically allocate on the disk. A filesystem's block size determines the efficiency with which it transfers large amounts of data, with larger block sizes yielding faster transfer rates for large files. However, transfer rates are not the entire story. Fast disk I/O is always desirable, but until disk drives are significantly less expensive, storage efficiency is also an issue. Large block sizes use the disk less efficiently.

The original System V filesystem supports block sizes of 512, 1024, or 2048 bytes; the latter is only supported via an optional package. The BSD filesystem supports block sizes of 4, 8, 16, 32, and 64 KB, giving much better throughput. To avoid wasting space, the designers of the BSD filesystem introduced the concept of a disk *fragment*. Fragments make it possible to store smaller files efficiently. Each block is split into two, four, or eight (usually eight) fragments. When allocating disk space, the BSD filesystem always allocates full blocks, except for the final block of a file. The last block may be partial—that is, the filesystem may use a group of contiguous fragments to make up the final block. Figure 5-3 shows a filesystem with an 8-KB block size and a 1-KB fragment size. On this filesystem, a 25-KB file consists of three blocks and one fragment.

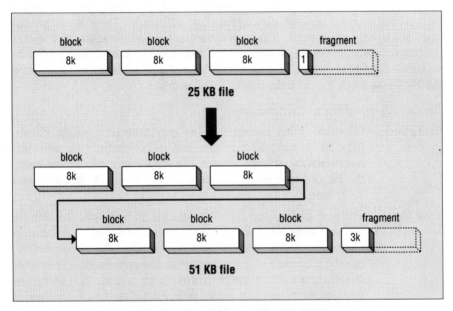

Figure 5-3. Blocks and fragments in the BSD filesystem

If you later expand the file to 51 KB, the filesystem copies the fragment to an empty block, adds some more blocks, and then adds three fragments at the end. Now the file has eight full blocks and three fragments. All blocks except for the last are full blocks. A 1-byte file always occupies an entire fragment, be the fragment size 1 KB (with an 8-KB block size) or 8 KB (with a 64-KB block size). The smaller the fragment size, the more efficiently the disk will be used.

To optimize disk performance, you must reach a compromise between storage efficiency and I/O throughput. A large block size will give the best I/O speed for large files. A small fragment size (and hence a small block size) gives storage efficiency. The best way to make this compromise varies for every filesystem, depending on what kinds of files it holds. As a general rule, filesystems used for large files should have a large block size. For large files, the balance between storage efficiency and I/O efficiency shifts. As file size increases, the amount of unused space wasted at the end of the file becomes relatively small. But if you are working with huge files, you probably want to need to access your data rapidly.

The issues for System V are almost exactly the same. A 2048-byte block size usually provides better performance than a 1024- or 512-byte block size but wastes more disk space. The standard block size (1024 bytes) usually represents the best compromise between performance and efficiency. There is one special case, however. Interactive's 386/ix provides a high-performance disk driver (HPDD) option that only supports the 1024-byte block size. For many applications, the 1024-byte block size with the HPDD will give better performance than the 2048-byte block size with the standard device driver.

Here are other specific recommendations:

Executables Filesystems that contain a lot of executable files should have a large block size. Executables tend to be relatively large, which minimizes the efficiency issue. The faster access associated with the larger block size minimizes startup time and paging (swapping) time.

Data files The best approach to data files depends on how large the files are and how they are used. If a filesystem contains many small data files, it should have a small block size. Under these circumstances, storage efficiency is more important than performance. As a rule of thumb, small files are not performance-critical. If a filesystem contains many large data files (many times the block size) and if applications programs tend to read these files sequentially rather than seeking back and forth within the file, the filesystem's block size should be large. Storage efficiency is not a concern with large files; disk throughput while accessing large files often is.

Code development

Source code, object modules, makefiles, test data files, and other files associated with developing applications programs are best placed in a filesystem with a small block size. These files are often small, so storage efficiency is important. Source code control is often used in development directories, increasing the importance of storage efficiency, and maximizing performance usually isn't a concern until you are out of the development phase.

This description is backward since block sizes apply to filesystems rather than to individual files. Almost any practical filesystem mixes all of these different types of files. However, by careful planning you should be able to place code development projects on one filesystem, production data files on another, and executables on a third. If you cannot, remember that system performance tuning is always a matter of compromises.

The block size of any filesystem is set when *mkfs* creates it. It is impossible to change the block size without destroying the filesystem and creating a new one. Under BSD UNIX, the simplest way to create a filesystem is to use the *newfs* command, which reads its arguments, computes a dozen or so disk parameters, and then calls *mkfs* appropriately. If you use *mkfs* on your own, you are forced to remember all sorts of inconvenient disk trivia. The syntax of the *newfs* command is described in the sidebar "*newfs* in a Nutshell." Here's an example of how to use it. Assume that you want to create a filesystem with a 32-KB block size on the disk partition */dev/disk2e*. The disk drive (*disk2*) has type *cdc-9715*, which you would find by looking in your */etc/disktab* file.* The *newfs* command below creates a new filesystem on this partition, accepting defaults for all parameters other than the block size:

```
# newfs -s 32768 /dev/rdisk2e cdc-9715
```

If you are using System V, you don't have a simple *disktab* command. Instead, you must use *mkfs*. Fortunately, there are nowhere near as many disk parameters to worry about. We've described the syntax of System V *mkfs* in the sidebar "*mkfs* in a Nutshell;" let's proceed to an example. Let's assume that you are building a filesystem on partition 3 of disk 0 on controller 1 (your second controller). This corresponds to the special file */dev/rdsk/d1d0s3*. Look up the partition's size in */etc/partitions*; we'll assume it says that the size is 204800 512-byte blocks (roughly 100 MB). You want the new filesystem to have a block size of 2048 bytes and the default number of inodes. To accomplish this, give the command:

```
# mkfs /dev/rdsk/c1d0s3 204800 -b 2048
```

386/ix implementations provide an administrative management tool (called *sysadm*) that uses a menu-based system to format a new disk drive, partition it, and create new filesystems for it.

---

*If your system supports changeable partition sizes, the */etc/disktab* file is obsolete, at least in a technical sense. However, many vendors have retained */etc/disktab* as a human-readable repository of information about the supported disk types. Others, like Sun, can derive the disk's type from the disk itself.

BSD newfs In A Nutshell

---

newfs [**-Nv**] [*parameter-options*] *raw-dev disk-type*

arguments

raw-dev The raw special file for the disk partition on which you want to build a filesystem.

disk-type The type of disk you are using. Many systems omit this argument— check your documentation.

options

-N Print all the disk parameters on standard output but don't touch the disk

-v Verbose; show all commands that *newfs* executes.

-a *apc* Number of alternates per cyclinder (SCSI only, not all manufacturers)

-b *block* The block size for the filesystem, in bytes. Default: 8192 bytes

-c *cpg* The number of cylinders per group. Default: 16. Don't change this.

-d *rot* Rotational delay, in milliseconds.

-f *frag* Fragment size for the filesystem, in bytes. Default: 1024. Must be 1/2, 1/4, or 1/8 of *block*.

-i *bpi* Bytes per inode. Default: 2048 bytes per inode.

-m *free* Reserved free space, in percent. Default: 10%.

-o Optimization type. Must be "space" or "time". Default depends on *free*.

-r *rpm* Rotational speed, in RPM. Never change this.

-s *size* The filesystem's size, in sectors. Never change this.

-t *tps* The number of tracks per cylinder. Never change this.

-n *nrot* The number of distinguished rotational positions per track. Default: 8. Never change this.

5.3.3 Inodes

An *inode* is a data structure that describes a file. Each file, directory, special file, link, socket, named pipe—in essence, absolutely any entity that can appear in a UNIX filesystem—is associated with an inode. The number of inodes that any filesystem has is determined when *mkfs* creates it. You can't get more inodes without scrapping the filesystem and rebuilding it. The number of inodes created when the filesystem is first generated is the maximum number of files (directories, and so on) that the filesystem can hold, regardless of how much disk space is free. In the worst case (thousands of 0-byte files), you could conceivably run out of inodes on a disk that was practically empty.

Inodes occupy some disk space (roughly 200 bytes, but the actual size varies from vendor to vendor), so there is a tradeoff between the number of files a filesystem can hold and the filesystem's usable capacity. This tradeoff is traditionally resolved in favor of inodes. The standard BSD UNIX tools, *newfs* and *mkfs*, create one inode for every 2048 bytes, which assumes that the average file size is greater than 2K. This is a generous assumption; it is rare for a filesystem to run out of inodes. I have only seen filesystems run out of inodes in two situations:

- If you receive a lot of UUNET news, the filesystem that holds the news spooling directory (usually */usr/spool/news*) may run out of inodes. If you have problems with the news directory, reducing the expiration time for news articles may be a better approach than increasing the number of inodes. Reducing the expiration time also decreases the disk space that your news directory requires.

- If you make extremely heavy use of links, you may run out of inodes. Complex version management systems layered on top of SCCS or RCS tend to use links profusely and can therefore cause inode shortages.

System V mkfs In A Nutshell

---

mkfs *special blocks*[:*inodes*] [*gap bpc*] [**-b** *block*]

arguments

special	The raw special file for the disk partition on which you want to build a filesystem
blocks	The size of the filesystem, in 512-byte blocks.
inodes	The number of inodes to create for the filesystem
gap	The rotational gap
bpc	The number of blocks per cylinder
block	The blocksize for the filesystem, in bytes: 512, 1024, or 2048

Consult your documentation for appropriate values for *gap* and *bpc*.

Reducing the density of inodes may be a reasonable option for filesystems that will be occupied by large files. The System V defaults are less generous but still ample: roughly one inode for every four logical blocks, subject to some round-ing. Thus, a filesystem with 1024-byte blocks will have one inode for every 4096 bytes, while a 2048-byte block size gets one inode for every 8 KB. Even with the largest block size, you will rarely run out of inodes before you run out of space.

The BSD command *df -i* will show you how many inodes exist and are in use on any filesystem. Under 386/ix, use *df -t* to find out how many inodes are available; XENIX systems can use *df -i* (the same as BSD UNIX). If you choose to change the number of inodes, use *newfs* to generate a new filesystem. For example, the com-mands below create a filesystem with one inode per 12000 bytes on device */dev/rdiskl e*:

```
# BACKUP THE FILESYSTEM
# /etc/umount /dev/rdiskle
# /etc/newfs -i 12000 /dev/rdiskle cdc-9715
# /etc/mount /dev/rdiskle
# RESTORE THE FILESYSTEM
```

CAUTION

Before running *newfs*, remember to backup the filesystem. *newfs* and *mkfs* destroy the data on the filesystem.

For System V, you need to run *mkfs* (or your system's disk management program) rather than *newfs* to change the number of inodes; otherwise, the procedure is the same.

5.3.4 Rotational Delay

Under the BSD fast filesystem, each filesystem has a *rotational delay* parameter. This parameter estimates the amount of time required for the CPU to service a transfer completion interrupt and initiate the next transfer. This information helps the operating system allocate blocks more efficiently. If the rotational delay is zero, the filesystem will allocate blocks contiguously. If possible, two consecu-tive blocks from a file will be physically adjacent. While this allocation style is good for systems that can service interrupts quickly, it yields bad performance for slower systems. If the rotational delay is zero and the time needed to service a disk interrupt is significant, the disk will have spun past the beginning of the next block before the system is ready to read the new block. In this case, the system has to wait for a full disk rotation before the data you need is in position again. If the rotational delay is nonzero, the filesystem will skip one or more blocks between consecutive blocks from the same file. By skipping blocks, the system minimizes the possibility that the disk will have to spin a full revolution before reaching the next block in the file. In this case, the system reads a block, skips a block while processing the disk interrupt, and then reads the next block from the file.

By default, the rotational delay is set to 4 milliseconds. If you have high-performance disks (SMD or IPI-2 disks on a high-speed bus) you may get significantly better performance by setting the rotational delay to 0, particularly if the filesystem has a large block size (32 or 64 KB). If reducing the rotational delay is appropriate for your system, you will see a significant increase in the speed of large read operations. The speed of write operations will probably remain unchanged. On filesystems with a smaller block size, the effect of rotational delay is not as clear. You may want to do some experimentation first. Try measuring how long it takes to copy a number of files (of whatever size you think is typical for the filesystem) before determining which approach is optimal. Rotational delays other than 4 and 0 should never be considered.

NOTE

Rotational delay affects read operations and write operations differently. Make sure your experiments cover both cases.

Under BSD UNIX, the rotational delay can only be set by using *tunefs*. If you are starting from scratch, use *mkfs* to create the filesystem, followed by *tunefs* to set the delay. If the filesystem already exists, you only need *tunefs*. For example, to set the rotational delay to 0 for the *disk1e* filesystem, use this series of commands:

```
# umount /dev/disk1e
# tunefs -d 0 /dev/disk1e
# mount /dev/disk1e
```

You do not need to backup the filesystem before using *tunefs*.

If you are running System V, the *mkfs* command lets you specify the rotational gap explicitly, as the number of sectors to skip between writing consecutive blocks of the file. However, you probably won't use *mkfs* directly. Instead, you will probably use an installation or disk management utility to initialize new disks. Under 386/ix, these utilities ask you for an interleave factor, which is yet another way to ask the same question. Choose the smallest interleave factor recommended for your disk controller.

Under System V.4, you can use the *dcopy* utility to change the rotational gap without creating a new filesystem. We will discuss *dcopy* later.

5.3.5 Fragmentation Control (BSD Only)

With time, any filesystem tends to become fragmented. As the filesystem becomes full, pieces of files tend to be scattered over the disk; the system cannot find enough contiguous blocks to store a new file in one place, so it must fit the file in empty spaces between other files. As files are added, deleted, truncated, and expanded, the filesystem becomes increasingly disorderly. Performance suffers because the disk drive cannot read a file with a sequential group of operations. Instead, it must constantly seek for different pieces of the file.

The BSD filesystem is designed to avoid disk fragmentation and, hence, to give consistent performance that doesn't degrade with time. We won't discuss the techniques used to avoid fragmentation; if you are interested, see "A Fast Filesystem for UNIX," reprinted in the *UNIX System Manager's Manual*. We will discuss how these techniques effect overall filesystem performance and storage efficiency.

Two parameters control the system's ability to reduce fragmentation: the *minimum free space* and the *optimization style*. The BSD filesystem's algorithm for finding free blocks becomes extremely slow as the filesystem becomes full. To prevent performance from degrading, BSD UNIX reserves a certain amount of free space on each filesystem. When the amount of free space in a filesystem reaches this lower bound, UNIX declares the filesystem full. Users cannot allocate any more file storage and attempts to do so will receive the "Filesystem full" error message.

At this point, the filesystem isn't really full—there is still a minimum quota of free space, which the superuser can allocate. As a result, *df* will occasionally show you filesystems that are more than 100 percent full. This means the superuser has allocated more disk space and the actual free space has dropped below its minimum limit. As far as mortal users are concerned, the filesystem is full and attempts to grab more storage will fail. File I/O will be extremely slow until the disk's free space returns to a more reasonable level. In addition, a lot of things start to fail when you run out of disk space. It may be difficult to clean the filesystem satisfactorily because there is no room in which to work. Don't rely on the root's ability to use every last block of storage. It is a very bad idea to wait until the filesystem is out of space before starting to clean up.

The *minimum free space* parameter sets the amount of space that will be reserved. This is normally 10 percent of the filesystem. It can be modified with the -m option to *tunefs* or *newfs*. Increasing the minimum free space probably will not increase disk performance; 10 percent is optimum for most situations. Reducing the minimum free space reclaims some disk storage, but sacrifices performance. It is legal to set the minimum free space to zero, but this will significantly compromise I/O performance.

The UNIX filesystem also lets you choose between two different optimization styles: space and time. *Space optimization* asks UNIX to optimize disk usage (i.e., to minimize fragmentation) and is the default whenever you request less than 10 percent free space. Under these conditions, the operating system tries to preserve throughput by taking more care (and time) allocating disk blocks. *Time optimization* asks the system to use a faster but less picky allocation algorithm and is the default whenever the minimum free space is greater than or equal 10 percent. Under these conditions, it is relatively easy to allocate disk blocks well, so the less fussy algorithm will do an adequate job.

The example below shows how to use *tunefs* to set the minimum free space to 12 percent and to select *time* optimization:

```
# umount /dev/diskle
# tunefs -m 12 -o time /dev/diskle
# mount /dev/diskle
```

You can also use *newfs* to set the minimum free space and optimization style: In addition to changing the minimum free space, *newsfs* is building a completely new filesystem and destroying the old. Therefore, it will eliminate fragmentation completely. Here's how to give the *newfs* command:

```
# BACKUP THE FILESYSTEM
# /etc/umount /dev/rdiskle
# newfs -m 12 -o time /dev/rdiskle cdc-9715
# /etc/mount /dev/rdiskle
# RESTORE THE FILESYSTEM
```

The BSD filesystem reduces the problem of fragmentation but doesn't eliminate it. Over time, the filesystem will gradually become fragmented, no matter how much free space you give it or what optimization style you prefer. And consequently the performance of any filesystem will degrade over time. If you don't have an extent-based filesystem, the only way to eliminate fragmentation is to start from scratch: backup the filesystem, create a new filesystem with *newfs*, and restore the filesystem.

5.3.6 Fragmentation Control (System V Only)

The biggest problem with the System V filesystem is vulnerability to fragmentation. With time it becomes impossible to devote a contiguous series of disk blocks to a file. The *free list* (the list of unused disk blocks) contains individual blocks here and there but no large contiguous sequences.

The System V *fsck* utility inspects the filesystem upon startup and repairs it if necessary. It can also reorganize the free list to minimize fragmentation. To do so, take these steps:

1. Put the system in single-user mode (with *shutdown*).

2. Dismount the filesystem that you are interested in.*

3. Run *fsck -S* to rebuild the free list.

4. Reboot the system as soon as *fsck -S* finishes.

Reorganizing the free list helps minimize fragmentation but can only do so much. Files that were created before you ran *fsck* will remain fragmented. You can't undo fragmentation that has already occurred unless you have System V.4. (See *dcopy* later in this chapter.) The only way to eliminate fragmentation completely is painful but possibly worth the effort: backup the filesystem, use *mkfs* to reinitialize the filesystem, and then restore the filesystem. When you restore the filesystem, every file will consist of a series of contiguous blocks. The system's disk performance will improve noticeably but it will eventually refragment itself.

System V.4 provides some additional tools for dealing with disk fragmentation. The utility *dcopy* copies an old-style (System V) filesystem to cartridge tape, then restores the filesystem optimally. It eliminates fragmentation (both within the file and on the free list) and reduces directories to their minimal size. You can't use *dcopy* for new-style (BSD, UFS) filesystems.

NOTE

I have seen one V.2 system that supported an early version of *dcopy*. While it would repack your filesystem properly, the situations under which you could use it were very restrictive. I have seen no other versions for either V.2 or V.3. Therefore, you probably don't have *dcopy*, and even if you do have it, you might not be able to use it. But check your manuals first.

Use *dcopy* with these commands:

```
# umount fs1
# umount fs2
# dcopy -F s5 options fs1 fs2
```

where *fs1* is the raw special file for the filesystem you're copying and *fs2* is the block special file for the filesystem you're restoring. As we've shown, both

---

*You can't dismount the root filesystem. In this case, you must put the system into single-user mode before proceeding. It is absolutely crucial that filesystem activity stop while *fsck* or *dcopy* are running.

filesystems must be unmounted. *fs1* and *fs2* can be the same. For example, the following command copies and restores the filesystem */work*, which is located on partition 3 of disk 1:

```
# umount -F s5 /work
# dcopy -F s5 /dev/rdsk/1s3 /dev/dsk/1s3
```

dcopy provides a few useful options:

-V   Print the commands that this *dcopy* invocation will generate but don't take any action. Use this option to ensure the *dcopy* command line is correct.

-o   The following options are system-specific. This option must precede the options that are listed below.

-sb:g Reorganize the filesystem using a cylinder size of *b* blocks and a gap of *g* blocks between successive blocks in the same file (rotational gap).

-an   Put files that have not been accessed within *n* days at the end of the filesystem, after the filesystem's free blocks. Normally, all files are placed at the beginning of the filesystem, followed by the free blocks. With this option, *dcopy* will cluster your frequently used files at the beginning of the filesystem.

-d   Don't change the order of files within a directory.

For example, the following command places files that have not been accessed within five days at the end of the filesystem and does not reorder directories:

```
# umount -F s5 /work
# dcopy -F s5 -o -a5 -d /dev/rdsk/1s3 /dev/dsk/1s3
```

Always do a full backup before running *dcopy*. It is destructive and something like a tape error in midstream could kill you. After reorganizing a filesystem with *dcopy*, run *fsck* before remounting.

NOTE

dcopy and the underlying program, *compress*, are not available on all systems. AT&T says that it only works on the 3B2, but we hope that other systems manufacturers will follow suit. In addition, you must have a cartridge tape drive. And a warning: We have not been able to test this command. What happens if the filesystem can't fit onto one tape? The V.4 manuals don't say. One hopes that *dcopy* knows about multivolume tape sets but it would not be the first UNIX tool that didn't.

5.4 Balancing I/O Workload

The BSD tool *iostat* prints a number of I/O statistics that will help you to balance disk load. Use it this way:

```
% iostat drives interval count
```

where:

drives   An optional list of disk drives about which you want reports. For *ios-tat*, disk drive names have the form *dkn*, where *n* is an integer. By default, *iostat* reports on drives *dk0* through *dk3*.

interval   The sampling interval, in seconds; *iostat* reports statistics every *interval*. While *interval* is optional, it is hard to get any meaningful statistics without it. A good sampling interval is 5 seconds.

count   The number of samples to take. If omitted, *iostat* will loop indefinitely (i.e., until you stop it with a CTRL-C).

Here is a typical *iostat* report, with a sampling interval of 5 seconds:

```
% iostat 5i
...            dk0              dk1              dk2              dk3          cpu
... bps tps msps bps tps msps bps tps msps bps tps msps us ni sy id
...  63   4  0.0    8   1  0.0   14   2  0.0   17   3  0.0  28  0 10 62
...  18   2  0.0    0   0  0.0   73   2  0.0   15   2  0.0  90  0 10  0
... 115   6  0.0   27   4  0.0    0   0  0.0    3   1  0.0  79  0 21  0
... 237  14  0.0    6   1  0.0    0   0  0.0    4   1  0.0  49  0 51  0
... 102   6  0.0   11   2  0.0    0   0  0.0   12   2  0.0  94  0  6  0
...  94   6  0.0   17   3  0.0    0   0  0.0    0   0  0.0  90  0 10  0
... 120   7  0.0    6   1  0.0    0   0  0.0   31   4  0.0  94  0  6  0
...  39   2  0.0    0   0  0.0    0   0  0.0   16   3  0.0  89  0 11  0
...   1   0  0.0    0   0  0.0    0   0  0.0    3   0  0.0  63  0 11 26
```

The statistics reported are:

tin, tout   Number of characters waiting in the input and output terminal buffers. These statistics have no impact on filesystem optimization.

bps   The average number of kilobytes per second during the previous interval for disk *dkn*.

msps   The average number of milliseconds per seek. This figure is highly unreliable and is not even computed by some vendors; ignore it.

tps   The average number of transfers per second during the previous interval for disk *dkn*.

cpu   Not of interest for filesystem optimization.

The first line of the report attempts to show some sort of statistical average since the system was booted; ignore it. The remaining lines show the I/O statistics for the previous sampling interval. The most difficult thing to understand is the relationship between disk numbers and your actual disk drives. The disks are numbered according to the following rules:

- *dk0* is always your system's root disk drive.

- The next drives in this list are the drives that have dedicated swapping partitions. They appear in the order in which they are listed in the configuration file.

- The remaining drives are listed in the order in which they are checked by *fsck*. This is controlled by */etc/fstab*.

In the report above, most of the I/O activity was on disk 3 and disk 0. Disk 2 had a single burst of activity at the start of the sampling period, and disk 1 had more consistent (though less intense) activity throughout the period. Ideally, a long-term average of the statistics for each drive would show roughly equal activity. In practice, this never happens. Disk 0 (always the root disk) usually shows the most activity by a fairly large margin. The standard system executables are stored on the root filesystem. Because these are the most commonly invoked programs, the root disk drive is usually the most heavily used.

Under System V, *sar -d* is supposed to show you how much activity is taking place on each disk drive. Unfortunately, it doesn't work on any 386/ix system. As far as we know, it requires special features that are only supported by the AT&T 3B-series disk controllers, so we suspect that it doesn't work on any systems (aside from the 3B). Unfortunately, without *sar -d* you're reduced to looking at the blinking lights on the disk drive that show when accesses are taking place. Once you know how heavily each disk drive is being used, you can try reorganizing the filesystem to balance the load more equitably. That's more easily said than done. It's easy to give some hints, like we did earlier in the chapter, but very hard to succeed. Here's a quick recap of the hints:

- Put site-specific executables on some disk other than the root disk.

- Put */usr* on some disk other than the root.

- Distribute swap space evenly among all fast disk drives.

- Use an in-memory filesystem for */tmp* if you have a lot of memory and your system supports it.

- Assign working groups to filesystems in a way that spreads the anticipated workload out; for example, if two groups of users stress file I/O, put their material on different disk drives.

No doubt, some inequities still remain. To smooth these out, here are some further hints:

- If per-process throughput is your goal, put the filesystem with the largest and most performance-critical data files on the disk drive with the best raw transfer rate. When single-process throughput is the issue, raw data rates govern I/O performance.

- If aggregate throughput is your goal, put the root filesystem on the disk drive with the best seek time. When aggregate throughput is at stake, seek times become the dominant factor in disk performance.

If you have only one "fastest disk," you must decide whether you want to optimize per-process or aggregate file performance.

It is hard to strike the best compromise between storage requirements, equitable distribution, and maintaining a clear and reasonable filesystem layout that will help (rather than hinder) your users. Let's look at a brief example of how you might do this. Consider a system that is used by three groups of physicists:

theory   This group does a lot of programming but doesn't handle large data sets and doesn't perform a lot of I/O.

astro   This group does less programming but uses the computer to analyze data from a radio telescope. It has very large data files and I/O bandwidth is often a problem for them.

nuclear   This group does about as much programming as *astro* and also uses the computer to analyze data. Its applications differ in that their data requirements are smaller. Its jobs tend to be CPU-bound rather than I/O-bound.

Now let's look at the hardware available. Assume that you have three disk drives. The root disk drive contains the root filesystem, standard executables, spooling areas, and other administrative areas. The other two disk drives are free for general purpose use.

To balance the workload, you might want to give *astro* its own disk drive with a single filesystem. This filesystem should have a large block size to provide the best single-process access to large files. Let the other groups, *theory* and *nuclear*, share the second disk drive. These two groups have smaller I/O requirements, so they should be able to coexist peacefully. Their disk can be split into two filesystems with a relatively small block size. If your system supports multiple I/O subsystems, giving the astronomers their own VMEbus will prevent their I/O workload from affecting the system's other users. The astronomers will get the best possible per-process performance. They won't swamp the other disks with I/O requests, enabling the system's other users to get satisfactory aggregate response and they will have sufficient storage for their large files.

5.4.1 Disk Locality

System V includes a tool called *sadp* for gathering statistics about disk references. If you are trying to cluster heavily used files together, you can use *sadp* to find out whether you are succeeding. As I have said elsewhere, I am not a great believer in these clustering techniques. But if you choose to follow this path, you will find *sadp* indispensable and may be able to use it to prove me wrong. Unfortunately, *sadp* is not a part of 386/ix, at least for V.3 and probably not for V.4—it requires a lot of information that is specific to the AT&T's 3B2 I/O architecture. It may be available with System V implementations that run on other architectures.

sadp produces two kinds of data: data about which disk cylinders you access and data about the seek distance (the number of cylinders between successive disk accesses). You can't get one report without the other, but you can get the reports either in tabular or histogram form. We'll assume that you want a histogram, which gives you a quick visual check of disk performance. To get a histogram, invoke *sadp*:

```
% sadp -h options interval reports
```

where *interval* is the length of time (in seconds) that will be covered by each *sadp* report and *reports* is the number of reports to generate. The *interval* must be greater than 10 seconds; the number of reports is optional and defaults to 1. The *options* are:

-d type   The disk's type. This may be *sdsk* for SCSI disks, *fdsk* for floppy disks, or *hdsk* for all others.

-n   The disk's number. Alternatively, you may have two numbers separated by a hyphen (e.g., 3-5, meaning all disks from disk 3 to disk 5) or a set of numbers separated by commas (e.g., 3,5,7, meaning disks 3, 5, and 7). If omitted, *sadp* prints a set of reports that covers all disk drives. If this option is specified, the *-d* option must also be present.

For example, to create one pair of histograms summarizing usage of hard disk 2 for more than 20 minutes, use the command:

```
% sadp -h -d hdsk -2 1200
```

The report from the previous command will look something like this:

```
CYLINDER ACCESS HISTOGRAM
disk=2
Total transfers = 1009
12%|
   |
10%|
   |                          *
 8%|                          *
   |                          *   *
 6%|                          **  *
   |                          ****          *
 4%|*                         ****          *
   |*                         ****          **
 2%|*                         ****          ****
   |**........*...*......****...............****......*......
 0%                         Cylinder number
        1       2     2     3     4     4     5     5
        4       0     7     3     0     6     2     9
        4       8     2     6     0     4     8     0
```

The horizontal access shows disk cylinders. Cylinder 0 is at the inside of the disk. The vertical axis shows how often any group of cylinders is accessed. This histogram shows that the inside of the disk (where system-critical information is stored) is accessed fairly often. There's a heavily used area a third of the way out and a third heavily used area roughly two-thirds of the way out on the disk. By looking at the setup of this disk (i.e., the disk cylinders assigned to each filesystem; you should record this when you format the disk), you can figure out which filesystems correspond to the heavily accessed areas. The "localize access" school of thought says that, ideally, this disk should be organized so that there's only one peak of activity. In other words, there should be one big cluster of stars on the histogram. You may be able to accomplish this by placing the heavily used files in the same filesystem.

Even if you don't believe in the localize access school, there is an obvious worst case that you should take care to avoid. If *sadp* shows that you have two peaks of activity at the inner and outer edges of the disk, you have something to worry about.

Along with the cylinder access histogram, *sadp* gives you a *seek distance histogram* that looks like this:

```
SEEK DISTANCE HISTOGRAM
disk=2
Total seeks = 1009
12%|*
   |*
10%|*
   |*
 8%|*
   |*
 6%|**
   |**
 4%|***
   |****
 2%|*******
   |********
 0%****************** . . . . . . . . . . . . . . . . . . . . . . . . . . . . . . . . . . . . . . . . .
      1       2       2       3       4       4       5       5
      4       0       7       3       0       6       2       9
      4       8       2       6       0       4       8       0
```

In this display, the horizontal axis shows *seek distances*, or the number of cylinders between successive disk accesses. The vertical axis shows the percentage of the total disk seeks that required a given seek distance. Ideally, the seek histogram should show one large spike on the left side (very small seek distances), tapering off as quickly as possible. This means that most disk accesses require only a minimal movement of the disk's heads.

5.5 Filesystem Buffers

The filesystem manages a large cache of I/O buffers, commonly called the *buffer cache*. This cache allows UNIX to optimize read and write operations. When a program writes data, the filesystem stores the data in a buffer rather than writing it to disk immediately. At some later time, the system will send this data to the disk driver, together with other data that has accumulated in the cache. In other words, the buffer cache lets the disk driver schedule disk operations in batches. It can make larger transfers and use techniques such as seek optimization to make disk access more efficient. This is called *write-behind*.

When a program reads data, the buffer cache can often eliminate disk accesses entirely. When a program reads, the system first checks the buffer cache to see if the desired data is already there. If the data is already in the buffer cache, the filesystem does not need to access the disk at all. It just gives the user the data it found in its buffer, eliminating the need to wait for a disk drive. The filesystem only needs to read the disk if the data isn't already in the cache. To increase efficiency even further, the filesystem assumes you're going to read the file consecutively and reads several blocks from the disk at once. This increases the likelihood that the data for future read operations will already be in the cache. This is called *read-ahead*. All in all, the buffer cache allows the disk drivers to convert many random I/O operations, performed by many different processes, to a few coordinated transfers. Figure 5-4 illustrates this process.

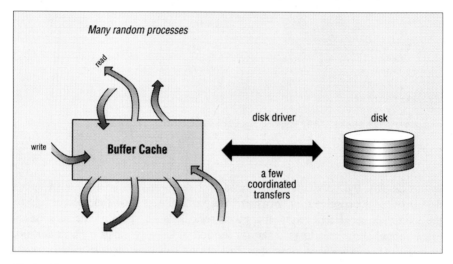

Figure 5-4. The buffer cache

The size of the buffer cache has an important effect on performance. Increasing the size of the buffer cache increases the chance of finding data in the cache, eliminating the need to access the disk itself. It also increases the filesystem's ability to optimize disk accesses. The buffer cache is particularly important if you access a small group of files repeatedly. In this case, increasing the cache's size will help disk throughput considerably. The cache's size is less important if you work with extremely large files. Granted, you may be willing to devote most of memory to filesystem buffers, but this is usually impractical. The most difficult tradeoff in performance tuning is between memory and file I/O. If you expand the cache, you squeeze memory. If you squeeze memory too much, paging and swapping overload both the CPU and the I/O subsystem.

On System V.4 and SunOS Release 4.0 and following, the buffer cache plays a much smaller role. The kernel manages file access by mapping files directly into its virtual address space and letting the memory management machinery take care of the rest; however, the kernel still needs to manage a cache of buffer headers. System V.4 lets you control the number of buffer headers that will be allocated at one time and the maximum amount of memory that will be devoted to buffer headers. By restricting the cache's maximum size, you can guarantee that a certain amount of memory will be reserved for users. If your system spends a lot of time paging, you should decrease the maximum cache size.

BSD UNIX doesn't give you any indication of how efficient the cache is. You will have to take our word that making the cache larger may improve your I/O performance. With System V, the *sar* utility can give you cache statistics:

```
% sar -b

ora ora 3.2 2 i386     05/21/90

00:00:01 bread/s lread/s %rcache bwrit/s lwrit/s %wcache
01:00:03       3      51      94       4      15      69
02:00:02       4      57      94       4      14      69
03:00:01       3      45      93       4      14      68
04:00:01       2      34      93       4      12      69
05:00:02       2      27      93       3       8      68
06:00:00       0       7      96       0       1      63
07:00:00       0       8      96       0       1      63
08:00:00       0       8      97       0       1      64
08:20:00       1      12      94       1       2      65
08:40:00       1      15      94       1       3      64
09:00:00       0       6      95       0       1      59
09:20:01       2      44      95       3       9      64
09:40:00       3      65      95       5      14      65
10:00:00       1      18      92       2       6      66
10:20:01       1      21      95       2       5      66
10:40:01       1      20      94       3       8      66
11:00:01       3      43      94       3      10      68
11:20:01       4      70      94       3      11      68
11:40:01       2      27      93       4      10      66
12:00:01       8      65      88       6      19      66

Average        2      31      94       3       8      67
```

The fields in this report are:

bread/s   The average number of read transfers, per second, from a disk to a buffer.

lread/s   The average number of read transfers, per second, from a buffer to an application.

%rcache   The percentage of read operations that were able to read from the cache rather than directly from the disk.

bwrit/s   The average number of write transfers, per second, from a buffer to a disk.

lwrit/s The average number of write transfers, per second, from an application to a buffer.

%wcache The percentage of write operations that were able to write to the cache rather than the disk.

The report above shows extremely good cache utilization (more than 90 percent for reading and around 65 percent for writing). You can ignore the physical (or raw) operations; by definition, these don't go through the cache. If **%rcache** falls significantly below 90 percent or if **%wcache** falls much below 65 percent, you should consider enlarging the buffer cache—provided that your system isn't also paging. If it is paging and your buffer cache is too small, you should seriously consider buying more memory.

If you use the RFS (Remote File Sharing) facility, you should be aware of an important variation: *sar -Db*. This command separates cache activity for local and remote file access, allowing you to fine tune local and remote access separately. Kernel customization allows you to reserve portions of the buffer cache for exclusive-local or exclusive-remote use.

Under 386/ix, filesystems with a 2048-byte block size use a separate set of buffers. Unfortunately, *sar -b* combines the data for both sets into one report; there is no way to segregate 2048-byte data from 1024-byte data.

5.5.1 Disk Updates (System V)

In addition to letting you control the number of buffers reserved for different filesystem types, the configuration process for V.3 lets you control the algorithm for updating disks. We describe the configuration process in detail in Chapter 8, *Kernel Configuration*; for the time being, we'll look at how the disk gets updated.

As we've said, when a program writes data into a file, it is actually putting data into a buffer. Some time later, a daemon (*bdflush*) comes along, gathers a group of data buffers, and sends the entire group to the disk driver. This allows the driver to look at the transfers in each batch, figure out the physical location of each data block, and make the transfer in the best possible order rather than randomly jumping back and forth on the disk. This is called *seek optimization*.

Problems occur when the system crashes. Data that is in the buffer cache but has not yet been flushed to the disk is usually lost. It is obviously in your best interest to minimize the amount of data that could get lost during a crash. You don't want to flush the buffers too rarely, leaving you prone to lost data and disk corruption if the system crashes. But you do want to minimize disk activity and let the system make a large number of coordinated transfers at once. Flushing data to the disk more often increases the system's reliability by minimizing lost data but decreases performance efficiency.

Two configuration parameters control the flushing process. *BDFLUSHR* (renamed *FSFLUSHR* in V.4) controls the interval at which the flush daemon runs. By default, the daemon runs once per second. The standard System V.3 configuration files don't let you change the flush interval, though you can force a greater interval if you really want to. An equally important constant is *NAUTOUP*. This is the number of seconds after which any given buffer will be flushed to disk. When it runs, the flush daemon checks the age of each buffer (the amount of time since the buffer was written). If the buffer's age is greater than *NAUTOUP*, the daemon copies the buffer to the disk. If the buffer's age is less than *NAUTOUP*, the flush daemon leaves it alone: it will be written later. Typical values for *NAUTOUP* are 10 to 15 seconds, which means that data doesn't arrive on the disk safely until 15 seconds after you write it. Setting *NAUTOUP* to zero flushes all buffers to disk as soon as the flush daemon runs. This gives the best reliability but the poorest performance: it prevents the disk driver from optimizing disk access patterns.

Depending on the reliability of your system, you can do a lot to improve performance by increasing *NAUTOUP* and *BDFLUSHR*, particularly if the system is dedicated to file-intensive applications, such as database management. *NAUTOUP* can be as high as 120 (flush buffers that are older than 2 minutes), while *BDFLUSHR* could reasonably be 60 (run the flush daemon every minute). Try these extreme values only if your system is reliable—that is, if you can count on it running for days at a time without crashing. The less reliable your system is and the more important your data is, the less you can afford to play with these parameters. You are trading speed against the amount of data you will lose during a crash.

5.6 In-memory Filesystems

A number of UNIX systems now support *in-memory* filesystems, often called RAMdisks by vendors. These systems include the most recent version of SunOS (4.1), XENIX, and Interactive's 386/ix (only with the high-performance disk driver option). An in-memory filesystem lets you create filesystems that never exist on disk. As a name implies, the data only exists in memory, which is used to simulate a disk drive. Accessing an in memory filesystem is extremely fast. Data transfers take place at the speed of memory, rather than at the speed of your disk drive and I/O bus.

While in-memory filesystems are extremely fast, they have several major draw-backs:

- They are temporary. An in-memory filesystem disappears whenever the sys-tem reboots. They cannot be used for permanent data and are only good as substitutes for /tmp. Depending on your application mix, this may be all you need. Programs that spend a lot of time reading and writing temporary files will be able to take good advantage of an in-memory filesystem.

- They are small. Obviously, an in-memory filesystem can't be larger than your system's physical memory. In reality, it has to be a lot smaller: you need room in memory for the kernel, you need room to run user-state programs, and so on. Unless your system has a huge amount of memory, an in-memory filesystem will be at most a few megabytes.

- They reduce the amount of physical memory that is available. Space used by an in-memory filesystem can't be used to run programs. With an in-memory filesystem, your system will be more prone to paging. We do not recommend creating an in-memory filesystem if your system spends a lot of time paging. You will only make your memory shortage worse.

Sun's in-memory filesystem is the most flexible we have seen. The memory required for the filesystem is variable. Unlike other implementations which per-manently reserve a piece of memory, Sun's memory filesystem only takes up as much space as is required. The memory filesystem can also be paged or swapped if the system's memory requirements grow. Performance will suffer when this happens, but the additional degree of flexibility may be important in some situa-tions.

To create a memory filesystem under SunOS, use the command:

```
# mount -t tmp swap mount-point
```

where *mount-point* is the name of a directory. If you want these filesystems to be created automatically, put the requisite *mount* commands in the /etc/rc.local startup script or place this entry in /etc/fstab:

```
swap            mount-point tmp rw 0 0
```

For example, to place the /tmp filesystem in memory, make sure that /etc/rc.local contains the command *mount /tmp* (or an equivalent) and add this line to /etc/fstab:

```
swap /tmp tmp rw 0 0
```

Interactive's memory filesystem for 386/ix (called RAM disk) is part of the high-performance disk driver option. To install it, use the *kconfig* utility. Start by running *kconfig* and selecting the "Configure kernel" and the "Configure high performance disk driver" menus. As you proceed through the configuration questions, *kconfig* will eventually ask if you to create a RAM disk. Reply *y*; *kconfig* will then ask how much memory you want to reserve for the RAM disk, in 4-KB blocks.

Under 386/ix, all of the memory reserved for a RAM disk is allocated at once and isn't available to the rest of the system. You cannot create a RAM disk on a system with limited memory, and you should be extremely conservative in the amount of memory you allocate. Make sure that enough memory is left to run the applications that you need.

5.7 Striped Filesystems

Disk striping is a technique for increasing per-process disk performance. A striped filesystem is composed of two or more physical disk drives. Each file is spread across all of the disk drives that make up the filesystem. Because files are spread across many disks which can work in parallel, per-process performance is significantly better than for a standard, single-disk filesystem. Therefore, striped filesystems can help you improve performance for programs that stress disk I/O to very large files. Whether a striped filesystem will help aggregate I/O throughput (rather than single-process I/O) depends on how your vendor implements striping.

Many UNIX systems in the mini-supercomputer class support striping, but it is not standard by any means. The tools for creating and maintaining striped filesystems vary from manufacturer to manufacturer. If you want to set up a striped filesystem, consult your vendor's system administration manual.

5.8 Conserving Disk Space

The prior discussion has stressed disk throughput and tended to neglect storage efficiency. You can do several things to conserve disk space:

- Configure filesystems with small block sizes. This entails a performance penalty if your system stresses per-process throughput. However, it is not a bad option if you can decide which filesystems really need good performance.

- Configure filesystems with less free space. This will free up some storage but not much (at most 10 percent, assuming you're starting from a standard configuration). In turn, it will have a negative effect on disk performance.

- Use the *compress* utility to shrink files that you don't access often. *compress* typically makes ASCII files 30 to 50 percent smaller.

- Institute some form of rationing by enabling disk quotas or limiting the size of files users can create.

- Clean out filesystems regularly. It is surprising how much trash occupies a typical filesystem: core dumps, checkpoint and backup files created by editors, old object modules, and other stuff. By using *cron* and *find*, you can automate the cleaning process.

- Delete files that aren't used. If no one plays the UNIX games, there's no reason to keep them on the system. If no one uses *yacc*, you might consider deleting it. Be careful, though. If you delete a popular game, sooner or later every user will have a private copy, and you'll have even less free disk space than when you started. And there's no way to tell when you might find a use for *yacc* (or any other tool). You may even discover that you've been using it all along without knowing it; many UNIX tools are invoked by other seemingly unrelated programs. Deleting system files (aside from games) is a risky business.

The first two options have already been discussed, we won't belabor the point further. We will devote some attention to techniques for rationing disk storage and for purging useless files from the filesystem.

Before discussing ways to conserve disk space, we must first discuss ways of measuring how much space is available and who is using it. Two tools, *df* and *du*, report how much disk space is free and how much is used by any given directory.

5.8.1 Filesystem Free Space

For each filesystem, the *df* utility tells you how much disk space is available, how much is free, and how much is in use. By default, it lists both local and remote (i.e., NFS) filesystems. Under BSD UNIX, the output from *df* looks like this:

```
% df
Filesystem    kbytes    used    avail   capacity  Mounted on
/dev/disk0a   889924  724308    76620      90%    /
/dev/disk3d   505463  376854    78062      83%    /benchmarks
/dev/disk5e   635287  553121    18637      97%    /field
/dev/disk2d   505463  444714    10202      98%    /research
/dev/disk1e   956094  623534   236950      72%    /homes
toy:/usr      498295  341419   107046      76%    /usr
toy:/           7495    5883      862      87%    /root
...
```

This report shows information about five local filesystems and two remote filesystems (from the system *toy*). The *research* and */field* filesystems are close to capacity (97 and 98 percent, respectively), while the other filesystems still have a lot of room left. You might want to take some action to free up some storage on these two filesystems. On most systems (but not all), *df* deducts the minimum free space before computing the capacity. The superuser can always allocate disk space until the disk is completely full. Therefore, a filesystem that is 100 percent full really has 10 percent free space (unless you have changed the minimum free space)—but this last 10 percent is only accessible to the superuser.

df can be invoked in several other ways:

- If you already know that you're interested in a particular filesystem, you can use a command such as *df /homes*; this reports usage statistics for the filesystem */homes*. To specify a filesystem, you may give its root directory name (e.g., */homes*) or its special file name (e.g., */dev/disk1e*).

- If your system uses NFS and you are only interested in local filesystems, use the command *df -t 4.2*. You should always use this command if remote file servers are down. If you have mounted remote disks that are unavailable, *df* will be extremely slow.

- If you are interested in inode usage rather than simple filesystem capacity, use the command *df -i*. This produces a similar report showing inode statistics.

If you are using the older System V filesystem, the report from *df* will look different. The information it presents, however, is substantially the same. Here is a typical report, taken from a XENIX system:

```
% df
/        (/dev/root ):    1758 blocks    3165 i-nodes
/u       (/dev/u    ):     108 blocks   13475 i-nodes
/us      (/dev/us   ):   15694 blocks    8810 i-nodes
```

There are 1758 physical blocks (always measured as 512-byte blocks, regardless of the filesystem's logical block size) and 3165 inodes available on the root filesystem. To find out the filesystem's total capacity, use *df -t*. The command *df -l* only reports on your system's local filesystems, omitting filesystems mounted by NFS or RFS. The *dfspace* command (available on Systems V.3 and V.4) produces a significantly nicer report that's similar to the BSD-style *df*. For each filesystem, *dfspace* shows the amount of free storage both in kilobytes and as a percentage of the filesystem's size.

5.8.2 Filesystem Usage

It is often useful to know how much storage a specific directory requires. This can help you to determine if any users are occupying more than their share of storage. The *du* utility provides such a report. Here's a simple report from *du*:

```
% du /homes/workgroup
107      ./joe
94       ./john
217      ./mary
577      ./sally
18       ./howard/stuff1
14       ./howard/private
33       ./howard/work
868      ./howard
258      ./susan/code
769      ./susan
2634     .
```

This command shows that the directory *lhomeslworkgroup* and all of its subdirectories occupy about 2.5 MB (2634 KB). The biggest users in this group are *howard* and *susan*, who have a total of 868 and 760 KB each, respectively. The report also shows storage occupied by subdirectories (*lhowardlwork*, etc.). *du* does not show individual files as separate items, unless you invoke it with the *-a* option. Note that System V reports disk usage in 512-byte blocks, not KB.

The *-s* option tells *du* to report the total amount of storage occupied by a directory; it suppresses individual reports for all subdirectories. For example:

```
% du -s /homes/workgroup
2634
```

This is essentially the last line of the previous report.

It's a common technique to write a shell script that runs *du* and sends nasty mail to users whose storage has exceeded some amount. This could be called a poorman's quota system. However, in my experience this technique creates more anger than compliance—even if your mail message is more polite than the one in the sample script below:

```
# !/bin/sh
# Script to flame at users with large home directories.  This
# could be modified to check other directories (work spaces).
# We assume the SunOS 4.0 convention for home directories.
#
targetdirs=/home/`hostname`
users=`ls $targetdirs`
#
# set this to some suitably large chunk of the disk
limit=40000
#
for user in $users
do
     storage=`du -s $targetdirs/$user | awk  '{ print $1 }' -`
     if [ $storage -ge $limit ]
     then
          mail $user <<@
```

```
You have over $limit blocks of disk space, you
antisocial slob.  In fact, you have $storage.
Why don't you clean up?
@
     fi
done
```

5.8.3 Disk Rationing

No matter how much disk space you have, you will eventually run out and probably much sooner than you expect. Files have a way of expanding to fill the disks that are available. Users rarely archive their old, unused files without some coercion. If disk space is available, users will generally keep their old stuff around, "just in case." And if disk space isn't available, they will fight tooth and nail to keep their data.

One way to force users to clean up is to impose quotas on disk usage. BSD UNIX supports a disk quota system which will enforce the quotas you establish. Prior to V.4, System V had no quota system at all. In Release V.4, System V supports quotas for BSD-style (UFS) filesystems. Quotas are maintained on a per-filesystem basis. They may be placed on disk storage (the number of blocks) and on inodes (the number of files). The quota system maintains the concept of *hard* and *soft* limits. A user who exceeds a soft limit gets a warning but can continue to accumulate more storage. The warning will be repeated whenever the user logs in. At some point (i.e., after some number of sessions in which the storage stays above the soft limit), the system loses patience and refuses to allocate any more storage. At this point, the user must delete files until he or she is again within the soft limit. Users are never allowed to exceed their hard limit. This design allows users to have large temporary files without penalty, provided that they do not occupy too much disk space long-term.

Like anything else, quotas are a tradeoff. Enabling quotas adds some additional overhead to filesystem operations, slightly increasing the system's workload. This overhead is small and may not be noticeable (except when you are logging in), but it's there. To minimize the overhead, you might want to impose quotas on filesystems where storage is critical, leaving others alone. For example, you may want to impose quotas on the filesystem that has personal home directories, leaving filesystems that support particular development projects alone. This will allow official business to go on uninterrupted while preventing users from filling a disk with old mail (a common problem) and other personal files.

To enable quotas on your system, take these steps:

1. Become superuser, *cd* to the filesystem's root directory, and use the command *touch quotas*. This creates the file *quotas*, if it does not already exist.

2. Edit the */etc/fstab* file. If you are running NFS, add the option *quota* to the filesystem's *options* field. You must also add this option to the appropriate entry for all remote hosts that mount the filesystem—otherwise, the remote hosts won't observe your quotas. If you are not running NFS, change the option *rw* to the option *rq*. Here are two examples; one shows the *fstab* entry for a system running NFS, while the other shows the old-style *fstab*:

```
/dev/disk1e /w 4.2 rw,quota 1 3 # NFS fstab entry, with quotas
/dev/disk1e:/w:rq:1:3          # pre-NFS fstab entry, with quotas
```

3. For each user, use the command:

```
# /etc/edquota username
```

To give the same quota to a group of users, use the command:

```
# /etc/edquota -p user1 user2 ...
```

NFS users may find that the *edquota* command has been moved to */usr/etc/edquota*.

4. The *edquota* command creates a temporary quota file and invokes an editor on it. By default, it will invoke *vi*, but it will check your *EDITOR* environment variable to find out which editor you prefer. Initially, the temporary file looks like this:

```
fs /w blocks (soft=0, hard=0) inodes (soft=0, hard=0)
```

The limit 0 means no limit (i.e., infinity). Edit this file, replacing the zeroes with whatever limits you consider appropriate for disk blocks and file count. When you have finished editing, save the file and exit from the editor.

5. To ensure your quotas are syntactically correct and consistent with current disk usage, use the command:

```
# /etc/quotacheck filesystem
```

6. Make sure that */etc/rc* executes the command */etc/quotaon -a*, which starts quota checking.

7. To enable quotas, reboot the system or manually execute */etc/quotaon*.

Some other techniques can prevent users from creating large files. You can use the *limit* command to restrict the size of files that a user can create. To set a maximum filesize, use the command:

```
% limit filesize max-size
```

For example, the command below prevents a user for creating any files larger than 2 MB:

```
% limit filesize 2m
```

With this command, UNIX will refuse to allocate more disk space to any file that grows larger than 2 MB.

Similarly, you can use *limit* to restrict the size of core dump files. This is relatively painless, since most users don't want core dump files. Core dumps are generally large files and are often generated for innocuous reasons, such as invoking commands incorrectly. To set a maximum size for core dumps, execute the C shell command:

```
% limit coredumpsize max-size
```

To eliminate core dumps entirely, use the command:

```
% limit coredumpsize 0
```

limit commands such as this can be placed in the *.cshrc* file for every user. If a program tries to dump core but would require a dump that exceeds the limit, the core file is not created. Because core dumps are essential for effective debugging, any users who are actively debugging programs should know the command *unlimit coredumpsize*, which removes this restriction.

5.8.4 Disk Housekeeping

No matter how good your users are at cleaning up, the disk will periodically accumulate trash that get overlooked. Core dump files, checkpoint files created by editors, old object files and executables, etc., are all prime examples of disk trash. The most basic tool for locating these files is *find*. It can be used in two ways:

- **For the timid**: *find* can produce a list of files that you suspect aren't needed. You can go over this list and decide which files aren't needed.

- **For the bold**: You can define the files that you consider extraneous and program *find* to delete them automatically. You can automate the task completely by running *find* through *cron*.

Among experienced UNIX administrators, the latter approach is quite common. Let's discuss how to implement it, making the following assumptions:

- The gnu-emacs editor is in common use at your site. This editor creates checkpoint files by adding a tilde (~) to the name of the file you are editing. You want to delete backup files that are more than a day old.

- Another editor in common use creates checkpoint files by preceding the filename with *.CKP*. These are particularly insidious because they are invisible to the default *ls* command; users may not even know that they exist. You want to delete these files if they are more than a day old.

- You want to delete all core dump files that are more than a day old.

This *find* command searches the filesystem for files that match these characteristics:

```
find / \( -name core -o -name '*~' -o -name '.CKP*' \) -atime +1 -exec rm {} \;
```

This command means "look for files named *core* (*-name core*) or (*-o*) whose name ends in ~ or whose name begins with *.CKP*, AND haven't been accessed within the past day (*-atime +1*), and delete all files that match these criteria (*-exec rm {} \;*)." Start searching at the system's root directory (*/*)." The *-o* option combines the two adjacent parameters with a logical OR; by default, adjacent parameters are ANDed together. AND normally takes precedence over OR; quoted parentheses, \(and \), are used to group operations.

It's obviously a bad idea to use a command such as this until you're certain it will work correctly—that it will delete files you don't want without touching anything you do want. Try it by hand first, replacing *-exec* with *-ok*. With the *-ok* option, *find* prompts you before taking action on any file. Enter *y* if you want to execute the action (in this case, deleting the file) and *n* if you don't.

Once you are confident that the command won't accidentally delete any files you want to save, you can execute it regularly via the *cron* facility. Under BSD UNIX, the *crontab* entry below executes a somewhat simpler *find* command at 1:15 a.m. daily:

```
15 1 * * *   root   find / -name core -atime +1 -exec rm {} \;
```

Under System V, the *cron* facility is set up differently; a different *crontab* is maintained for each user. Given the command:

```
# crontab root
```

the system will invoke an editor on the root's *crontab* file. Add the following line, then save the file and quit the editor:

```
15 1 * * *  find / -name core -atime +1 -exec rm {} \;
```

The *crontab* command then installs the new version of the crontab file, executing *find* daily at 1:15 a.m.

NOTE

The latest release of SunOS has converted from a BSD-based *cron* to a System V-based *cron*.

find has many features and options, almost all of which are useful for filesystem cleanup. For a complete discussion, refer to the discussion of *find* in Section 1 of the *UNIX Programmer's Reference Manual* or enter the command *man find*.

6

Network Performance

UNIX Networking
Introduction to TCP/IP Problems
Basic Network Etiquette
Network Performance Issues
Networks and CPU Load
RFS: System V Remote File Sharing
Special Considerations for STREAMS

In the past few years, users have come to rely on distributed networked filesystems, easy access to remote systems, and other network-based amenities. As networks become more important to computing systems, they become a larger part of system performance as a whole. The network can become the limiting factor for I/O performance; if a group of systems relies heavily on a network, the network can (in the worst case) become the dominating factor in overall system performance. Unfortunately, understanding network performance is extremely difficult. You are looking at interactions between computer systems, not just at single computers. Problems with other systems in the network can cause below-par performance on your system. Your computer may be totally innocent, while the guilty party may be rooms, floors, or even buildings away. The tools that measure different aspects of network performance give voluminous, though generally unhelpful, data.

6.1 UNIX Networking

UNIX networking is mercifully standard. TCP/IP networking entered the BSD UNIX world with Release 4.1C. The network tools that were included with Release 4.2 (*rlogin*, *rsh*, *rcp*, etc.) have become omnipresent throughout the UNIX world. Berkeley's TCP/IP implementation has been ported to almost all System V implementations, where it is available as an option. Sun Microsystem's Network File System (NFS) became an extremely popular way to share files between different systems. It has been ported to System V (in addition to DOS, VAX/VMS, and several other operating systems) and is available as an option. In Release 4 of System V, NFS and TCP/IP are fully integrated into System V. Therefore, we can cover virtually all of UNIX networking by discussing Berkeley's TCP/IP and Sun's NFS. And the X window system, which can place a significant load on the network, is completely standard across many operating systems.

There is one other group of tools to contend with: AT&T's RFS (Remote File Sharing) facility, which is an option available with System V.3 and the most recent release of SunOS. System V.4 includes RFS alongside NFS. We must admit we have rarely seen RFS in use. Even among confirmed System V users, NFS seems to be the file-sharing mechanism of choice. Toward the end of this chapter, we will give some attention to RFS and the issues it raises.

Most TCP/IP packages for System V are implemented via the STREAMS facility rather than using the original BSD socket mechanism. If you use System V, the STREAMS package may require some attention.

6.2 Introduction to TCP/IP Problems

From a user's point of view, there is one easy way to tell when networking is affecting system speed. Operations that use the network seem slow, while operations that do not use the network seem to take place at normal speed. If an *rlogin* session echoes characters several seconds after they are typed, while a direct *login* echoes normally, network performance may be behind the delay. If you are editing a file on a remote system via NFS and the file takes an abnormally long time to save, network performance may again be causing the delay.

Determining an appropriate course of action is tricky, though. If the concept of "acceptable badness" applies anywhere, it applies to networking. Even a badly overloaded network only runs at maximum capacity for seconds (at most minutes) at a time. Most of the time, only a small fraction of network bandwidth is in use. It may be reasonable to ask users to tolerate such delays. Ten seconds may seem like an eternity when an editor is saving a file but it is certainly not a crucial loss of time. In such situations, you are better off asking users to tolerate the system's performance rather than taking on the task of restructuring the network to optimize its behavior. If, however, it takes minutes (rather than seconds) to save a file or if saving a file produces "NFS server not responding still trying" messages before succeeding, you have more significant network problems (possibly a faulty network or a faulty file server) and will have to take some action.

6.3 Basic Network Etiquette

A few simple rules of etiquette will help users get a lot more out of your installation. If you understand how a network functions, these rules will be common sense. Observing these rules will minimize network traffic and, in many cases, will solve significant performance problems without requiring any configuration changes.

The Network File System (NFS) has allowed virtually transparent access to files across Ethernet. This is a tremendous advantage, but it has its dark side. It is easy to forget or to stop caring about where files are physically located. This quickly leads to network performance problems, for two reasons:

1. The Ethernet is shared by every user of every system on the network. Therefore, it is a relatively limited resource with many users. This situation can be alleviated somewhat by adding subnetworks (we will discuss network topology later), but no matter how complex the network's topology, a network basically consists of many systems communicating through a single piece of wire. If one user is accessing a very large file across the network, he or she may be slowing down the network for all users: other users on his system, other users on other systems, users of diskless workstations, etc.

2. Accessing a file via Ethernet can never be faster than doing a remote login and locally accessing the same file. You still have to read or write to the disk drive. No matter how fast the network, it can only add overhead.

Users should be aware of the tradeoffs they make when they access remote files. If a program reads or writes a tremendous amount of data, it is better to log in to the system where the data is local than transfer the data across the network using NFS—better for both the user who is running the program and all the other users on the network.

The point is not that users should avoid NFS but that a network is a tool and, like any other, has appropriate and inappropriate uses. It is an excellent tool for moving files between systems, for general browsing, for remote editing, and for file sharing. If several workstations can share the /usr filesystem, you've managed to free a lot of disk space. This may be well worth additional network congestion and slow access. But NFS is not an appropriate tool for sustained high-speed data access or for remote tape access. If a lengthy program is I/O-bound, there is no good reason to make the program slower by incurring additional network overhead. If a program is I/O-bound but runs very quickly, the convenience of the network may well be worth the additional overhead, provided that you don't run it hundreds of times per day. Editing, compilation, and other tasks that are not I/O-bound are ideal for the network. Limit diskless workstations to remote editing and *login*.

If you need to transfer huge amounts of data between different computer systems, Ethernet may not be the appropriate medium to use; the basic Ethernet cable is limited to 10 MB per second (less than 1 MB per second, after accounting for network overhead). Other media are now available that offer significantly higher sustained transfer rates.*

As a system manager, your share in basic network etiquette is to make sure that any diskless workstations at your site have enough memory to run efficiently. A diskless workstation uses the network for all paging and swapping activity. If the workstations don't have enough local memory to minimize paging and swapping, they can easily consume a lot of network bandwidth, even if the users obey the etiquette we discussed above. Workstation users will certainly notice sharply degraded performance whenever their workstation is paging (regardless of the overall network load). The memory requirements of any workstation depend primarily on the manufacturer and the manufacturer's operating system release.

---

*We will only mention two of these here; a full discussion is far beyond the bounds of this book. HPPI (high-performance peripheral interface) is a 100-MB/second 32-bit parallel link. While HPPI is fundamentally point-to-point, star couplers, and ring networks will greatly increase its flexibility. FDDI is a high-speed fiber-optics link. Both FDDI and HPPI are still in the very early stages, although some equipment is beginning to appear on the market.

6.4 Network Performance Issues

For optimal network performance, the network must meet three conditions:

- It must be able to transfer data correctly (that is, it must have *data integrity*). If it cannot, you must isolate the faulty equipment (a network interface, transceiver, connector, or cable).

- It must provide enough bandwidth to satisfy the needs of the network's users. If the network does not have enough bandwidth, the amount of time needed to transfer data between any two points gets excessively long.

- Each system on the network must be fast enough to handle the network traffic addressed to it.

6.4.1 Unreachable Hosts

The simplest network tool is a utility named *ping*. It sends one packet to a specified *host*, requesting a response. If a correct response arrives, *ping* prints the message "host is alive." Some versions of *ping* also print the time required to receive the response. If the response doesn't arrive, *print* prints the message "host is unreachable." In the latter case, there is no valid path between your system and the *host* you are trying to reach. If so, one of the following must be true:

- Your system is not connected to the network. Make sure you can *ping* other hosts on your network.

- If your system has a network coprocessor, the coprocessor may have crashed. Make sure you can *ping* other hosts on the network.

- The host you are trying to reach has crashed. *ping* should work after the host has rebooted.

- Some portion of the network between your system and *host* is broken. The problem may range from a bad piece of cable to a network gateway that is dead.

- Your system's routing tables are incorrect or incomplete.

The *ping* command is as simple as it sounds. It is normally given as:

```
% /etc/ping host timeout
```

The *timeout* argument is optional. It specifies the amount of time that *ping* will wait before deciding that the *host* is unreachable. By default, *ping* decides that hosts are unreachable after 20 seconds.

NOTE

On some systems (in particular, SunOS), *ping* and other network commands are in the directory */usr/etc*.

If you suspect intermittent problems, invoke *ping* this way:

```
% /etc/ping -s host packetsize count
```

This tells *ping* to send one request per second, up to a total of *count* requests. The size of each request is *packetsize*—64 bytes is a good value (and it's the default). *ping* reports each response as it arrives, allowing you to see whether the *host* is periodically disappearing from the network. If you omit *count*, *ping* continues to send packets until you enter CTRL-C. When *ping* terminates, it summarizes the total number of packets that it received, the total number of errors, and other data.

If *host* returns most of the packets but misses a few, you have to make some hypotheses about what is wrong. It is possible that *host* is badly overloaded and cannot respond within a reasonable time. This is unlikely (the default 20-second timeout period is rather long), but you should check into it. It is more likely that network interface or a connector is intermittently bad.

6.4.2 Data Corruption on the Network

The network protocols that are used for Ethernet and other communications media incorporate several levels of error detection and correction. When a system receives a bad packet from the network, it detects the error and asks the sender to send another packet. The exact mechanism for deciding that something is missing and requesting a replacement depends on the protocol you are using. If you are using the TCP protocol, the protocol itself is responsible for replacement. If you are using UDP (a related protocol), the application program handles replacement. Fortunately, the packet replacement mechanism is carefully hidden. If you are not writing your own network software, you can assume that you always get reliable data from the network. However, data corruption leads to performance problems. When a large percentage of network packets are damaged en route, performance declines for two reasons. The network software has to request a retransmission and wait for the retransmitted packet to arrive. In turn, retransmission increases the overall network load, which increases the probability of collisions, requiring more retransmissions.

Therefore, network integrity problems appear as performance problems—the network appears abnormally slow. In the worst case, the network may stop working altogether. It may be impossible to access remote systems and programs using the network will time out.

The simplest tool for diagnosing network problems is the command *netstat -i*. Here's a sample report:

```
% netstat -i
Name Mtu  Net/Dest   Address    Ipkts    Ierrs Opkts    Oerrs Collis
en0  1500 bld1_e1-ne mysys      18852493 0     17449167 0     1
sl0* 1006 none       none       0        0     0        0     0
sl1* 1006 none       none       0        0     0        0     0
sl2* 1006 none       none       0        0     0        0     0
lo0  1536 loopback-n localhost  4666628  0     4666628  0     0
```

This report shows:

Name   The name of the interface. It identifies a particular Ethernet board. *enk* indicates Ethernet board *k* on your system, which corresponds to the special file */dev/enk*, and *lo0* is the *loopback interface*. The loopback interface is a convenience for testing network software. Packets sent to this interface do not go out over the network but are immediately reflected back to the sender. *sln* indicates a "SLIP" interface (IP protocol over an asynchronous serial line). On this system, the SLIP interface is unused.

Mtu   The maximum transfer unit or the maximum packet size for this interface.

Net/Dest   The network to which this interface is connected.

Address   The Internet address of this interface. This field contains the name used to address this interface on the network. It is usually a hostname, such as *mysys* in our example. Look up the actual Internet address in the */etc/hosts* database.

Ipkts   The number of input packets received by this interface since the system was booted.

Ierrs   The number of input errors that have occurred at this interface since the system was booted. This should be extremely low—under 0.025 percent of the input packets. Input errors include virtually all checksum errors.

Opkts   The number of output packets sent by this interface since the system was booted.

Oerrs   The number of output errors that have occurred at this interface since the system was booted. This should be extremely low—under 0.025% of the output packets.

Collis   The number of collisions that have been detected at this interface since the system was booted. This may be relatively high— conceivably as high as 10 percent of the output packets.

To diagnose gross network problems, look at **Ierrs** and **Oerrs**. Input errors includes all errors that occurred as a result of receiving packets from the network. If an input error occurs, the network interface just discards the packet and trusts the software to replace it. A large number of input errors usually means there is faulty hardware on the network. Faulty hardware can mean anything from another computer system that is generating packets improperly to a bad connector or terminator. It is also possible that your system's device driver cannot receive packets fast enough. Check to make sure that your system responds well to a burst of packets from *spray* (which we will discuss shortly).

A large number of output errors means that your system's network interface is faulty. The problem may be in your system's network controller, the Ethernet drop, or virtually anything between your CPU and the main Ethernet cable. Output errors aren't caused by other systems. If you see output errors, the problem is local.

In normal operation, the acceptable number of input or output errors is extremely low: 0.025 percent of the total number of input or output packets. You can expect to see higher numbers if you are actively playing with the network hardware (plugging and unplugging cables) or if a power failure or some other situation causes all of your systems to boot simultaneously. In these situations, a large number of output errors is normal.

netstat -i also reports collisions. Collisions occur when your system starts sending data at the same time as another system on the network. When your system detects a collision, it waits a random amount of time and retransmits the packet. Collisions are normal events and don't indicate hardware problems. However, the probability of two hosts transmitting at the same time increases the more heavily the network is used, so collisions are an extremely good indicator of network load. The number of collisions should be, at most, 10 percent of the total number of output packets. If the number of collisions is consistently greater than (or close to) 10 percent, the network overloaded. Your only solution for this problem is to rearrange the network in a way that reduces traffic.

NOTE

I have seen some lazy network implementations that don't differentiate between output errors and collisions. In this case, **Collis** will be zero and the **Oerrs** will for all practical purposes reflect the number of collisions.

The drawback to *netstat* is that its counters reflect your system's activity since the last time it booted. If you're lucky enough to have reliable systems that run for months without crashing, the numbers from *netstat* will be incredibly large and probably meaningless. Statistics that are weeks old will drown out any important trends. It's easy to fix this problem with a simple shell script. The short program below takes *netstat* readings at regular intervals, looks at a single network interface, and reports the changes between the current reading and the previous one—i.e., the number of input packets during the last interval, the number of collisions during the last interval, and so on:

```
# !/bin/sh
# get a series of netstat reports and normalize
# invoked as: program-name interval interface-name
( while true # simulate vmstat behavior:  one report every
  do          # interval seconds
      sleep $1
      netstat -i
done ) | awk \
  "BEGIN { printf \"%12s%12s%12s%12s%12s\n\",\"New Ipkts\",\
        \"New Ierrs\", \"New Opkts\",\"New Oerrs\",\"collis\";
        pipkts=0; pierrs=0; popkts=0; poerrs=0; pcollis=0
        }
  # find the line describing the interface we care about
  /^$2/ { ipkts=\$5 - pipkts; ierrs=\$6 - pierrs; opkts=\$7 - popkts
        oerrs=\$8 - poerrs; collis=\$9 - pcollis
        printf \"%12d%12d%12d%12d%12d\n\",ipkts,ierrs,opkts,\
            oerrs,collis
        pipkts=\$5; pierrs=\$6; popkts=\$7; poerrs=\$8;\
            pcollis=\$9
        }" -
```

6.4.3 Gathering Network Integrity Data from NFS

Systems that are running NFS can also get useful data about network corruption by using *nfsstat -c*, which reports the system's client-side NFS statistics (i.e., statistics about NFS requests that this system originated). Here's a typical report:

```
% nfsstat -c
Client rpc:
calls      badcalls   retrans   badxid    timeout    wait     newcred
19678      0          74        8         74         0        0
```

```
Client nfs:
calls       badcalls   nclget    nclsleep
19661       0          19661     0
null        getattr    setattr   root       lookup      readlink read
0   0%      2260 11%   33  0%    0    0%     3083 15%    116  0%  11200 56%
wrcache     write      create    remove     rename      link     symlink
0   0%      2154 10%   119 0%    46   0%     3   0%      17   0%  0    0%
mkdir       rmdir      readdir   fsstat
1   0%      0   0%     523 2%    106 0%
```

The **retrans** field (under **Client rpc**) indicates the number of packets that this host had to retransmit as an RPC client: that is, the number of retransmissions it made while reading or writing an NFS file. If this field is greater than 5 percent of the total number of client NFS calls, suspect trouble. Compare the number of retransmissions to the **badxid** field. If **badxid** and **retrans** are roughly equal, one or more of the network's NFS servers is having trouble keeping up with the client's demands. Using *spray* (we'll discuss this later) to send a large number of packets from the client to the server will probably confirm this. This isn't a data corruption problem, but a performance problem on the part of the server. We discuss slow servers in Section 6.5.1. If **retrans** is high but **badxid** is relatively small or zero, the problem is in the network itself—the network is either slow or suffering from data corruption. In this example, retransmissions are only about 0.3 percent of total number of RPC calls, an acceptably low figure.

nfsstat can do one thing that *netstat* lacks: it lets you zero the counters at any time. Therefore, you don't have to look at data gathered over the last month—it's easy to collect data for a day or so. To zero the counters, become root and give the command *nfsstat -z*. It may be useful to zero the *nfsstat* counters regularly. To zero the counters at 2 a.m. daily, add one of the following entries to your system's *cron* files:

```
0 2 * * * root nfsstat -z # add to /usr/lib/crontab for BSD systems
0 2 * * *      nfsstat -z # add to root crontab file for System V
```

6.4.4 Tracking Down Network Problems

Reflected signals (echoes, if you will) are the fundamental cause of trouble on any cable. Reflections are caused by *impedance bumps*, which are sudden changes in the cable's characteristic impedance. When a signal reaches an impedance bump, part of it is transmitted normally; the other part is reflected. Of course, it is impossible for a network interface to distinguish reflected signals from real signals, which therefore interfere with other traffic. The network interfaces start discarding many packets and performance drops to zero.

There are many different causes for an impedance bump. Sharp bends or kinks in the cable cause impedance bumps, so all Ethernet installation manuals will tell you to avoid sharp turns. A bad piece of cable, connector, terminator, or Ethernet tap can also cause an impedance bump. (A terminator is nothing more than a 50-ohm resistor that prevents a reflection from occurring when the signal reaches the end of the cable.) In practice, badly soldered connectors and poorly installed Ethernet taps are very common problem sources. Learn to not trust your connectors, even if they were professionally built. Using preterminated cable will help you to avoid trouble. Avoid "stinger" or "vampire" Ethernet taps (the kind that puncture the cable jacket). They are convenient but prone to problems. And only install taps on the 2.5-meter boundaries that are marked on all standard Ethernet cables.

If any part of the network is faulty, the network (or at least the subnetwork) as a whole will not work properly. There are two ways to track down the problem: the right way (which is expensive) and the wrong way (which may not work). The right way to isolate a network problem is to buy a network cable analyzer, which costs $10,000 or so. The analyzer sends signals down the network and waits for them to *reflect* (i.e., to bounce back). By measuring the interval between the initial signal and the reflection, it can tell you how far away the problem is. You then have to get out your tape measure and start measuring your cable. A network analyzer can usually pinpoint a problem to within a few inches. It can also give you important information about the nature of the problem: Is the network shorted? Is it open? Or is the problem more subtle, such as a kink in the cable?

The wrong way to proceed is to start at one end of the network and gradually disconnect systems, one at a time, until the network begins to work again. When the network starts to work again, you can assume that the last link that you disconnected was faulty; however, this assumption can very easily be false. The network might be working because you bumped an intermittent connector or flexed a faulty cable. For the time being, it will work. If you're lucky, you won't have trouble again. If you're unlucky, you will be doing the same thing again next week. We won't deny that this method is useful, but lost efficiency and repeated attempts to solve the same problem can quickly become more expensive than the tools needed to do the job correctly.

6.4.5   Data Corruption at a Gateway

Gateways between networks are an additional source of errors. To find out whether gateways are causing data corruption, use *netstat -s*. The complete report looks like this:

```
% netstat -s
ip:
        267130 total packets received
        3 bad header checksums
        0 with size smaller than minimum
        0 with data size < data length
        0 with header length < data size
        0 with data length < header length
        967 fragments received
        0 fragments dropped (dup or out of space)
        0 fragments dropped after timeout
        0 packets forwarded
        0 packets not forwardable
        0 redirects sent
icmp:
        21 calls to icmp_error
        0 errors not generated 'cuz old message was icmp
        Output histogram:
                echo reply: 1
                destination unreachable: 21
                time stamp reply: 231
        0 messages with bad code fields
        0 messages < minimum length
        0 bad checksums
        0 messages with bad length
        Input histogram:
                destination unreachable: 2
                echo: 1
                time stamp: 231
        232 message responses generated
tcp:
        0 incomplete headers
        4 bad checksums
        0 bad header offset fields
udp:
        0 incomplete headers
        0 bad data length fields
        0 bad checksums
        0 socket full drops
```

All counts reflect the total number of packets that were transmitted since I system was last booted. The **bad checksums** fields under **ip, icmp, tcp,** and **udp** indicate packets that were corrupted while flowing through a network gateway. Gateway corruption should be an extremely small percentage of the total number of packets received: hundredths of a percent or even less. If your system shows a significant number of bad checksums, you should determine which gateway is faulty.

Isolating a faulty gateway is difficult. *netstat* can show that you have problems but does not tell you where they are. The best way to proceed is by transferring a large file across each gateway and noting when the **bad checksums** field increments. Gateway errors should be extremely rare. If you want a reasonable chance of seeing an error occur, you need to transfer thousands of network packets (which carry several hundred bytes of data each). This means you must transfer a file that is at least several megabytes in length, and preferably longer. Copying the file to */dev/null* saves disk space on the receiving end. Better yet, most network analyzers have a mechanism for sending packets across a gateway.

For example, assume that running *netstat* on the system *host1* shows a significant number of gateway errors. Assume that transfers between *host1* and *host2* cross the gateway *g1*, and transfers between *host1* and *host3* cross the gateway *g2*. The following sequence of commands would help you to isolate the gateway that is corrupting data:

```
% netstat -s | grep "checksum"
...
% rcp host2:bigfile /dev/null
% netstat -s | grep "checksum"
...
% rcp host3:bigfile /dev/null
% netstat -s | grep "checksum"
...
```

If the **bad checksums** count increases after copying the file from *host2*, then gateway *g1* is bad; if the **bad checksums** count increases after copying the file from *host3*, then gateway *g2* is bad.

The following shell script is a simple attempt to automate this process:

```
# !/bin/sh
# LOOK FOR ERRORS WHILE CROSSING GATEWAYS
# invoke as program-name host1 host2 ... hostn
myself=`hostname`
bigfile=/vmunix      # pick any large file you want,
                     # the bigger the better
                     # or even better, create a file
                     # that's even larger
netstat -s | grep "checksum"      # get initial report
for host in $*
do
    echo "Testing copies from $host to $myself"
    rcp $bigfile $host:/tmp
```

```
      rcp $host:/tmp/$bigfile /dev/null
      netstat -s | grep "checksum"   # has anything changed?
      rsh $host "rm  /tmp/$bigfile"
  done
```

When you have isolated a faulty gateway, you must determine exactly what is wrong with it. The problem is usually some form of memory corruption, which can occur within the network interface itself, the system's I/O memory, the system's main memory, etc. Because almost any computer and many other kinds of communications hardware can serve as a gateway, we can't make any general comments about how to isolate the problem. Consult the gateway's manufacturer for more help.

6.4.6 Network Congestion

Like any other communications medium, the network has a finite bandwidth; it can only carry data at a certain limited rate. For Ethernet, the theoretical maximum rate is 10 MB per second. Even on a lightly loaded network, actual transfer rates are significantly lower. Inefficiencies in the network controllers plus the overhead required for the layered network protocols reduce the actual transfer rate significantly.

When a network is too crowded, *packet collisions* occur. Packet collisions take place when two systems on the network try to transmit at the same time. Their two transmissions collide, resulting in completely garbled data. After detecting a collision, the network hardware waits for a period of time and tries transmitting the same data again.

The easiest way to detect collisions is to look at *netstat -i*. We've already discussed this report; here's a quick review:

```
% netstat -i
```

Name	Mtu	Net/Dest	Address	Ipkts	Ierrs	Opkts	Oerrs	Collis
en0	1500	bld1_e1-ne	mysys	18852493	0	17449167	0	1
sl0*	1006	none	none	0	0	0	0	0
sl1*	1006	none	none	0	0	0	0	0
sl2*	1006	none	none	0	0	0	0	0
lo0	1536	loopback-n	localhost	4666628	0	4666628	0	0

For looking at collisions, only the **Collis** field interests us. The number of collisions may be as large as 10 percent of the total number of packets. Every network has periods of high activity during which there will be many collisions. A problem exists only if your network spends a lot of time in this state or if it is commonly in this state. Network loads are generally characterized by short periods of peak activity, which should not be frequent enough or long enough to be a problem. Don't determine that your network is congested on the basis of a single report. Before you decide there is a problem, run *netstat -i* repeatedly and note how the number of collisions changes over time. If the number of collisions tends to be high, you must reorganize your network to minimize network traffic.

Another way to find out whether a network is heavily loaded is to look at the active connections report. *netstat* produces this report when it is invoked without any options:

```
% netstat
Active Internet connections
Proto Recv-Q Send-Q Local Address   Foreign Address  (state)
tcp      0      0 localhost.3297  localhost.sunrpc TIME_WAIT
tcp      0      0 localhost.3296  localhost.sunrpc TIME_WAIT
tcp      0      0 mysys.1020      somewhere.1021   ESTABLISHED
tcp      0      0 mysys.shell     somewhere.1023   ESTABLISHED
tcp      0      0 localhost.3295  localhost.sunrpc TIME_WAIT
tcp      0      0 localhost.3294  localhost.sunrpc TIME_WAIT
tcp      0      0 localhost.3293  localhost.sunrpc TIME_WAIT
tcp      0      0 mysys.1023      somewhere.1021   TIME_WAIT
tcp      0      0 mysys.login     nowhere.1022     ESTABLISHED
tcp      0      0 mysys.login     elsewhere.1017   ESTABLISHED
...
```

This report shows one line for every currently active connection using the Internet protocol family. Each line shows the protocol in use, the number of characters in the send and receive queues for each connection, the address of the connection on the local and remote hosts, and the state of the connection. The important statistic is the number of packets in the send queue. At any time, this number should be 0 for most of the connections that are listed. If the send queue is large for many of the connections, the network is significantly congested. Again, occasional periods of heavy traffic are normal and to be expected. If network traffic remains heavy for a long period or if invoking *netstat* repeatedly at random times generally shows congested traffic, you should consider changing your network configuration.

To reduce traffic on a congested network, divide it into two or more subnetworks connected by a gateway. Gateways are systems that belong to two or more networks. They detect packets on one subnet that are destined for another and forward those packets between the two nets. You can buy dedicated gateways to connect two networks, but it is more common to use a general purpose computer system with two network interfaces as a gateway. Once you have partitioned the network into two subnetworks, systems on each subnetwork will be able to communicate without interfering with the other subnetwork. The only traffic that flows through the gateway is the traffic that needs to get to the other subnet.

Before reconfiguring your network, carefully decide what the new configuration should be. You can do a lot to reduce network traffic by thinking about how your network is used. Your goal is to isolate as much traffic as possible on individual subnetworks. The following rules of thumb will help you to accomplish this goal:

- Diskless workstations should always be on the the same subnetwork as their file server.

- Systems that mount each other's disks via NFS should be on the same subnetwork, unless the actual NFS activity between the two systems is relatively low.

- Systems shared by the same group of people should be on the same subnetwork.

- Systems that handle a lot of network traffic should have a lot of memory. Such systems include large file servers and other systems that support several diskless nodes. No matter what kind of networking you are using (BSD-style or STREAMS-based), proper network operation requires a lot of memory.

Here is an example that shows how restructuring a simple network can reduce traffic and improve performance. Assume that you have the following systems:

chem1   A large mainframe (minisupercomputer) used for computational chemistry.

chem2   Another mainframe used for computational chemistry.

eng1   A mainframe for structural analysis.

admin   Another system running UNIX used for administration.

helium A diskless workstation, booting from *chem1*, used by a chemist.

neon   A file server, used by the chemistry group.

argon   A diskless workstation, booting from *neon*, used by a chemist.

ford   A diskless workstation, booting from *eng1*, used by a mechanical engineer.

edsel   A diskless workstation, booting from *eng1*, used by a mechanical engineer.

The chemistry file server (*neon*) is used to boot the chemistry group's workstations, hold home directories, etc. The group's large data files reside on the two mainframes that run the group's major applications programs. The engineering mainframe, *eng1*, doubles as a file server for the group's workstations. In practice, a network this small would not be likely to suffer network congestion problems; however, this small network will demonstrate the techniques that are used to reduce traffic.

Organizing a network along departmental lines is usually a good way to reduce total traffic and this network is no exception. Place *chem1*, *chem2*, and the chemistry workstations on one network; place *eng1* and the mechanical engineering workstations on the other. The administrative system, *admin*, can be placed on either network; however, putting it on the mechanical engineering network may balance the workload a little better. Then use *neon* (the chemistry file server) as the gateway between the two networks. The redesigned network would look like Figure 6-1.

This network isolates the chemistry-related traffic on one subnetwork and the mechanical engineering and administrative traffic on the other. It is a good assumption (and easily verified) that the chemists will use files on *chem1* and *chem2* and will often use *rlogin* to work on these machines. Similarly, it's a good assumption that the mechanical engineers will use *eng1* most heavily. While the engineers and chemists may use each other's systems and all will access *admin* from time to time, we expect this sort of usage to be relatively small.

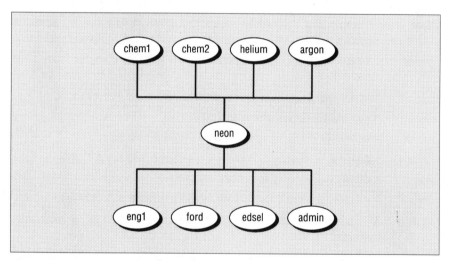

Figure 6-1. The redesigned network

Partitioning the network reduces the traffic on each subnetwork and minimizes the traffic flowing across the gateway. Implementing this new network requires adding an additional network interface to the gateway and changing the cabling appropriately, changing the */etc/networks* and */etc/hosts* databases to reflect the new subnetwork and the new network addresses, and modifying each system's *ifconfig* and *routed* commands (which should be in one of the */etc/rc* startup files) to enable the network interfaces and route packets appropriately between the subnets. You can improve system performance further by adding a dedicated file server for the mechanical engineering workstations. Particularly for large networks, dedicated file servers are much more efficient at handling network traffic than systems designed for high-performance computation.

One final consideration about network congestion. If network performance is really important to you, you should very seriously consider buying a local disk for every workstation. A small disk is relatively cheap, but lost productivity quickly becomes very expensive. If you must use diskless workstations, try to limit them to four or five per file server. If you will be using the workstations primarily as superintelligent terminals (that is, if you don't plan on running any applications programs other than editors and simple utilities such as *cat* and *ls*), you may be able to get away with one file server for every eight workstations or so. Don't try to get away with 15 or 20 workstations per server. You are only asking for trouble.

Most installations that I've seen haven't obeyed these rules and have paid the price—particularly if a power failure or some other catastrophe takes down the entire network at once. Chaos results when 18 or 20 workstations try to boot from the same file server at the same time. When the servers are badly over-loaded, the workstations will start timing out packets, requiring the server to resend perfectly good data twice, 10 times, or 100 times. It may take hours (or may even be impossible) for the overloaded servers to get everyone running again. Booting the entire network at once is a worst-case situation, but you will notice severe congestion problems even during normal operation. Placing each file server on a dedicated subnetwork with its diskless workstations will help, regardless of the ratio of file servers to workstations. But do yourself a favor: try to maintain a reasonable ratio of diskless workstations to file servers. Your life will be miserable otherwise.

6.5 Networks and CPU Load

Systems on the network are allowed to "drop" a packet because they are unable to handle it at the moment. If it is important, the network protocol or the application program will eventually request a replacement. While they aren't bad in themselves, dropped packets can be a symptom of several problems:

- The system's network software and hardware are not capable of responding to incoming network data fast enough to handle the packet.

- The system's CPU is under heavy load, preventing the network software from responding fast enough, even though it would normally be adequate.

- The network software temporarily doesn't have the buffer space needed to handle the incoming packet. This is usually a consequence of CPU load. It means that the higher-level software using the network hasn't been able to read the incoming data.

A system is most likely to drop packets if a large number arrive at once. Most systems can't really handle a sudden barrage of Ethernet traffic as well as they should. If a system that can generate packets very quickly sends a lot of data to a system that can't receive packets quickly, the receiving system will probably drop a lot—maybe even most—of the incoming packets. However, most dropped packets must eventually be replaced, and the replacement packets add to the network's workload. Also, dropped packets may indicate that system is suffering from other problems.

Use the program *spray* to find out whether or not a system is prone to dropping packets. *spray* sends a sudden burst of network traffic from one network host to another:

```
% /etc/spray host options
```

If there are no options present, *spray* sends roughly 100000 bytes to the given *host*. By default, this data consists of 1162 packets, each with 86 bytes of data. Here is a typical report from *spray*:

```
% spray otherhost
sending 1162 packets of lnth 86 to otherhost ...
        226 packets (19.449%) dropped by otherhost
        68 packets/sec, 5890 bytes/sec
```

The important statistic here is the number of packets that were dropped. If the percentage of packets dropped is small (under 5 percent), there is no cause for concern. If the percentage of packets dropped is large, as it is here, it means that the system running *spray* can generate packets much faster than the other system can receive them. This usually means that *otherhost* is suffering from an abnormal load or that it is just not as fast at responding to the network. It can also mean that something is corrupting data *enroute*, but this is less likely.

How do you differentiate between data corruption and a slow Ethernet server? Running *uptime* or *vmstat* (*sar -upw* for System V users) on the remote system will show you how heavily loaded it is. If you want to find out what the network is doing in more detail, you can watch for evidence of data corruption while running *spray*. Here's how:

- Log in to the remote system and run the command:

```
% netstat -s | grep "socket full drops"
```

and note the number. This counts the number of times the system has dropped a UDP packet (Universal Datagram Protocol, part of the TCP/IP protocol group) because it didn't have time or buffer space to handle it.

- Run *spray* on your local system, and note the number of dropped packets.

- On the remote system, run the *netstat* command again.

- If the number of socket full drops has increased by the number of dropped packets that *spray* reported, the remote system cannot read the incoming data stream fast enough.

- If the number of socket full drops has increased by a smaller amount, the remote system's network interface is rejecting packets because they are incorrect. Somehow your network is corrupting data. In this situation, you would expect *netstat -i* on the remote system to show input errors. Get out your network analyzer and start working.

Another technique, which we've already mentioned, is to look at the client NFS statistics by giving the command *nfsstat -c*:

```
% nfsstat -c
Client rpc:
calls       badcalls   retrans    badxid     timeout    wait   newcred
19678       3          948        883        1242       0      0
...
```

First look at the number of retransmissions. If this is small (under 5 percent of **calls**), you have nothing to worry about. If it is large and if the **badxid** and **timeout** fields are roughly equal (within a factor of 2 or 3), then one of the network's NFS servers is slow and dropping packets. In the report above, these two fields are within 50 percent—that's good enough to assume that dropped packets are a problem. If **badxid** is much lower than **timeout**, get out your network analyzer because the network itself is causing trouble.

You may be surprised at which of your systems are good network servers and which aren't. Workstations tend to be excellent servers, though they may be limited in other ways; after all, workstation manufacturers live or die based on their network efficiency. Large multiuser systems often aren't optimized for network work. You will find that many superminicomputers and mainframes can be surprisingly slow on the network, even though they have much more CPU capacity.

However, before you get too concerned about dropped packets, remember that they aren't as bad as they sound. It should be obvious that we can force any system to drop packets at just about any time. Take the fastest network system you have, load its CPU heavily with a few compute-bound applications, and blast a few thousand packets at it—you'll see loads of dropped packets. *spray* is particularly good at forcing systems to drop packets because it uses the network in the worst way possible. Real applications don't load the network with a stream of

1000 or so packets carrying virtually no data. You can make *spray* somewhat more realistic by sending 1000-byte packets:

```
% /etc/spray host -l 1000
```

But the results are still flawed. Therefore, you can't take *spray* seriously as an indicator of overall network performance—all it shows you is which systems react well to heavy network loads and which don't or, more precisely, whether the system receiving the data is faster than the system sending it.

6.5.1 Living with Slow Servers

Once you have found out that you have some slow systems on your network, what can you do? If your analysis indicates that these slow systems are suffering from CPU or memory problems, look at these first. If you don't have CPU or memory problems, there is one simple, although somewhat painful, solution. Spending some time with *spray* will reveal fairly quickly which systems are good network performers and which aren't. If you are planning to reorganize the network, this is an extremely important piece of information. A network will run most efficiently if its major disk servers (i.e., the systems that export NFS filesystems) are relatively fast on the network. Remember, these systems are resources shared by everyone; it makes sense that they should be fast. If you have really minimized traffic between two subnetworks, it may be tolerable for your gateway to be a poor network performer, but we would be more comfortable using a good network system for a gateway. You can also buy dedicated pieces of hardware to serve as bridges between two networks. This may be a cost-effective alternative to using a general purpose computer as a gateway. If you can organize your network in this way, you will minimize the total number of dropped packets network-wide.

Of course, these suggestions may fly in the face of reality. A workstation with good network response may also have relatively slow disks, may not support the large disk drives you need for some applications, and so on. (We will remind you, though, that NFS is far from optimal for sustained high-speed file access.) It may be impossible for you to justify the expense of a dedicated Ethernet bridge or router. Once again, system optimization is a matter of achieving the best possible compromise among many different factors.

Reducing the NFS Workload

If you are forced to use systems with poor network performance as network file servers, all is not lost. You can take some steps to reduce the NFS server's workload. NFS allows you to specify the buffer sizes for read and write operations in the client system's */etc/fstab* file. How does this help the server? The client sends out a burst of packets whenever its NFS buffers are full. Therefore, reducing the buffer size reduces the length of these bursts. The client may get off a short stream of packets, but it will soon empty the buffer. The client will then have to wait for the buffer to become full before it can send another burst of packets. However, reducing the buffer size isn't a clear-cut win because it will tend to increase the CPU overhead required for NFS processing on both the client and the server. For the best results, set the size of the read buffer (**rsize**) to the memory page size of the client and set the size of the write buffer (**wsize**) to the memory page size of the server. For example, assume you notice that the system named *server* is slow, and that your system mounts one remote filesystem from *server*. Furthermore, assume that both systems have a page size of 4096 bytes. Then you should have the following entry in your */etc/fstab* file:

```
server:/remfs/dataspace /space nfs rw,hard,wsize=4096,rsize=4096 0 0
```

This entry minimizes the number of packet bursts that *server* will receive, without increasing the NFS overhead too badly. Consult your system's documentation to find its memory page size or use the *pagesize* command if it is available. UNIX systems often have a page size of 8 KB but there are many exceptions. Furthermore, NFS can be used to share files with many non-UNIX systems.

NOTE

The **rsize** and **wsize** fields are only applicable to remote filesystems. Don't use them for local filesystems.

Timeouts

If an NFS client (i.e., the system accessing a remote disk) does not receive a response to an NFS request within a certain time, the client *times out*—it assumes the data was mishandled somewhere and generates another request. If there are a lot of timeouts when the NFS server (the host supplying the filesystem) is under a heavy load, the host may simply be unable to respond to NFS requests fast enough. In this case, it is appropriate to increase the timeout period. The responses will arrive eventually, if given enough time.

Check the number of timeouts with the command *nfsstat -c*:

```
% /etc/nfsstat -c

Client rpc:
calls     badcalls retrans badxid  timeout  wait     newcred
35943     356      941     95      1283     0        0

Client   nfs:
```

```
calls     badcalls  nclget   nclsleep
35455     3         35554    99
null      getattr   setattr  root    lookup    readlink  read
0   0%    3282  9%  32  0%  0   0%   7192 20%  910  2%   15946 44%
wrcache   write     create   remove  rename    link      symlink
0   0%    6753 19%  167  0%  101  0  13   0%   3   0%    14 0%
mkdir     rmdir     readdir  fsstat
2   0%    0   0%    741  2%  299  0%
```

If the number of timeouts is a large percentage of the number of calls (i.e., greater than 5 percent), you may be having problems. Try copying a very large file across the network, look at whether the number of timeouts increases, and try to determine whether the problem is serious. It is useful to clear the *nfsstat* statistics before performing this experiment. To do so, run *nfsstat -z*, which sets all of the counts to zero. This command may only be given by root (i.e., superuser). If experiments show that your system chronically suffers a large number of timeouts, you should take some action; however, remember that it is normal for networks to be congested from time to time. You only have a problem if the situation is chronic.

If a system suffers from a lot of timeouts, you may want to increase the NFS *timeo* parameter. This parameter specifies how long the system should wait (in tenths of a second) for a response before assuming that the response is not coming. It is set in client host's */etc/fstab* entries for remote filesystems. A typical *fstab* entry looks like this:

```
toy:/mf /toy/mf nfs noquota,hard,bg,intr,timeo=15 0 0
```

This entry mounts the remote filesystem */toy/mf* with a timeout period of 1.5 seconds. To double the timeout period, change *timeo=15* to *timeo=30*, dismount */toy/mf*, and remount it.

NOTE

Increasing the timeout period will also increase the time users have to wait before NFS decides that a system is not responding. This never pleases users. By setting the parameters *retrans* (number of retransmissions before determining that the access has failed) and *timeo* (timeout period), you can limit the extent to which your users are inconvenienced. The default values for these parameters vary from manufacturer to manufacturer and should be given your system's documentation for *mount*. It is also annoying to boot a system when one or more remote hosts are down. To reduce the pain, ensure remote filesystems have the option *bg*.

6.5.2 NFS Workload and Kernel Table Size

There is another way in which NFS interacts with general CPU performance. On an NFS server, you would expect to see more files open at any given time than you would on any other system. After all, you're allowing users from other computers to use your files. This means that the kernel's inode and file tables for an NFS server should be larger than for a non-NFS system. If the inode table runs out of space, the system's performance will suffer. The kernel will have to swap entries in and out of the table, increasing the overhead required to access a file. You also have to account for additional system daemons, additional timeout table entries, etc. Therefore, it's a good idea to increase the size of the kernel tables for systems that are NFS servers. This requires you to build a new kernel (we'll discuss the mechanics in detail when we discuss kernel configuration.) Right now, the question is, "How much should I increase the size?" As far as performance is concerned, the size of the inode table is the most important factor.

For Berkeley UNIX systems, the *MAXUSERS* configuration constant determines the size of the important tables, including the inode table. A good rule of thumb for an NFS server is to allow for one extra user for each diskless workstation that the server supports and allow another extra user for each two additional clients that mount the server's files. For example, consider an NFS server *servr*. Three diskless workstations boot from this server and five additional systems (other than the workstations) mount filesystems from *servr*. Therefore, you should allow for six extra users (five and a half, rounded up, although you could probably get away with five). If *MAXUSERS* was previously 16, you should change it to 22 and build a new kernel. If your system is chronically short of memory, you may not want to resize the kernel tables for NFS. You may be better off living with poor network performance or rearranging the network so the system is no longer an NFS server.

Under System V, you can independently set the sizes of the kernel tables. Using whatever configuration method is appropriate for your system (most implementations of System V come with a menu-driven vendor-dependent configuration tool), increase the settings for *ninodes* (for descendants of System V.3) or *inodes* (for descendants of V.2).

6.6 RFS: System V Remote File Sharing

Remote File Sharing (RFS) is an alternative to the Network File System (NFS). RFS is an option on most versions of System V and will be a standard part of System V.4. It is also an option for some descendants of Berkeley UNIX (SunOS). Like NFS, it allows systems that are on the network to mount each other's filesystems, allowing users to access remote files as easily as local files. RFS can use a number of different transport media: System V manuals generally assume that you will run RFS over STARLAN (another local area network), but it can also run over Ethernet and other networks that are compatible with AT&T's "Transport Interface Specification." Whichever network medium you use, the same considerations about network congestion and data corruption apply.

If you use Ethernet with TCP/IP to run RFS, you can use the network monitoring tools we discussed earlier (*netstat*, *spray*, etc.) to detect network problems. If you are using some other network or protocol, you will need to find out what tools are applicable to your installation.

The same considerations involving network load apply, too. Local disk access will always be faster than network access, barring some great disparity in disk speed. Try to set up your network so that the users on each system will spend most of their time accessing local disks.

On System V, *sar* provides a number of reports to help you analyze network performance. These reports tell you whether your system is overloaded by remote RFS requests and will give you some ideas about what you can do to solve the problem. The command *sar -Du* will show you the percentage of time the CPU spends servicing RFS operations. This statistic is interesting, but not really useful. If you have problems, you will need to look at the *-Db* and *-Dc* reports to understand what is going wrong and why. The *sar -Du* report looks like this:

```
% sar -Du
ora ora 3.2 2 i386    05/21/90

00:00:01     %usr    %sys    %sys    %wio    %idle
                     local   remote
01:00:03      25       6       2       2       65
```

This system is only spending 2 percent of its time servicing RFS-related system calls. This is reasonable; we don't suspect any problems.

6.6.1 Filesystem Organization with RFS

The report from *sar -Dc* tells you how many system calls are being made on behalf of RFS requests. You can use this data to determine whether your system is overloaded by RFS traffic. If it is overloaded, consider reorganizing your network so users are closer to the files they need. Here's a sample from such a report:

```
% sar -Dc
ora ora 3.2 2 i386    05/21/90

00:00:01 scall/s sread/s swrit/s  fork/s  exec/s rchar/s wchar/s
```

```
01:00:03
   in          1       2       3               0.00     300     200
   out         4       5       6               0.00    1000    2000
   local      84      23       9      0.21     0.26    9581    4364
```

The **in** line summarizes statistics for incoming requests (i.e., requests made by other systems for data on your system); the **out** line summarizes statistics for outgoing requests (i.e., requests made by your system for remote data). The **local** line summarizes purely local operations. The columns are:

scall/s   The number of system calls per second, excluding read and write system calls.

sread/s   The number of read system calls per second.

swrit/s   The number of write system calls per second.

fork/s   The number of fork operations per second.

exec/s   The number of exec operations per second. Remote exec operations put a particularly heavy load on the system.

rchar/s   The average number of characters read per second. To compute the average number of characters read per system call, divide this number by **sread/s**. If the quotient is small, read operations are being performed inefficiently.

wchar/s   The average number of characters written per second. To compute the average number of character written per system call, divide this number by **swrit/s**. If the quotient is small, write operations are being performed inefficiently.

The number of remote operations should usually be much smaller than the number of local operations, unless your system is primarily a server with few local users. Consider rearranging the network if this isn't true. Furthermore, the total number of remote system calls should always be relatively small. AT&T suggests that systems shouldn't handle more than 30 per second (**scall+read+writ**). If the average number of characters transferred per operation is relatively low, try to get users to write their I/O software more efficiently. Transferring a few bytes with each operation is inherently inefficient. Rewriting the program will increase its performance dramatically, in addition to improving the system as a whole.

Another tool that will help you balance your network's structure is *fusage*. This program reports the total amount of data transferred from each disk partition on behalf of your own system and on behalf of its RFS clients. Here is a typical report:

```
% fusage
FILE USAGE REPORT FOR ora
```

```
/dev/dsk/0s1                /
                            /
                       ora        12345KB
                   Clients          678KB
                   TOTAL          13023KB
```

This report shows that local users accessed 12345 KB on the root filesystem of *ora*. Remote users (clients) access 678 KB of data. This is what we like to see. If your network is structured reasonably (i.e., structured so that users can do most of their work locally), local usage should be significantly greater than remote usage.

6.6.2 RFS Buffer Usage

When you configure a kernel, you can specify the percentage of your system's buffer cache that is reserved for RFS operations (*nremote*). To tune this parameter appropriately, you must look at how efficiently RFS is using the cache. The report from *sar -Db* will give you this information:

```
% sar -Db

ora ora 3.2 2 i386    05/21/90

00:00:01 bread/s lread/s %rcache bwrit/s lwrit/s %wcache pread/s pwrit
01:00:03
   local      3      51      94       4      15      69       0       0
   remote     1      11      92       1       1       0
```

This is similar to the report for *sar -b*. Look at the percentage of cache hits for remote read operations (**%rcache**); you can ignore data for write operations. Increasing the absolute size of the cache (*nbuf*) or the percentage of the cache that is reserved for RFS (*nremote*) will increase the cache's efficiency. Conversely, decreasing either parameter will decrease the percentage of cache hits. With a cache efficiency of 92 percent, we have nothing to worry about. We might even consider decreasing the cache's size to save memory.

6.6.3 Server Usage

The report *sar -S* shows the number of server processes that are available. RFS server processes are similar in concept to the NFS daemons. However, the number of RFS server processes varies dynamically between a maximum and minimum set by the *MINSERVE* and *MAXSERVE* configuration parameters. Here's the report from *sar*:

```
% sar -S

ora ora 3.2 2 i386     05/21/90

00:00:01 serv/lo-hi   request   request   server    server
              3 - 6     %busy  avg lgth   %avail  avg avail
01:00:03          6    100.0        25      0.0           0
```

If there aren't enough server processes available (i.e., the number of processes has increased to the maximum limit), RFS performance will suffer. When all of the servers are in use, new RFS requests have to wait in a queue until a server becomes free. The sample above shows that the number of servers can vary between three and six. Currently all six servers are in use; there are no servers available. If the system spends a lot of time in this state, you should consider increasing the maximum number of servers.

Conversely, if the number of servers in use is usually at or near the minimum, you can try decreasing the minimum number of servers. This will decrease the system's CPU overhead.

6.7 Special Considerations for STREAMS

If you are running System V, your network software is built on top of the STREAMS package. The configuration of the STREAMS package can play an important part in overall network performance. STREAMS configuration is particularly important for System V.2, System V.3, and XENIX, which have fixed-size stream parameters. In V.4, the important STREAMS parameters are controlled dynamically, so you can ignore this aspect of tuning.

The command *netstat -m* shows whether there is any room in the crucial STREAMS tables and will help you decide whether you need to increase any of the kernel configuration parameters. Here is a typical report:

```
% netstat -m
             alloc     inuse      total     max     fail
streams:       256        60       2125      64        0
queues:       1024       344      12732     368        0
mblocks:      2150       263    5308936     398        0
dblocks:      1720       263    4626872     392        0
dblock class:
    0 (    4)    256         0     286287       5        0
    1 (   16)    256        48     699347     138        0
    2 (   64)    256        27    3398892     125        0
```

3 (128)	512	188	155741	214	0
4 (256)	128	0	29061	12	0
5 (512)	128	0	17752	23	0
6 (1024)	64	0	31550	36	0
7 (2048)	64	0	6012	5	0
8 (4096)	56	0	2230	11	0

For overall system performance, the most critical parameters are the number of data blocks available for each block size (4 bytes, 16 bytes, 64 bytes, and so on). These are set by the NBLKn parameters, where n is the buffer size (in bytes). Statistics on the usage of each block size appear beneath the label *dblock class*. This report shows that the system has 256 4-byte blocks, of which none are currently in use and at most 5 have been in use at one time. There are also 256 16-byte blocks, of which 48 are currently in use and at most 138 have been in use at one time. There are 512 128-byte blocks, of which 214 have been in use at one time, and so on.

This system does not require any significant tuning. The number of blocks allocated to each class is already significantly larger than the defaults and is appropriate to a system with a relatively heavy network load. If the number of data blocks in any class is too small, you will see that all or most of the blocks are in use and that the number of failed attempts to allocate data blocks is nonzero. A good approach to tuning is to try doubling the number of blocks in each size class where you have had trouble. If the system is short of memory, you might try reducing the number of 4096-byte and 2048-byte blocks substantially. This system could probably get by with 20 4-KB blocks, which would save 144 KB. You could obviously reduce the number of 4-byte blocks, but why bother? There is little to be gained here.

If your site uses the network heavily, you may also need to increase the number of streams and the number of queues, which are controlled by the *NSTREAM* and *NQUEUE* parameters. There are usually four queues for each stream, so the value of *NQUEUE* is typically four times the value of *NSTREAM*. The number of streams your system needs depends entirely on what network applications you are running, how they are designed, and how heavily they are used. *netstat -m* will show you whether your settings for these parameters are appropriate. Our example shows that the system is configured with 256 streams, of which 60 are currently in use and at most 64 have been used. The system has never run out of streams or queues, so there is no need to increase either parameter. However, these settings are significantly higher than the default values, which assume relatively little network usage.

If you want to compute how many streams and queues you really need, here's how to get a start. NFS only requires one stream. Each terminal that is in use (including virtual terminals, or *ptys*) requires one stream. Remember that *rlogin* sessions and shell windows opened by *emacs* editors use virtual terminals.

Finally, each window that X users have open requires one stream. Add any streams used by home-brew applications and you're done. If you are on a single-user workstations, the number of streams needed for X will be small—probably eight at the most. If you support many users with X terminals, the number of streams can explode. It will be roughly the number of users times the average number of windows per user.

As we've said, System V.4 dynamically allocates the STREAMS data structures. However, you can control the maximum amount of memory that can be allocated to STREAMS (data structures, buffers, etc.) at any time. The *STRTHRESH* parameter sets the maximum amount of physical memory that can be allocated to STREAMS. It is commonly set to a relatively large value—for example, one-quarter to one-half of the system's total memory. Although this should be sufficient to handle heavy network loads, you may want to experiment with larger values if your site uses X and and other network services heavily.

Chapter 8, *Kernel Configuration*, describes how to modify these and other kernel configuration parameters.

6.7.1 STREAMS and SunOS

The STREAMS facility is included in SunOS 4.0 and 4.1. It is used for terminal drivers, including pseudo-terminals (*ptys*) and RFS, but not *per se* for TCP/IP, NFS, or X. However, *rlogin*, *xterm*, and many other network applications rely on pseudo-terminals. So you can't strictly say that SunOS networking is independent of STREAMS.

However, you need only worry about STREAMS configuration if you're running SunOS 4.0, which is similar to System V.3. STREAMS buffers and tables are statically allocated. Therefore, if you are running SunOS 4.0, you should make sure that you have enough streams (*NSTREAM*), enough queues (*NQUEUE*), and enough small data buffers (*NBLK*). As for System V, the command *netstat -m* will show you whether or not you have enough buffers. Here's a typical report:

```
% netstat -m
409/896 mbufs in use:
```

...Other information about mbufs, which we'll omit...

```
streams allocation:
                                 cumulative   allocation
              current    maximum      total     failures
streams            29         39        176            0
queues            109        149        695            0
mblks              60        282    2727416            0
```

total dblks	60	282	2727416	3833
size 4 dblks	0	104	919121	3833
size 16 dblks	10	139	216987	0
size 64 dblks	1	88	817067	0
size 128 dblks	49	71	578392	0
size 256 dblks	0	2	78927	0
size 512 dblks	0	1	5845	0
size 1024 dblks	0	2	22183	0
size 2048 dblks	0	3	88894	0
size 4096 dblks	0	0	0	0

The first part of the report shows statistics about *mbufs*, or network buffers. You can ignore this. *mbufs* are dynamically allocated. The second part of the report shows the STREAMS tables. Note that this system could use some additional 4-byte buffers: the value of *NBLK4* should be increased.

SunOS 4.1 is similar to System V.4. STREAMS buffers and tables are allocated dynamically, so you don't need to worry about them.

7

Terminal Performance

Chattering Terminal Lines
Disabling a Bad Terminal Line (BSD)
Disabling a Bad Terminal Line (System V)
Character Lists
Terminal Drivers and STREAMS

Terminal performance is not generally a problem. If users report poor interactive performance (most likely, delays between the time they type a character and the time the character is "echoed" on the terminal), the problem is usually not the I/O subsystem *per se*; check the system's load average and determine whether or not the system is paging. Above all, determine whether or not the user is directly connected to the computer or if he is using *rlogin*, the X window system, a network terminal server, or some other mechanism to access a remote computer. If the user is using a remote system, network congestion is almost always the culprit. You will find that terminal performance is rarely an issue when the user is working locally.

7.1 Chattering Terminal Lines

However, a malfunctioning terminal line can drag down system performance as a whole. A noisy terminal line can generate thousands of random characters. The system must process each of these characters. The flood of many characters arriving much faster than any user can type quickly overwhelms the terminal controller and the CPU. Performance, particularly interactive performance, degrades quickly.

This problem is easy to solve but tricky to spot. Malfunctioning terminal lines are often intermittent; furthermore, the terminal line may work properly when it is in use. Under BSD UNIX, there are two ways to detect chattering terminal lines: using *iostat* and *pstat* to check the terminal queues and using *ps* to look at the *getty* processes. Under System V, you can still use *ps* to check *getty* activity; to check raw terminal data, you need to look at *sar -y*.

7.1.1 Detecting Chattering Terminals (BSD)

We will cover the BSD tools first. The report from *iostat* looks like this:

```
% iostat 5
        tty ...
 tin tout ...
...
   1  299 ...
   5   44 ...
...
```

The first two columns indicate the number of characters in the terminal input and output queues, respectively. The number of characters in the output queue may be quite large. This is of no significance; a program may be dumping pages of output to someone's screen. The number of characters in the input queue should be fairly small; no matter how many users your system has, they generally type fairly slowly and intermittently. If the **tin** column shows many characters in the input queue, a terminal line may be chattering.

Use *pstat* to find out which terminal line is causing the trouble. With the *-t* option (not supported under SunOS), *pstat* produces a report like the following:

```
% /etc/pstat -t
1 cons
```

#	RAW	CAN	OUT	MODE	ADDR	DEL	COL	STATE	PGRP	DISC
0	0	0	0	140540f0	0	0	95	O C H	15	

```
64 gtt lines
```

#	RAW	CAN	OUT	MODE	ADDR	DEL	COL	STATE	PGRP	DISC
0	0	0	0	e0	0	0	-47	O C X ·H	0	
1	0	0	0	0	0	0	0		0	
2	0	0	0	0	0	0	0		0	
3	0	0	0	0	0	0	0		0	
4	0	0	0	0	0	0	0		0	
5	0	0	0	0	0	0	0		0	
6	0	0	0	0	0	0	0		0	
7	0	0	0	0	0	0	0		0	
8	0	0	0	14054cd8	0	0	0	W	0	

```
...
```

```
128 pty lines
# RAW CAN OUT    MODE     ADDR DEL COL    STATE  PGRP DISC
0   0   0    0 140500d8    0    0  22  0 C       18849 ntty
...
```

The report is divided into three sections: one for the console terminal (**cons**), one for standard terminals (**gtt lines**), and one for pseudo-terminals (**pty lines**). Virtual terminals are used by remote login sessions, shells started within an *emacs* editor, and other terminal sessions that don't correspond to a physical terminal port. Pseudo-terminals cannot suffer from noise problems, so you can ignore them.

The first column (**#**) shows the terminal's number. Use the terminal number to generate the name of its *tty* file. For example, terminal number 8 is associated with the special file */dev/tty08* and terminal number 16 is associated with the special file */dev/tty16*. You will need to know this filename to perform any administrative operations on the terminal.

The second column (**RAW**) shows the number of characters in the *raw input queue*. The next column shows the characters in the *canonical input queue* (**CAN**). The raw input queue shows the total number of characters that have been typed; the canonical input queue shows the number of characters that have been typed but discounts characters that have been deleted (by backspace, CTRL-U, etc.). Neither of these numbers should be large, and both will probably be zero most of the time. If the terminal currently isn't in use, the number of characters in the input queue should always be zero. If it isn't, the terminal line is generating spurious characters.

7.1.2 Detecting Chattering Terminals (System V)

System V should be able to detect chattering terminal lines and disable them automatically. If you are a System V user, you should (we hope) be able to ignore this section. However, nothing works perfectly, even the best schemes for detecting and disabling a bad terminal line fail from time to time.

System V doesn't support *iostat* or *pstat*. Use *sar -y* to get the data you need. Unlike the BSD tools, *sar* provides some long-term averaging. This should help you find intermittent problems—you don't have to catch a bad terminal line in the act. Here is the *sar* report:

```
% sar -y

ora ora 3.2 2 i386    05/21/90
00:00:01 rawch/s canch/s outch/s rcvin/s xmtin/s mdmin/s
01:00:03     49       0      39       0       0       0
```

02:00:02	1	0	36	0	0	0
03:00:01	1	0	32	0	0	0
04:00:01	1	0	23	0	0	0

The columns in this report are:

rawch/s   The average number of raw characters received per second. This is the total number of characters received prior to any processing.

canch/s   The average number of canonical characters received per second. This is the number of characters received after interpreting deletions, two-keystroke combinations, etc.

outch/s   The average number of output characters printed per second. This is often quite high. It is easy for the computer to produce hundreds of characters per second; for example, this happens whenever you refresh the screen while editing.

rcvin/s   The average number of receive interrupts per second.

xmtin/s   The average number of transmit interrupts per second (i.e., output interrupts).

mdmin/s   The average number of modem interrupts per second.

This report gives us something to be concerned about. The first time slot shows an average of 49 raw characters per second, which is way too high for a small system. It will take some additional research to find out what is going on, but there appears to be some kind of terminal problem.

7.1.3 Other Techniques

There is another way to find bad terminal lines that is applicable to both BSD and System V UNIX. It isn't as precise but is usually just as effective. A program named *getty* monitors the terminal lines for attempts to log in. There is always one *getty* process for each enabled terminal that is not in use. *getty* should not accumulate any time, since it only has work to do when the terminal is generating characters. If any *getty* processes have accumulated CPU time, they are probably monitoring a terminal that is generating spurious characters. To watch *getty*, BSD users should give the command *ps -ax*:

```
% ps -ax | grep getty
  226 03  IW    0:00  (getty)
  227 04  IW    0:00  (getty)
18410 08  I     0:00  (getty)
18583 10  I     0:00  (getty)
 6278 co  IW    0:00  (getty)
18676 p4  S     0:00  grep getty
```

The System V equivalent is *ps -e*. The number of *gettys* is usually much smaller than the number of terminals because *getty* only runs when the terminal isn't in use (that is, when no one has logged in). The report above indicates that terminals 3, 4, 8, and 10 and the system console are enabled but not currently in use. None of the *getty* processes have accumulated any time; therefore, none of these terminal lines are noisy. If a terminal line were chattering, one of the *getty* processes would have accumulated a significant amount of time. A second or two is nothing to worry about, but any larger accumulation is cause for concern.

7.2 Disabling a Bad Terminal Line (BSD)

Once you have isolated a noisy terminal line, you must disable it. Under BSD UNIX, you must change the terminal's entry in */etc/ttys*. There are several different versions of this file, depending on which version of UNIX you are using. The line below shows a typical entry in */etc/ttys* for BSD 4.3 UNIX:

```
tty16      "/etc/getty std.19200"   unknown        on secure
```

This line controls terminal 16 (special file */dev/tty16*). The terminal's type is "unknown," and the terminal is currently enabled (i.e., "on"), which means this terminal may be used to log in. The additional qualifier "secure" states that users may log in from this terminal as root (i.e., superuser). To disable this terminal line, merely change the word "on" to "off." After making this modification, force *init* to read the file again by giving the command:

```
# kill -HUP 1
```

This dangerous-looking command has no effect on the system aside from forcing *init* (always process 1) to reread the terminal descriptions. It will not have any effect on anyone who is using the system. After giving this command, disconnect the bad terminal line and determine why it is noisy.

If your system runs XENIX or a version of BSD UNIX prior to 4.3, the */etc/ttys* file will look much different. The entry for */dev/tty16* is shown below:

```
1mtty16
```

The 1 at the beginning of the line indicates that terminal 16 is enabled. To disable it, change the 1 to a 0 and give the command *kill -HUP 1*.

The format of the */etc/ttys* file (whatever it may be on your system) is described in Section 5 of the *UNIX Programmer's Reference Manual*.

NOTE

SunOS 4.1 has added to the confusion. For this version of UNIX, */etc/ttytab* is now the "master" list of terminals. Its format is the same as the BSD 4.3 for */etc/ttys*, which we described above. However, SunOS also has a file named */etc/ttys*, which is identical to the "old-style" (Berkeley 4.2 and earlier) version of */etc/ttys*. If you are a Sun user, edit */etc/ttytab* and ignore */etc/ttys*. The latter file is generated automatically; it is used for compatibility with some older programs.

7.3 Disabling a Bad Terminal Line (System V)

Most System V implementations use a file named *inittab* to enable and disable terminals. For V.3 (including 386/ix), this file is in the directory */etc*. V.4 moves *inittab* to */sbin*. Assume that *tty34* appears to be malfunctioning. The *inittab* entry that controls this terminal will look something like the following:

```
1034:23:respawn:/etc/getty:tty34:19200
```

This line tells *init* to start a *getty* process for terminal */dev/tty34* at 19200 baud whenever the system enters multiuser mode and whenever a user logs off. The last field in this entry isn't the baud rate itself, it is an identifier that corresponds to an entry in */etc/gettydefs*.

To disable the terminal, you must tell *init* not to start *getty* process for this terminal. To do this, replace the word "respawn" with the word "off":

```
1034:23:off:/etc/getty:tty34:19200
```

After modifying the *inittab*, force *init* to read the new file by giving the command:

```
# init q
```

These actions disable terminal line *tty34*. No one will be able to log in from it until you change *inittab* and give the *init q* command again.

The 386/ix implementation of V.3 rebuilds the *inittab* file whenever you reconfigure the system. Therefore, you either have to edit */etc/inittab* whenever you build a new kernel or you can make these changes permanent by modifying */etc/conf/cf.d/init.base*. Any changes you make here will be preserved whenever you regenerate the system. Of course, we very much hope that you don't permanently disable terminal lines whenever one fails. It is much better to change *inittab*, find the problem, and then re-enable the terminal. But if you don't think you will get around to debugging terminal lines for a while, and if you are rebuilding the kernel regularly for some reason, you may want to make your changes permanent (even if only "permanent" in a temporary sense).

7.4 Character Lists

Under BSD UNIX, the character list table is a pool of terminal buffers. If you add many users to the system without increasing the number of character lists in the kernel, the system may run out when it is under a heavy load. When the kernel runs out of character lists, it will start dropping characters that users type. The characters will still be echoed on the terminal, but the shell or application program will never receive them. There is no good way to measure the availability of character lists. The only way to know there is a problem is to be aware of the symptoms.

To get more character lists, you need to rebuild the kernel. The best way to increase the number of character lists is to increase the value of *maxusers*. You probably ran out of character lists because you added several new terminals or modems and didn't increase *maxusers* accordingly. You can also edit the *param.c* configuration file to change the definition for the *clist* variable.

7.5 Terminal Drivers and STREAMS

At the end of Chapter 6, which discusses network performance issues, we discussed the effect that STREAMS can have on network performance. In this section, we mentioned that the terminal drivers under System V, SunOS 4.0, and SunOS 4.1 also use the STREAMS facility. Therefore, if STREAMS is badly configured, your terminal performance can suffer. As we said earlier, you don't need to worry about STREAMS for System V.4 and SunOS 4.1. Both of these versions manage the important STREAMS configuration parameters dynamically. System V.3, XENIX, and SunOS 4.0 require you to configure STREAMS "by hand" if you want anything other than the default settings.

We'll refer you to Section 6.7, "Special Considerations for Streams," for a more thorough discussion of how to configure STREAMS. We'll hit some of the high points with respect to terminal drivers here. Here's what you should watch out for:

- Are there enough small data buffers? You should not see any allocation failures for 4-, 16-, 64-, or 128-byte buffers. You may need to increase the number of buffers if you add more terminals or modems to the system. High-speed modems (i.e., modems running 9600 baud or more) can easily drain a lot of buffers. The number of STREAMS data buffers are set by the parameters *NBLK4* through *NBLK4096*.

- Are there enough streams? Each terminal and each pseudo-terminal requires one stream. Remember that if you have a windowing system (X, SunView, or even shell windows within *emacs*), every window is a pseudo-terminal. Therefore, if you have a large system that supports many X terminals, you may need a lot of streams. Other applications that use STREAMS may require streams of their own. The parameter *NSTREAM* sets the number of streams.

- Are there enough queues? There are usually four queues for each stream. The parameter *NQUEUE* sets the number of queues.

8

Kernel Configuration

Why Build a Custom Kernel?
Configuring a BSD Kernel
Configuring a System V Kernel

The *kernel* is the heart of the UNIX operating system. It is the program that manages memory, schedules processes, manages I/O, and does all of the other low-level tasks that make the system work for you. The kernel is not a "process," like the programs you run from the keyboard. It pre-exists all processes and is responsible for starting the first process. It is the life-support system that allows everything else to work.

Because it is so important, the kernel has some key privileges. On most UNIX systems, it is *always* resident in the processor's physical memory.* Other programs can be swapped or paged to disk, but not the kernel. Therefore, the kernel should be as small and compact as possible, and at one time, it was. But like most

---

*The only exceptions of which I am aware are systems that have the MACH kernel, developed at Carnegie Mellon University. OSF's forthcoming version of UNIX will be the first commercial version to include the MACH kernel.

software, the UNIX kernel grew with time: new features and compatibility modes were added, bug-fixes were larger than the code they replaced, and so on. If you have ever developed software, you know the story. As a result, the kernel and its tables can require a significant portion of the system's total memory particularly on small systems.* One important reason to create a custom kernel is to make it as small as possible: to trim away unneeded features, to make its tables as small as comfortably possible. For a very small system, this can be almost as effective as buying more memory and much cheaper.

There are also many situations in which you want to make the kernel larger. If you buy more memory, you may want to live without some of the restrictions you have imposed on your system. You may want to support more users, allow programs to have more files open at one time, etc. You may also want to add new I/O devices or optional features which require kernel modifications. As always, performance management involves making tradeoffs between different aspects of performance. Do you want flexibility or speed? Is it more important to support additional users or to have more memory available for a small number of users?

8.1.1 How We'll Proceed

We will discuss BSD UNIX configuration first, followed by System V. In each case, we will discuss the configuration process, followed by the configuration options and parameters that you can set. For System V, we have to discuss three configuration processes (there are significant differences between XENIX (V.2), V.3, and V.4). We'll treat these in order, followed by one discussion of the configuration parameters for all System V versions.

We won't cover how to add additional software packages or how to configure new devices. Any additional software package that you buy or order should have its own installation instructions. If a commercial software package requires kernel modifications, it should provide an installation script that performs these modifications automatically. Adding a new device (particularly if it is not a device supported by your vendor) is well beyond the bounds of this book.

---

*Plan 9, an AT&T research project lead by the original UNIX developers, has reversed this trend. Its kernel is extremely small. However, Plan 9 probably won't have any impact on commercially available systems for several years.

8.1.2 A Word on BSD and System V Kernels

BSD and System V take fundamentally different approaches to system configuration. These differences have to do with the fundamental structure of BSD and System V software. You should be aware of these approaches before you start.

BSD UNIX typically comes equipped with a "generic" kernel. The manufacturer guarantees that the generic kernel will run on any supported system configuration. The generic kernel includes most possible options and device drivers for every supported device and has generously large tables. You can run this kernel, but probably don't want to. Because it is large, it will be inefficient. For BSD UNIX, kernel tuning is usually a matter of trimming away fat. Some manufacturers (Sun among them) ship a minimal kernel in addition to the generic kernel, plus correct configuration files to build kernels that are adapted to several different applications. This lessens the need for customization but doesn't eliminate it.

System V takes a more minimal approach to kernel customization. The standard System V kernels are typically small. Customization is a matter of adding features and increasing table sizes. Most versions of System V also provide some kind of kernel customization program, which provides a menu-driven interface to modification. For XENIX, it's called *configure*; for Interactive's 386/ix, it's called *kconfig*; for HP-UX, it's called *sam*. If such a program is available, USE IT! It will help to prevent mistakes and may prevent you from overriding settings that are needed for optional software packages. BSD UNIX manufacturers don't provide such help.

8.1.3 Measuring Memory

One important reason to build a custom kernel is to reduce its memory requirements, leaving more memory free for the jobs you want to run. Therefore, after making any modification, you'll want to know how much memory the new kernel requires and how much memory you have saved.

It's possible to do a number of fairly messy calculations and compute the kernel's memory needs. You have to know the size of the basic kernel executable (which you can measure), you have to know how much space is taken by various options (which you often have to guess, though your manufacturer may have been gracious enough to supply you with a table showing how much room each option requires), and you have to compute the size of a dozen or more memory-resident tables. For all the work that's required, the result ends up being fairly inexact. Labor and intricacy give this process the appearance of precision, but not the reality.

There's a much easier way to get precise information on your kernel's memory requirements. One of the first things that any kernel does is compute the total amount of memory that exists, allocate memory for itself and its tables, and compute the amount of memory remaining for user's processes. It reports the results during its initialization messages. Therefore, you can find out how much memory is available and how much the kernel requires by booting the system and looking at the messages that appear on the console. If you don't want to reboot the system, you should be able to find these messages in */usr/adm/messages*. Here are some figures for a supercomputer running 4.3BSD UNIX:

```
Mar 31 14:38:00 mysys vmunix: real mem = 67108864
Mar 31 14:38:00 mysys vmunix: avail mem = 57483264
Mar 31 14:38:00 mysys vmunix: using 255 buffers containing\
4186112 bytes of memory
```

This system has 64 MB of memory present. Roughly 10 MB are used by the kernel and its tables, including the 4 MB (or so) that are used by the buffer cache. These measurements were taken on a system that routinely supported 40 or so users and had 10 GB of disk or so of disk space. On a personal computer or workstation, you would expect to see much smaller numbers. Here's another display from a XENIX system running on a well-configured 80386-based personal computer:

```
L4L5L6MNOPmem: total=9216k, reserved=4k, kernel=1224k, user=7988k
kernel: drivers=4k, 10 screens=68k, 600 i/o bufs=600k, msg bufs=8k
nswap=6000, swplo=0, Hz=50, maximum user process size=9788k
QRSTUVWXYZ
```

This system has 9 MB of memory on line. Roughly 1.2 MB are used by the kernel, which includes 600 KB of buffer cache. XENIX is unusually verbose in the amount of information it provides about memory usage. While XENIX is gradually being superseded, we can only hope that its successors will follow suit.

8.1.4 Words to the Wise

As with any serious operation, you should take the proper precautions before you start. You wouldn't start a big woodworking project without putting on safety glasses unless you like to collect medical insurance. Therefore, we'll dispense some wisdom before proceeding any farther. They've been gleaned from many sad experiences building custom configurations.

Manufacturers periodically issue new releases of their operating system. Some new releases fix bugs. Some add significant new features, together with their own new bugs. You should welcome and install these new releases, even though they require additional work (if you have built a nonstandard kernel, you'll have to go through the configuration process again). However, don't assume that a new kernel release will run efficiently just because an older one does, particularly if you have the minimum memory configuration for your system. Like all other software, UNIX kernels grow with time. It is not uncommon for a manufacturer to upgrade the kernel and announce, simultaneously, that they no longer support configurations with small memory. If you suddenly find that your memory configuration is no longer supported, you may find that the new system is abysmally slow. Careful tuning may help to alleviate this problem but usually won't solve it. Your only real choices are to make do with bad performance, go back to the older version of your operating system, or buy more more memory. And here's a warning: No matter what anyone tells you, the System V.4 kernel will be much larger than any previous System V kernel.

Documenting the configuration process is critical to maintaining a healthy system. As we've said, you'll have to go through configuration again whenever your system manufacturer ships an update. When you repeat the process for the new system, you will want to know what you did last time. After running the new kernel for six months, you may suddenly find out that the assumptions you made when building it were invalid, or that the system's usage patterns aren't what you thought they were. You may even have a long-suffering user that has patiently lived with some problem that you introduced. In these cases, you need to know what changes you made and what you were thinking about when you made them. Documentation is easy for BSD UNIX, where you can add comments to the configuration files directly. For System V, you will have to keep your own notes. One drawback with configuration utilities is that they don't record why you made your changes.

Before even thinking about reconfiguring your kernel, make a spare copy of the current kernel:

```
# cd /
# cp vmunix vmunix.GOOD
```

Never leave yourself without a copy of the kernel that works correctly. You don't care whether or not this kernel is efficient—all you need to know is that it works. If your custom kernel has a custom bug, you will have something to fall back on. System V kernel installation utilities make a backup copy automatically, but why trust them? When you're dealing with something this important, paranoia is never inappropriate. A common convention for managing kernels is to give each kernel a name of the form *vmunix.nn*, where *nn* is 00 for the original kernel and is incremented by 1 for each kernel you build. Then link /*vmunix* to whichever kernel you want to run. Only restart the numbering sequence if your system manufacturer ships a new kernel. If you follow these conventions, *vmunix.00* will always be a standard and workable (if not ideal) kernel.

One more caution: ALWAYS do a complete backup before installing a new kernel. Why? Let's just say that if things go wrong, they can go very wrong. It is certainly possible for a slightly misconfigured kernel to scribble all over a disk drive. You don't need to worry so much if you're installing a kernel built from a configuration file that your manufacturer provided. But you should always do a complete backup before installing a software upgrade. Upgrade releases sometimes fool around with your disk in ways that are incompatible with previous releases. If you install the upgrade and can't use it for some reason, you may not be able to go back to your original version without doing a complete "cold" installation. The bottom line is: no matter what you do, make sure you can get the system back in working order.

8.2 Configuring a BSD Kernel

In principle, configuring a new kernel is relatively simple. A kernel configuration file describes the system you want to build. Configuration files are usually kept in the directory /sys/conf. The directory /usr/sys/conf is often a link to /sys/conf and is where you should do your work. Some manufacturers have rearranged the directory structure slightly, usually to account for different system architectures.

Once you have found the configuration directory for your system (and your particular architecture), look for the file named GENERIC. This file describes a default kernel which contains all possible options. We will assume that you start from this kernel, then configuration will mostly be a process of deleting things you don't want. Some manufacturers (Sun in particular) also include some standard makefiles for certain smaller kernels. If configuration files for smaller kernels are available, see whether or not any of them are appropriate for your system. If you can use one of these, do so. If a smaller kernel is close to what you want but not quite there, start by modifying the smaller configuration file rather than GENERIC. To get a feel for how configuration works, you may want to spend some time comparing the GENERIC configuration to some of the smaller standard configurations.

We'll assume that you're starting from the GENERIC kernel and that you want to name the new kernel MIKE1. Make a copy of GENERIC for your new kernel. Never edit GENERIC directly. Then create a "build directory" for your new kernel. The configuration utility creates this directory for you, but we prefer to make it by hand.

```
% cd /usr/sys/conf
% cp GENERIC MIKE1
% mkdir /usr/sys/MIKE1
% vi MIKE1
```

At this point, edit your configuration file *MIKE1* to reflect any changes you want. We'll discuss the structure of this file and changes you may want to make below. When your new configuration file is finished, take the following steps:

```
% config MIKE1
% cd /usr/sys/MIKE1
% make depend
% make MIKE1
```

The *config* command processes the configuration file, placing a number of files in your private build directory, */usr/sys/MIKE1*. The first *make* command computes dependencies for source code that has to be recompiled. You have to perform this step even if you don't have any source code around. (Some manufactures have changed the *config* program to run *make depend* automatically.) The final *make* command builds the new kernel, which it leaves in your build directory. The kernel's filename is controlled by the *config* file, but it will probably be called *vmunix*. *ps* and other programs will have problems if the kernel has some other name. Note that the kernel's filename (*vmunix*) and the kernel's name (*MIKE1*) differ.

At this point you can install and run your new kernel, according to your manufacturer's instructions. If any errors occurred during the configuration process, DON'T try to install the new kernel. You almost certainly won't like the results. Try to figure out what went wrong and generate a new kernel that builds without errors.

8.2.1 Structure of a Configuration File

A configuration file is a sequence of one-line entries specifying different aspects of the kernel's configuration. Fundamentally, there are 12 different kinds of configuration lines. We'll introduce them in the order in which you'll usually find them. With each line, we've included a sample line taken from a modified Sun 3 configuration file:

machine   Identifies the system's architecture. You won't need to change this.

```
machine       "sun3"    # system type
```

cpu   Identifies the particular model. In some situations, the same configuration file may be used to build kernels for several different and compatible models. You don't have to change it, but building a kernel that only runs on one type of system reduces the kernel's size.

```
cpu           "SUN3_160"  # Sun-3/160 or
                          # Sun-3/75 cpu
```

ident An identifier for the kernel. This should be the same as the name of the configuration file and the build directory (in our example, *MIKE1*). It is *not* the kernel's filename, which is usually *vmunix*.

```
ident        MIKE1     # build directory name
```

timezone The time zone in which the system will be running. Time zone setting has gotten very complex to take into account all kinds of international timekeeping rules. The simplest setting for *timezone* is to specify the number of hours you are west of Universal Coordinated Time (formerly Greenwich Mean Time, which is five hours different from the U.S. Eastern time zone) and add the qualifier *dst* if your area observes daylight savings time. If you need anything more complicated, consult your manufacturer's documentation.

```
timezone     5 dst     # U.S. Eastern time zone,
                       # daylight savings time
```

maxusers This is the most important kernel configuration parameter, as it controls the size of the most important kernel tables. It is an estimate of the number of users your system will service, taking into account additional load presented by NFS operation, etc.

```
maxusers     4         # kernel table sizes
```

We'll discuss *maxusers* further below, but we'll note one aspect of it here. *maxusers* is not a hard limit on the number of users who can use your system simultaneously. Such a limit may, and probably is, specified by your license agreement with the manufacturer. If the limit is enforced (and it often isn't), the enforcement mechanism is completely unrelated to *maxusers*.

options There may be any number of *options* lines. They request certain optional features (for example, disk quotas and network support) which otherwise won't be included in the kernel. We will discuss these below in great detail.

```
options      INET      # Internet network protocols
```

config *config* lines specify the actual name of the kernel executable, the location of the boot partition, and the locations of the swapping partitions.

```
config       vmunix    swap generic # executable name
                                     # and swap spec
```

pseudo-device

> *pseudo-device* lines tell the kernel to include certain software options that are technically device drivers but that don't correspond to a physical device.

```
pseudo-device pty
```

controller, disk, tape, device

> These lines spell out the configuration of your system's peripherals in great detail.

```
controller    vme16d16 1 at nexus ?
```

Any characters to the right of a pound sign (#) are comments, which the configuration program ignores. It is a good idea to include copious comments. Later, you may need to remember what you did and why you did it.

8.2.2 The maxusers Parameter

The *maxusers* line determines the size of most important kernel tables (with the exception of the filesystem's buffer cache). It is an estimate of the effective number of users that will be on the system at any time. Contrary to what the name implies, it is not a limit on the maximum number of users for the system. *maxusers* merely determines whether or not the kernel has enough room to accommodate users comfortably.

To decide on a good value for *maxusers*, start with the number of users you expect to be using the system at any time. For a large shared system, this might be as many as 40 or 50; for a workstation, this might be only 1. Add 2 for basic administrative overhead; the system needs room to run daemon processes and the like. If the system is an NFS server, add 1 for every NFS client that boots from this system, and add 1 for every two additional NFS clients that mount filesystems from this system. The total is the recommended value for *maxusers*. On computers that run X or some other windowing system, you may also want to increase *maxusers*. Windowing systems encourage users to use more processes and thus may require larger kernel tables.

Because *maxusers* controls the size of the major kernel tables, reducing *maxusers* is one way to increase the amount of available memory. However, there are many tradeoffs involved. By decreasing *maxusers*, you are decreasing the number of users that the system can support effectively—you are decreasing the number of processes that the system can run simultaneously, you are decreasing the number of files that can be open, etc. Furthermore, you won't get any big savings by reducing *maxusers* unless your system is grossly overconfigured. Although these tables are very important, they are also relatively small. Prior to setting *maxusers* to an artificially small value, you should look at the buffer cache. If there are any big savings to be found, this is where you'll find them.

If you decide to modify *maxusers*, you should be aware of how your modifications will affect the system's performance. The system tables that are defined through *maxusers* are discussed thoroughly in the chapter on CPU performance. Here's a quick summary:

Table	Definition	BSD Default Setting
nproc	Size of the process table.	$20+8*maxusers$
ntext	Size of the text table.	$36+maxusers$
ninode	Size of the inode table.	$80+13*maxusers$
nfile	Size of the open file table.	$(nproc+16+maxusers)/10+64$
ncallout	Size of the callout (timer) table.	$16+nproc$
nclist	Number of character lists (terminal buffers). $60+12*maxusers$	
ndquot	Number of quota structures.	$ninode+(maxusers*nmount)/4$

If you are very bold and understand in detail how the UNIX kernel works, you can change the way these variables are defined in your kernel's copy of *param.c*, which *config* places in the build directory. Changing these definitions to increase the size of a table is, as a rule, harmless. Making the tables smaller is significantly more risky.

8.2.3 Devices

Device specification is by far the most complex and system-dependent part of kernel configuration. It is possible to reduce the kernel's memory requirements by leaving out devices that you don't need. However, this is tricky. Many systems have hidden devices that you don't know about that you *do* need. For example, it wouldn't be unreasonable for a floating point processor or an internal clock to be treated as a special kind of internal I/O device. It's tempting to say, "Go through the *device* specifications and delete any that you don't need," but that's obviously asking for trouble.

Without going into detail about how devices are specified (we'll leave that to your system's manufacturer), it is useful to know that there are four kinds of device specification lines:

controller   *controller* lines describe disk controllers, tape controllers, and bus interfaces (i.e., controllers that connect one bus to another).

disk   *disk* lines describe disk drives. A *controller* line by itself isn't sufficient. Most disk controllers can handle two or more disk drives, so you need a *disk* line for every disk drive that is present.

tape   As you might guess, *tape* lines describe tape drives. Again, most tape controllers can handle two or more tape drives.

device   *device* lines describe everything else (terminal controllers, Ethernet controllers, special graphics hardware, custom devices, etc.).

As you walk through the "device" section of a configuration file, you will see *controller* entries describing the addresses of disk and tape controllers and bus controllers. You will also see *disk* and *tape* entries that describe how particular disk and tape drives are connected, and you will see *device* lines to describe everything else. For example, in a Sun configuration file, we find these lines:

```
controller xyc0 at vme16d16 ? csr 0xee40 priority 2 vector xyintr 0x48
controller xyc1 at vme16d16 ? csr 0xee48 priority 2 vector xyintr 0x49
disk       xy0 at xyc0 drive 0
disk       xy1 at xyc0 drive 1
disk       xy2 at xyc1 drive 0
disk       xy3 at xyc1 drive 1
```

This says that two Xylogics disk controllers are connected to the system's VME bus in 16-bit address space (*xyc0* and *xyc1*), two disk drives are connected to each disk controller, disk *xy0* is connected to controller *xyc0* as drive 0, disk *xy1* is connected to controller *xyc0* as drive 1, and so on. For our purposes, we don't need to know how the controllers are connected (bus addresses and so forth). Check with your system's manufacturer if you need to understand this.

When you have become comfortable at reading this portion of the configuration file, map out what devices it is trying to configure. Then consult your system and see whether or not they exist. If you can get rid of a device type completely, great. You'll save memory because the device driver won't be included in the kernel. For example, if you don't have any SCSI disk drives and don't plan to have any, delete all references to SCSI disks. If you have to leave one SCSI disk drive entry, you might as well leave four. Given that the device driver has to be present, the additional memory needed to support some spare drives is insignificant. It's wise to configure a kernel so it can handle some extra (initially nonexistent) disk drives. You don't want to build a new kernel whenever you add more hardware. Keep in mind that the smallest possible kernel for your system is likely to be inflexible, and you must balance memory savings against flexibility. Make sure you don't delete any lines that describe your system's bus connectivity. On a Sun, names to watch for are *virtual* (sets up virtually-addressed devices), *obio* (sets up on-board I/O devices), and names that begin with *vme* (various parts of the VMEbus address space).

Your biggest problem will be figuring out how cryptic device names correspond to actual physical devices. There are no conventions for device names. It is common for the device names to reflect the company that manufactured the controller (as in the Xylogics disk controller above). Section 4 of the *UNIX Programmer's Reference Manual* should describe all the devices that your system supports.* Please consult this before taking a "slash-and-burn" approach to device configuration. This may prevent you from inadvertently deleting some devices that you otherwise need. Don't delete a device just because the cryptic name in the configuration file doesn't look familiar. It would be a shame to create a kernel that didn't know about terminals.

8.2.4 Pseudo-devices

Pseudo-devices are programs that interact with the kernel as if they were device drivers but that aren't connected to a physical device. Most pseudo-devices have to do with networking or windowing systems. In theory, you could eliminate them and save some space. In practice, you really can't. Networks and windowing are so basic to modern computer systems that it is almost inconceivable that you'd be willing to live without them. Some manufacturers may require some network pseudo-devices even on systems that aren't attached to a network.

There are a few standard pseudo-devices. These are:

ether   Some miscellaneous Ethernet software. Again, don't delete this pseudo-device unless you're sure you can live without networking.

imp   Intelligent message processor. You can do without this pseudo-device if you aren't an ARPANET site and have no intentions of becoming one.

loop   Ethernet "loopback" interface. If you want to live without networking, you could build a kernel without this device.

---

*Some good guessing will take you far. *wd* is a common designation for Winchester disks; *sd* and *st* are common designation for SCSI bus disks and tapes, respectively. *ie* is a fairly common designation for an Interlan Ethernet interface although it can also refer to Intel's Ethernet interface, and *le* often refers to some kind of on-board (local) Ethernet interface. If we saw a device named *cdc*, we wouldn't hesitate to guess that it was a CDC peripheral of some sort. And so on. But your manual is the final and ONLY authority for your system. Manufacturers change these designations at will.

nit   STREAMS NIT. Needed if you want to be a file server for a diskless node.

ns   Xerox network standard (XNS) software. The XNS network protocols were developed by Xerox and are an alternative to the Internet (TCP/IP) protocol suite. While XNS is rare within the academic and engineering environments at which UNIX developed, it is more popular within the business environment. It is reasonably likely that you can live without this. Your manufacturer may not even support it.

pty   Pseudo-terminals. Used almost everywhere by almost everything. For example, shell windows within *emacs* editors generally use pseudo-terminals. Don't try to do without this one.

This list is far from complete. Manufacturers are free to define their own pseudo-devices to do whatever they please. Any pseudo-devices that aren't on this list are probably specific to your system's manufacturer; consult the system's documentation for more information. We would certainly feel nervous about deleting any system-specific pseudo-device unless we knew exactly what it was for.

8.2.5 Root and Swap Configuration

The *config* line in a configuration file specifies the name of the UNIX executable. It also tells UNIX where to find the root and swap partition on the disks. A lot of complicated defaulting minimizes the amount you have to write here.

A typical *config* line would be:

```
config    vmunix    root on xy0 swap on xy0 and xy2
```

First, this line states that the name of the BSD UNIX executable is *vmunix*. Under BSD UNIX, many standard programs like *ps* assume the kernel is named */vmunix*. If you don't follow this convention, programs like *ps* won't work. Linking *vmunix* to the actual kernel is a way of obeying this convention without restricting your choice of kernel names.

The remainder of the line says the root filesystem is on disk *xy0* (which must be defined in a *disk* line). The root filesystem is, by default, assumed to be in partition *a* of this disk. There are swap partitions on disks *xy0* and *xy2*. By default, the swap partitions will be in partition *b*. One swap partition has to be on the root disk, and you may place other swap partitions on any disk drive you want.

Unless your system supports filesystem paging, this is the only mechanism available for controlling the size and location of your swapping areas. For the best performance, your swapping areas should be distributed as widely as possible among your disks and disk controllers. In the specification above, we've decided we need two partitions for swapping and placed them on disks 0 and 2.

Once you have decided to put a swapping partition on a disk, you have placed some constraints on how the disk can be used. In UNIX terminology, a disk partition is merely a predefined area on the disk. Disk organization is discussed in Chapter 5, *Disk Performance Issues*. If you're still uncomfortable with this topic, reread Chapter 5 and consult your system's documentation.

The *config* line can also have *dump* and *args* clauses, but the defaults (use the first swapping partition for kernel core dumps and *execve* argument passing) are reasonable for most situations.

8.2.6 Options

The *options* lines in a configuration file provide a catch-all mechanism for requesting optional software features, changing table sizes, and performing other miscellaneous duties. All an *options* line really does is generate a -*D* option (a preprocessor name definition) on the *cc* command line that generates the new kernel. For example, if you request the *QUOTA* option, you are really including the following code from *param.c* (one of the files that *config* will place in your build directory):

```
# ifdef QUOTA
struct   quota *quota, *quotaNQUOTA;
struct   dquot *dquot, *dquotNDQUOT;
# endif
```

Similarly, if you set the option *DFLDSIZ*, you are overriding the default definition for this parameter, which is made in the file *vmparam.h*:

```
# ifndef DFLDSIZ
# define DFLDSIZ   USRSTACK      /* initial data size limit */
# endif
```

Given the generality of this mechanism, the number of options that are available is almost infinite, particularly if you have the UNIX source code. We will only be able to hit the high points. If you are very bold and don't mind creating a lot of broken kernels, you can inspect your configuration header files and change some of the more obscure parameters. But don't say we didn't warn you.

Another consequence of this mechanism is that error detection is almost impossible. *config* will warn you if you try to do something obviously inconsistent, but there are many holes. For example, if you misspell the option *DFLDSIZ* as *DFLDSIX*, all *config* does is generate a slightly different (but incorrect) preprocessor definition. It doesn't know that you haven't added your own option named *DFLDSIX*. Likewise, when you build the new kernel, *DFLDSIX* will be treated like any other preprocessor definition. No one cares if a preprocessor definition is never used, so no warning will be given. Unless your typo generates something that is grossly incongruous, *config* probably won't notice.

Optional Software Features

First, we'll discuss optional software features. Eliminating an option saves some memory because code for that option isn't included in the kernel. The tradeoff is obvious: if you eliminate an optional feature, you can't use it.

The optional features below are standard to most BSD UNIX systems:

COMPAT   BSD 4.1 compatibility. Allows the system to execute 4.1 binaries without recompilation. 4.1 dates back to the early 1980s and predates most modern UNIX systems. You DON'T need this option. Recompile your ancient code.

INET   Internet network protocols. This option is basic to all Ethernet networking. Some systems require it even if you aren't using a network. Leave this option configured. If *INET* is configured, the *loop* and *ether* pseudo-devices must also be present.

NFS   Network File System. If you use the Network File System, you must include this option. If your site has Ethernet and more than one UNIX system that supports NFS, you probably want to include it. The ability to share files easily is well worth the additional overhead. NFS is an absolute necessity for sites with workstations. Sun has recently replaced this option with two others: *NFSCLIENT* and *NFSSERVER*. The first lets your system access remote filesystems via NFS. The second lets your system export filesystems to other NFS clients.

NS   Xerox network standard (XNS) protocols. These protocols have never caught on within the scientific world, though they are more common in other applications. If you don't use XNS networking, you can omit this option.

QUOTA   Disk quotas. If this option is present, the code for managing disk quotas (and the *nquota* and *ndquot* tables) is included in the kernel. You have to balance the importance of disk quotas against your system's memory requirements.

SYSACCT   System accounting. We've seen this option on Sun systems, though it doesn't appear to be standard. This option (if your system supports it) adds accounting code to the kernel. If your system doesn't provide *SYSACCT* as an option, accounting is always included in the kernel.

SYSAUDIT   C-2 security auditing. This is only available on some systems (recent Suns in particular). Don't include this option unless you require additional security. It adds a significant amount of overhead.

If you leave the *INET* option configured (and you almost always will), you may choose between the additional options below:

COMPAT_42   Another option for compatibility with BSD Version 4.2.

GATEWAY   The system can be a network gateway. This option is only needed if the system has two or more network interfaces. It allows the system to forward packets from one network to another.

TCP_COMPAT_42   This system allows BSD 4.3 UNIX systems to compensate for a bug in Version 4.2's network software. If your site mixes Versions 4.2 and 4.3, you should have this option. Even though 4.3 has been available for several years (and is soon to be replaced by 4.4), 4.2 systems are still fairly common.

If you leave the *NS* option configured, you have the following two options to consider:

NSIP   Allow the Internet software to transmit XNS packets through gateways. This option is only applicable if the *INET*, *NS*, and *GATEWAY* options are enabled.

THREEWAYSHAKE   Require a "three-way handshake" before considering a connection established. This increases the network's reliability. It is very rarely needed.

On many UNIX systems, a small group of options controls a number of System V interprocess communication features. Systems that support IPC include Concurrent, Hewlett-Packard, Pyramid, Sequent, Sun, and others. The trend towards merging System V and BSD features means you will probably see these options in other configuration files in the near future:

IPCMESSAGE   Include the IPC message facility.

IPCSEMAPHORE   Include the IPC semaphore facility.

IPCSHMEM   Include the shared-memory facility.

Listing these options in the configuration file builds a kernel that supports System V IPC. What you're really controlling is whether or not certain system calls are legal. Most BSD UNIX application packages do not assume that these features are present; therefore, it's usually safe to disable them. But don't be surprised if some local programs break. After all, programmers have no obligation to tell the system administrator whenever they find an interesting new system facility. If you decide to delete these features, it's your job to tell the system's users.

Finally, here are some other options that are available from Sun, but which we expect to leak into the rest of the BSD UNIX world with time:

CRYPT   Software support for the data encryption standard. If you want to use secure NFS or RPC (a recent enhancement) but don't have hardware encryption support, include the CRYPT option.

RFS   The System V "Remote File Sharing" facility, an alternative to NFS. You can probably get along without this option perfectly well. System V is integrating NFS, and while we've heard a lot about RFS, we have yet to find a site that actually uses it.

VFSSTATS   Also needed if, and only if, you are using RFS.

UFS   The standard BSD local filesystem. Under BSD UNIX, UFS supports local disk access. If you are running a diskless workstation, you don't have any local disks and can therefore omit the *UFS* option.

Options to Change the Buffer Cache

The size of the buffer cache has important effects on system performance. We discussed these effects in Sections 4.3.5, "The Buffer Cache," and 5.5, "Filesystem Buffers," and won't repeat that discussion here. In SunOS 4.0 (and later versions of SunOS), the size of the buffer cache varies dynamically. It still has an important effect on performance, but you can't control it. If you are running Version 4.0 of SunOS (or later), you can ignore this section.

If you don't specify the buffer cache's size explicitly, the generic kernel will set the cache's size when UNIX boots. After computing the amount of available memory (i.e., total physical memory minus the kernel and its other data structures), UNIX will reserve 10 percent of the first 2 MB plus 5 percent of any remaining memory for the buffer cache. If this figure is under 16 KB, UNIX will set the cache size to 16 KB. However, the minimum cache size is almost never an issue with modern systems. For example, suppose a system has 16 MB of memory. If the kernel and its data structures occupy 1 MB, the default buffer cache size is:

```
0.1*2 MB + 0.05*(16-1-2) MB = .85 MB
```

To specify the size of the buffer cache explicitly, add the *BUFPAGES* option to your configuration file. (This option will never be present in a *GENERIC* configuration file—such files will always accept your system's defaults.) A *BUFPAGES* configuration line has the form:

```
options BUFPAGES="npages"
```

where *npages* is the number of 1-KB pages to be allocated to the cache. For example, to allocate 16 MB to the cache, add the line:

```
options BUFPAGES="16000"
```

A buffer cache of this size would only be appropriate for a system with an extremely large memory. The buffer cache is typically between 5 and 15 percent of the system's available memory.

If you increase the buffer cache's size, you must also increase the size of the system page table (controlled by the constant *SYSPTSIZE*) to accommodate for the larger cache. If the page table is too small to map the entire buffer cache, *config* will print an error message telling you that it has reduced the size of the cache. There are several ways to handle this problem. You can recompute the size of the page table, you can simply increase the size of the page table and see whether or not the message goes away, or you can ignore it altogether, making do with the largest cache the current page table allows. All of these solutions are reasonable, including the last. Some systems won't let you change *SYSPTSIZE* through the configuration file, so you may be stuck with the final alternative.

You may also specify the number of buffer headers by using the *NBUF* option. This controls the actual number of buffers that can exist. If you don't specify this option, the system will compute a reasonable default, based on the amount of memory reserved for the buffer cache.

Program Size Options

Another group of options controls program size. These options limit the size of the text (i.e., executable), data, and stack segments. By increasing the values of these options, you can configure your system to run larger programs (if that's appropriate). By reducing their values, you can prevent your system from running large programs.

It's not clear what there is to be gained by preventing your system from running large programs. The page tables get much larger as the maximum size of a program's address space increases. Reducing segment size lets you get by with smaller page tables, thus saving memory, but the reason you need memory is so you can run large programs. Therefore, I am not convinced there is any great value in forcibly reducing program size. But don't forget about these parameters entirely. If you're in an environment that runs a lot of large programs (for example, simulations), you may need to increase the maximum segment sizes in order to support your system's users.

The options controlling program size are:

DFLDSIZ   Sets the system-wide soft limit for the size of a program's data segment. To set the system-wide soft data size limit to 10 MB, include the following *options* line:

```
options DFLDSIZE="(10 * 1024 * 1024)"
```

A user can override this soft limit by using the *setrlimit* system call (described in the *UNIX Programmer's Reference Manual*). C shell users can override this limit on the command line by using the *limit* command.

DFLSSIZ   Sets the system-wide soft limit for the size of the program's stack segment. To set this soft limit to 10 MB, include the following *options* line:

```
options DFLSSIZE="(10 * 1024 * 1024)"
```

The *setrlimit* system call or the C shell can be used to override the default maximum stack segment size.

MAXDSIZ   Sets the maximum size of the data segment. On some systems, the maximum text size is either 17 MB, 33 MB, or 64 MB. The system takes the value specified for this option and rounds it up. Other systems have removed this limitation. For example, to set the maximum data segment size to 64 MB, insert the following line into your configuration file:

```
options MAXDSIZ="(64 * 1024 * 1024)"
```

MAXSSIZ   Sets the maximum size for the program's stack segment. To set the maximum stack size to 64 MB, include the line:

```
options MAXSSIZ="(64 * 1024 * 1024)"
```

Some versions of BSD UNIX don't support this option. In these versions, the maximum stack size is always the same as the maximum data size.

MAXTSIZ   Sets the maximum size of the text segment. Programs with larger text segments aren't allowed to run. The maximum text size must always be smaller than the maximum data segment size. To set the maximum text size, use a line like the following:

```
options MAXTSIZ="( size-in-bytes )"
```

size-in-bytes is typically expressed as a product ($n*1024*1024$) to make it easy to read the maximum size in megabytes. For example, to set the maximum text size to 64 MB, use the line:

```
options MAXTSIZ="(64 * 1024 * 1024)"
```

8.2.7 Other Configuration Definitions

Some other important definitions are scattered throughout various header files. These aren't controlled directly by the configuration process. To modify these parameters, you must find and change the header file. The relevant files should be included with all systems, whether or not you have a source license. They will be in some subdirectory of */usr/sys*, normally either */usr/sys/h* or */usr/sys/machine*. The exact naming conventions have changed since the days of the VAX and may vary, depending on your system's manufacturer.

MAXUPRC   Defined in */usr/sys/h/param.h*. *MAXUPRC* sets the maximum number of processes any user can have.

NMOUNT   Defined in */usr/sys/h/param.h*. This parameter sets the maximum number of filesystems that can be mounted at one time. This includes both "local" and "remote" (i.e., NFS) mounts. Its initial value is usually 20; it can be increased to any value less than 255. SunOS 4.0 and later releases manage the number of mounted filesystems dynamically.

NOFILE   Defined in */usr/sys/h/param.h*. *NOFILE* sets the maximum number of files that any single process can have open at one time. Its initial value is usually 64. Increasing this value changes the size of the "user structure" (increasing it by one requires five more bytes in the user structure), which may require you to increase the *UPAGES* parameter accordingly.

On some BSD implementations, the maximum number of files is hard-coded into the run-time libraries. Yes, this is a mistake, but there is nothing we can do about it. If this is the case, changing *NOFILE* will break your system. Therefore, you shouldn't change *NOFILE* unless you really know what you're doing and are willing to deal with some breakage.

SYSPTSIZE Defined in */usr/sys/machine/vmparam.h*. UNIX uses separate page tables to describe virtual memory mappings for the system state and the user state. This parameter declares the number of pages that are reserved for the system page table. It is defined in different ways on different systems, but you will often see something like:

```
# define SYSPTSIZE size-of-mappable-area/constant
```

It may take some detective work to find whether *size-of-mappable-area* is specified in bytes or in pages. Note that some systems (Sun in particular) don't allow you to change *SYSPTSIZE*. They compensate by giving you a page table that can handle any reasonable configuration.

You should consider increasing *SYSPTSIZE* if you increase the size of the buffer cache. The system page table must always be large enough to map the entire buffer cache. If it isn't, *config* will give you a warning and part of the buffer cache will be unusable. You can guarantee that you have a sufficiently large cache by increasing *size-of-mappable-area* by the number of bytes (or blocks) you have added to the buffer cache.

UPAGES Defined in */usr/sys/machine/machparam.h*. This parameter defines the number of pages reserved for the "user structure." You may have to increase it to account for changes to *NOFILES*. *UPAGES* is almost always very small (typically between one and four pages); increasing it by 1 should do the trick in virtually every situation.

USRPTSIZE Defined in */usr/sys/machine/vmparam.h*. This parameter declares the number of pages that are reserved for the user-state page table. For VAX systems, the standard page table maps 256 MB of virtual address space. Most modern systems have increased the size of the page table significantly, often allowing you to map 4 GB of user-state virtual address space. Therefore, you probably won't have to touch this parameter.

Paging and Swapping Control

A final group of options control the paging and swapping algorithms.

DESFREE   The threshold at which desperation swapping begins. It is always less than *LOTSFREE*.

HANDSPREAD   The amount of memory between the two "clock hands" that determine when a page can be paged-out. Increasing the handspread increases the minimum time that a page will remain in memory after being "touched" by its process. Consequently, increasing the handspread makes it more likely that a given page will be touched and rendered invulnerable to paging. Increasing *HANDSPREAD* may improve the performance of large processes that access a lot of memory randomly.

LOTSFREE   The threshold at which paging begins. Paging starts when the amount of free memory dips below *LOTSFREE*.

MAXSLP   The amount of time, in seconds, that a process must be blocked before it is "very swappable"—i.e., before the process becomes a prime candidate for swapping. In other words, this is the system's definition of a long time.

MINFREE   The threshold at which the system considers itself "out of memory." At this point, the system will absolutely refuse to allocate more memory until it has freed some memory by swapping or paging. If the amount of free memory reaches *MINFREE*, the system is suffering a very severe shortage. It is not a good idea to reduce *MINFREE*. It guarantees the system a certain amount of memory to work with, even in the worst case.

SAFERSS   The minimum amount of memory, in pages, that a swapped-in process can have. If the working set of a program reaches this lower limit, no more pages will be paged-out. If the system wants to take any more memory from this program, it will swap the rest of the program out.

How you set these parameters depends on your goals. If you want to prevent swapping, you can increase *LOTSFREE*. You will spend more time paging, but you will also reduce the chance that the free memory will dip below *DESFREE*. Some administrators set *DESFREE* to zero to prevent swapping under any circumstances. This is only advisable if your system rarely suffers severe memory shortages. Conversely, you can reduce the time you spend paging by decreasing *LOTSFREE*. Is this a good idea? The later paging begins, the greater the chance that your system will resort to swapping or that memory will dip below *MINFREE*, at which point performance will be horrible.

At this point, you're about as low in the BSD configuration process as you can go without a source code license. Build your new kernel according to the instructions we gave above.

8.3 Configuring a System V Kernel

The configuration process for System V varies from release to release and from manufacturer to manufacturer. There are significant differences between each major version. However, the configuration parameters have remained more or less constant. The names have changed from time to time, and many parameters have disappeared from V.4. Always check the documentation supplied with your system before making any changes.

We'll discuss the configuration process for XENIX systems (most similar to V.2), Interactive 386/ix systems (a descendent of V.3), and the 3B2 version of System V.4 (the only one available as of publication) in some detail. Most System V implementations for 8086-series systems have menu-driven configuration tools. These programs make configuration much simpler and less error-prone. You don't have to worry about modifying the configuration files yourself. In fact, you shouldn't modify them yourself. The configuration process for AT&T's V.4 (at least the 3B2 version) has, unfortunately, taken a step backwards. We have been told that the *idbuild* family of configuration tools are part of the 80386 release of V.4. We hope that vendors like Interactive and SCO will take it upon themselves to provide higher-level tools like *kconfig*, as they have in the past.

8.3.1   Configuring a XENIX Kernel

XENIX configuration is essentially similar to configuration for Version V.2. Configuration is based on two files. A *master* file contains a description of all possible devices and gives the default values for all configuration parameters that aren't computed when the system boots. A configuration file (normally called *xenixconf*) describes any modifications you have made to this standard configuration. The new kernel you make will simply be called *xenix*. All of these files reside in the directory */usr/sys/conf*.

Changing Configuration Parameters

To build a new XENIX kernel, become superuser and give the command *lusr/sys/conf/configure*. It will display a menu describing several groups of performance tuning options:

```
1. Disk Buffers
2. Character Buffers
3. Files, Inodes, and Filesystems
4. Processes, Memory Management & Swapping
5. Clock
6. MultiScreens
7. Message Queues
8. Semaphores
9. Shared Data
10.    System Name
11.    Streams Data
12.    Event Queues and Devices
13.    Hardware Dependent Parameters
```

Enter the number of a category. *configure* will then cycle through the configuration parameters in this category. For each parameter, it will give you a prompt like the one below:

```
NBUF: total disk buffers.  Currently determined at
system start up:
```

This questions asks you to set the size of the buffer cache (using the standard buffer size). It states that the current value of *NBUF* is "currently determined at system startup," meaning that XENIX computes how much memory is available when the system boots and sets *NBUF* accordingly. If you are satisfied with this, enter a return. If you want to change this parameter, enter a new value, followed by a return. If the value you request is illegal or outside the acceptable range for this parameter, *configure* will print an error message and ask what you want to do next. When you have finished all the items in the category, *configure* will return to the main menu.

Once you're back at the main menu, you can work through another set of configuration options or enter *q* to quit. When you quit, *configure* will write a new version of *xenixconf*.

Device Drivers

The *configure* command lets you change configuration parameters but won't let you do anything about device drivers. Deleting device drivers shouldn't be an issue for XENIX. Unlike BSD kernels, System V kernels are additive. You add optional features as you need them, rather than removing features you don't want.

However, you may need to delete a device driver at some time. Assume you already know the name of the device (i.e., the inscrutable group of letters that serve as the "device name"); let's call it *hdt*. First, you need to find out the device's "major number." There are two ways to do this. Give the *ls* command below:

```
% ls -l /dev/hdt*
crw-rw-rw-   2 root      root       11, 32 Sep 24  1989 hdt0
```

The "major number" is 11. You will use this number to delete the device from the kernel. Unfortunately, this command only works if the device has been installed. If the device hasn't been installed, give the *configure* command below to find out the major number that has been assigned:

```
# /usr/sys/conf/configure -j hdt
11
```

Once you have found the major device number, give the command below to eliminate the device driver from the kernel:

```
# /usr/sys/conf/configure -d -m 11
```

configure will write a new configuration that deletes support for the device.

Finishing the Job

Once you have finished using *configure* to make your modifications, give the command:

```
# link_xenix
```

This will create a new XENIX executable. Copy the new executable to the root filesystem, shutdown the system, and reboot with the new kernel:

```
# cp xenix /xenix.new
# /etc/shutdown
...
Boot
: xenix.new
```

Now you're running the new kernel. If it works, congratulate yourself and use *hdinstall* to install this new version as */xenix*:

```
# hdinstall
```

This command automatically saves the old kernel as */xenix.old*. You *should not* trust this as your only method for saving the old kernel. If you mistakenly run *hdinstall* twice (easy to imagine—subtle kernel bugs can take a while to appear), you will destroy your working version of *xenix.old*.

If your new kernel doesn't work, reboot the old kernel (*/xenix* or *xenix.old*, depending on whether or not you ran *hdinstall*) and start debugging.

8.3.2 Configuring an Interactive 386/ix Kernel

386/ix configuration is, in many respects, similar to XENIX configuration. Configuration parameter tuning is based on two files: *mtune*, which contains default values and legitimate ranges for all parameters, and *stune*, which contains system-specific departures from these default values. A file named *mdevice* describes all legitimate device specifications, and the file *sdevice* describes the devices that are present. These files are in the directory */etc/conf/cf.d*.

You should never modify any of these files. The kernel configuration program, *kconfig*, will manage them for you.

Changing Kernel Parameters

To create a custom kernel, become superuser, go to the root directory, and run *kconfig*:

```
# cd /
# kconfig
MAIN MENU

1) CONFIGURE KERNEL
2) BUILD A KERNEL
3) INSTALL A KERNEL

Enter Choice [1-3,q]:
```

First, enter *1* to configure the kernel (customize kernel parameters and delete devices drivers you don't need). When you have finished, enter *2* to generate the new kernel. After that is finished, entering *3* will install the new kernel and shutdown the system.

When you enter *1*, *kconfig* will print a submenu:

```
CONFIGURATION MENU

1) ADD DRIVER
2) REMOVE DRIVER
3) ADD FACILITY
4) REMOVE FACILITY
5) ADD DEFAULT PARAMETERS FOR MEMORY SIZE
6) ADD TUNABLE PARAMETERS
7) CONFIGURE HIGH PERFORMANCE DISK DRIVE

Enter Choice [1-7,m,q]:
```

Entering *m* will ask whether or not you want to save the changes you have made, and return you to the main menu; entering *q* will exit immediately, forgetting your changes.

To change the kernel's configuration parameters, enter *5* or *6*. If you enter *5*, *kconfig* will generate a new set of default kernel parameters that should be ideal for your system's memory configuration. It will give you another menu:

```
CHOOSE THE CLOSEST MEMORY SIZE

1)  2MB
2)  4MB
3)  8MB
4)  16MB


Enter choice [1-4,m,q]:
```

Enter the number for the largest memory size that is *smaller* than your system's memory configuration. For example, if you have 10 MB, enter *3* (for 8 MB). By default, the system's configuration parameters assume a 2-MB memory configuration. Then enter *m* to return to the main menu. Of course, there is no reason to increase the system's parameters if you don't need to. If you have a single-user system with 10 MB, you can certainly get by with small kernel tables.

If you want to adjust the kernel configuration parameters on your own, enter *6* in response to the configuration menu. *kconfig* will then prompt you for the name of a configuration parameter and a new value. Continue this process until you are finished.

Removing Unneeded Devices

To remove an unneeded device driver, enter *2* in response to the configuration menu. *kconfig* will list the devices drivers that are currently installed. Enter the number of the device driver you want to remove. For example:

```
CHOOSE A DRIVER TO REMOVE FROM THE CURRENT CONFIGURATION

1)  AT serial I/O Driver
2)  AT hard disk driver
3)  Shell Layers Driver

Enter Choice [1-3,m,q]:
```

To remove the shell layers driver, enter *3*, then enter *m* to return to the main menu.

Removing Optional Software

You can also use *kconfig* to remove any optional software facilities that you have
added to the kernel. To do so, enter *4* in response to the main configuration menu.
You will see a menu like the following:

```
CHOOSE A FACILITY TO REMOVE FROM THE CURRENT CONFIGURATION

1) Inter Process Communication
2) Shared Memory

Enter Choice [1-2,m,q]:
```

The actual options available will depend on the facilities that you have added.
For example, if you have previously installed TCP/IP networking, you will see a
TCP/IP option in this menu. To delete any facility, enter its number. For example,
to delete the shared menu facility, enter *2*, then enter *m* to return to the main
menu. When you install the new kernel, any programs that make use of the
shared memory facility won't run.

Finishing Installation

After you have made all of your changes, you must build the new kernel and
install it. Return to the main menu:

```
MAIN MENU

1) CONFIGURE KERNEL
2) BUILD A KERNEL
3) INSTALL A KERNEL

Enter Choice [1-3,q]:
```

Enter *2* to build a new kernel from the configuration information you have just
entered. *kconfig* may ask you for more information about accepting certain
default values. Enter a carriage return to accept these defaults. When *kconfig* has
completed, it will print the messages:

```
Finished building unix system
Installing unix.n will shut down the system.
Do you want to install unix.n (y):
```

Enter *y* to continue with the installation process. You will next be asked for a
shutdown time:

```
Enter the number of seconds for shutdown user warning:
```

This is the amount of time *shutdown* will wait before the actual shutdown. A good figure here is 300 (5 minutes). Finally, *kconfig* will ask for confirmation:

```
This procedure will execute a shutdown to reboot the new
kernel unix.n.
Enter y to continue, n to terminate:
```

Enter *y* to go ahead, *n* if you have any reservations. After the system has shut down, reboot it. When you reboot, you will be running the new kernel.

If you want to return to an earlier kernel, run *kconfig* and select option 3 ("Install a kernel") from the main configuration menu. You will see the following message:

```
Installing a new kernel will shut down the system.
Do you want to install a new kernel (y):
```

Enter *y* to continue. *kconfig* will then list all the kernels that you have built:

```
CHOOSE THE KERNEL TO INSTALL

1) unix.1
2) unix.2

Enter Choice [1-2,m,q]:
```

The highest number is assigned to the kernel that you built most recently. Enter the number of the kernel that you want to install. *kconfig* will then ask you for configuration and a shutdown time. It will then shut down the system. When you reboot, you will be running the kernel you selected.

Using *kconfig* greatly simplifies kernel configuration. However, it has one basic problem: it is inherently difficult to document which features are included in which kernel. You never touch the configuration files and, therefore, don't have the opportunity to make comments. Documentation is an EXTREMELY important part of kernel customization. Make sure you keep detailed notes for every kernel you build. Otherwise, you will never remember whether *unix.25* was the kernel that worked or the kernel that destroyed your disks.

Here's one hint for keeping kernel documentation. The directory */etc/conf/kconfig.d/unix.n.d* contains a complete set of configuration files for the kernel *unix.d*. *n* is a serial number that is incremented with every new kernel you build. In this directory, write a file named *readme* or *comments* that exhaustively describes all changes you made to this kernel. Use this file to keep any notes about the kernel's behavior.

8.3.3 General V.3 Configuration Rules

For a general V.3 system, you can't assume the existence of a configuration program like *kconfig*. If your manufacturer supplies one, you should use it, but you can't assume it will be there. However, the standard AT&T release of V.3 provides several tools to help you with kernel configuration: *idtune* (to change configuration parameters), *idinstall* (to add or delete device drivers), and *idbuild* (to create the new kernel). *kconfig* is nothing more than a script that calls these (and a few other) tools.

Changing Configuration Parameters

The program *idtune* changes the value of any configuration parameter by modifying the *stune* file. It is used as follows:

```
# /etc/conf/bin/idtune option name value
```

where *name* is the name of a configuration parameter and *value* is the new value for the parameter. There are two mutually exclusive *options*:

-*m*   If the current value for the parameter *name* is greater than the new *value*, don't change it (i.e., set the value to the greater of the current value and the new value). For some inexplicable reason, AT&T calls this the "minimum" option.

-*f*   Force the change, even if *value* is outside of the legal range for the parameter *name*. Such changes don't necessarily have any effect. Some limits are built in to the software.

idtune prints the current value of the parameter (if there is one) and the new value and asks you to confirm that you want to make the change. Both -*f* and -*m* prevent *idtune* from asking the question.

For example, to change the *NBUF* parameter to 1000, give the command:

```
# /etc/conf/bin/idtune nbuf 1000
Tunable Parameter nbuf is currently set to 250.
Is it OK to change it to 1000? (y/n)
```

Entering *y* changes *NBUF* to the new value (1000).

Deleting Device Drivers

The program *idinstall* installs and removes device drivers by modifying your system's *sdevice* file. To delete a device driver, use it as follows:

```
# /etc/conf/bin/idinstall -d name
```

where *name* is the name of the device you want to delete. For example, assume that you want to remove the floppy disk driver. It's a good guess that this device will be named *fd*, though you should check by looking the proper name up in your manual. To delete this device driver from the kernel's configuration files, give the command:

```
# /etc/conf/bin/idinstall -d fd
```

Then use *idbuild* to generate a new kernel.

The actual name used for each device varies from manufacturer to manufacturer. Check your system's documentation for more information.

We won't discuss adding a custom device driver. If you have bought a new device, the vendor should provide an installation script that will run *idinstall* correctly. Developing and installing your own device driver is a topic beyond the limits of this book.

Building and Installing the New Kernel

When you are ready to build and install the new kernel, give the commands:

```
# cd /
# /etc/conf/bin/idbuild
```

This generates the new kernel according to the current configuration. To test the new kernel, shut the system down (with *shutdown*) and reboot it.

Swapping Devices

System V.3 allows you to specify a single swapping area in the configuration files. If you want to add more swapping areas, you don't need to modify the kernel. Instead, you should let the system boot with a single swap area, then add additional swap areas when the system enters multiuser mode by executing *swap* commands. To do this automatically, configure your disks for additional swapping areas and add appropriate *swap* commands to one of the */etc/rc2.d* initialization files. You could also add the *swap* command to */etc/rc2* itself, which is the script that executes the */etc/rc2.d* files.

8.3.4 Configuring a System V.4 Kernel

Under V.4, there are two UNIX kernels to worry about: the true UNIX kernel, which is running during normal operation, and mUNIX, which is a special kernel that is only used during configuration. With mUNIX, you shouldn't worry about speed or efficiency because it isn't the operating system you will run for normal work. You only care about reliability, and the best way to ensure reliability is to leave it alone. Therefore, we won't talk about mUNIX configuration in this book.

The Kernel Configuration Files

The configuration files for the 3B2 version of V.4 are located in the directory /etc/master.d. These files are:

hrt   Sets parameters for high-resolution timers.

kernel   Controls the important kernel tables.

log   Sets parameters for the STREAMS logging facility.

msg   Sets parameters for interprocess messages.

ports   Sets parameters for the "ports" facility.

prf   Sets parameters for kernel profiling.

s5   Sets parameters for the System V (old-style) filesystem.

sad   Sets parameters for STREAMS administration.

sem   Sets parameters for semaphores.

shm   Sets parameters for interprocess shared memory.

ts   Sets parameters for time-sharing scheduling.

ufs   Sets parameters for the BSD (Berkeley fast) filesystem.

Lines in these files have the format:

```
parameter-name = value
```

We have been told that the 8086-series version of System V.4 will retain the mtune and stune structure for configuration files. mtune holds the default value and upper and lower bounds for each parameter, while stune holds deviations from the default value.

The Configuration Process

To build a new kernel for System V.4, take these steps:

1. Save an old copy of the UNIX kernel:

    ```
    % cp /stand/unix /stand/oldunix
    ```

2. Go to the configuration directory:

    ```
    % cd /etc/master.d
    ```

3. Edit each configuration file that you want to change.

4. Go to the directory */boot*:

    ```
    % cd /boot
    ```

5. Give the command *mkboot* for each file in *master.d* that you modified. You must use the option *-k* if you modified the *kernel* file:

    ```
    % /usr/sbin/mkboot -k KERNEL
    % /usr/sbin/mkboot SHM
    ...etc....
    ```

    Note that the module names in the *mkboot* command are always capitalized.

6. Build a new kernel with the *cunix* command:

    ```
    % cunix -o /experimental
    ```

7. If *cunix* is successful, move your experimental kernel to */stand/unix*:

    ```
    % mv /experimental /stand/unix
    ```

8. Reboot the system running the new kernel.

Again, we are told that the 8086-series version will support the *idtune* and *idbuild* utilities for modifying kernel parameters and generating the new kernel. Vendors like SCO and Interactive will probably build their own configuration utilities on top of these low-level tools.

System Components

The file */stand/system* defines which components to include when building the system. By modifying this file, you can add or delete modules from the UNIX kernel. Deleting modules saves memory but limits the capabilities of your system.

The important lines in the file are the *EXCLUDE* and *INCLUDE* lines. They have the form:

```
EXCLUDE:   mod-name1 mod-name2 ...
INCLUDE:   mod-name3<n3> mod-name4<n4> ...
```

where the *mod-name*s are the names of kernel modules; these are files that are found in the */boot* directory, many of which correspond to configuration files in */etc/master.d*. The numbers *n3* and *n4* are integers that are only used when including device drivers. They specify the maximum number of devices that the system will support. We won't discuss configuring the system for new devices, so we will ignore these numbers from now on.

You can list any number of modules on an *INCLUDE* or *EXCLUDE* line. You may also have any number of *INCLUDE* or *EXCLUDE* lines. The system decides what to include and what to omit after processing the entire file.

Some modules you might wish to include (or exclude) are:

MSG   Messages. If you aren't interested in messages (an interprocess communications facility), exclude *MSG* from your system.

NFS   Network File System. If you don't use the Network File System (i.e., you don't share files at all or you use RFS for all file sharing), you can exclude *NFS* from your system.

PRF   Kernel profiling. If you aren't interested in getting a low-level picture of where the UNIX kernel spends its time, exclude *PRF* from your system.

RFS   Remote File Sharing. If you don't use AT&T's remote file sharing (i.e., if you don't share files or if you use NFS for all file sharing), you can exclude *RFS* from your system.

RT   Support for real-time processes. If your system is used for general purpose time sharing, you can exclude the *RT* module.

S5   The old System V filesystem. Theoretically, you can make your root filesystem a BSD-style (UFS) filesystem. If you can do this successfully and if you use the UFS filesystem for all other filesystems, you can exclude the *S5* module. However, System V.4's ability to boot from a UFS filesystem has been called into question. According to the AT&T documentation, it is possible.

SEM   Semaphores. If you aren't interested in semaphores (an interprocess communications facility), exclude *SEM* from your system.

SHM   Shared memory. If you aren't interested in shared memory (an interprocess communications facility), exclude *SHM* from your system.

UFS   The BSD "fast filesystem," which we have elsewhere called the "new filesystem." If you only use the standard System V filesystem, you can exclude *UFS*.

You can use this mechanism to exclude device drivers for peripherals you don't have.

For example, assume that you want to build a kernel without real-time processes and RFS but you want to make sure that the System V, UFS, and NFS filesystems are all included. First, check the *INCLUDE* and *EXCLUDE* lines to see where these features are mentioned. Delete *S5*, *NFS*, and *UFS* from any *EXCLUDE* lines, and delete *RT* and *RFS* from any *INCLUDE* lines. Then add the following to the *systems* file:

```
INCLUDE:  UFS NFS S5
EXCLUDE:  RT RFS
```

Of course, you don't need to list a facility if it already appears in an appropriate *INCLUDE* or *EXCLUDE* line.

We expect that the 8086-series version of V.4 will use the *idinstall* utility to add and delete these modules.

8.3.5 System V Configuration Parameters

This section presents the different configuration parameters for all three versions of System V: XENIX (V.2), V.3, and V.4. We have grouped the parameters by function. For each group of parameters, a table is listed that shows the name of the parameter for each version of the system (the names are often different), the file in which the parameter was defined, the "size" of the parameter per entry, and a typical value for the parameter (the default value, if one is defined). Following each table is a discussion of the parameters.

The size of a parameter per entry is a somewhat ambiguous concept. We mean the amount that the kernel's memory requirement increases if you increase this parameter by 1. Many parameters have no effect whatsoever on the kernel size. We indicate this with an asterisk.

Filesystem Parameters

This group of parameters controls the UNIX filesystem. It sets both user-visible features of the system (how many files you can have open, for example) and invisible but equally important features (the size of the buffer cache, which is critical to performance). The best settings for these parameters depend heavily on how you use your system. If you are short on memory or don't rely heavily on file I/O (for example, if you use your system mostly for editing), you can save memory and perhaps make your system more efficient by making these parameters as small as reasonably possible. If you use file I/O heavily (for example, if you do a lot of database work), you will want to make these tables larger and make do with the memory limitations. Table 8-1 lists filesystem parameters. After the table, we will discuss each parameter briefly.

Table 8-1. Filesystem Parameters

Name	Set In	Size Per Entry	Typical Value
V.2 Parameters:			
BUFFERS	xenixconf	varies	250
HASHBUF	xenixconf	12	64
MOUNTS	xenixconf	18	20
INODES	xenixconf	96	200
FILES	xenixconf	12	200
LOCKS	xenixconf	28	200
V.3 Parameters:			
MAXPMEM	stune	*	0
NBUF	stune	1076	250
NHBUF	stune	12	64
S52KNBUF	stune	2100	100
S52KNHBUF	stune	12	32
NMOUNT	stune	36	25
NINODE	stune	76	150
NS5INODE	stune	*	150
NFILE	stune	12	150
NOFILES	stune	*	60
FLCKREC	stune	28	100
BDFLUSHR	stune	*	1
NAUTOUP	stune	*	10
ULIMIT	stune	*	3072
V.4 Parameters:			
NBUF	kernel	88	100
NHBUF	kernel	12	64
BUFHWM	kernel	*	200
NINODE	s5	132	400
UFSNINODE	ufs	268	150

Name	Set In	Size Per Entry	Typical Value
NDQUOT	*ufs*	60	200
FLCKREC	*kernel*	*	300
FSFLUSHR	*kernel*	*	1
NAUTOUP	*kernel*	*	60
ROOTFSTYPE	*kernel*	*	*s5*
RSTCHOWN	*kernel*	*	0
NGROUPS_MAX	*kernel*	*	16

BUFFERS (V.2), *NBUF* (V.3, V.4)

> The number of buffers for block I/O (i.e., file I/O) operations. Decreasing the number of buffers limits I/O performance on heavily loaded systems; increasing the number of buffers uses a lot of memory but can improve I/O performance in some situations. The command *sar -b* will show how effectively you are using the buffer cache. By default, the system will choose a value for this parameter based on your memory configuration. (See also *NHBUF* and the *RFS* parameters.)
>
> In Version V.4, the *NBUF* parameter takes on a completely new meaning. The buffer cache itself has disappeared, but the system still needs to allocate buffer headers. These are managed dynamically, but in a restricted way. The system allocates headers in batches, *NBUF* at a time. Whenever it runs out of headers, it creates another batch. However, the system cannot return unused buffer headers to memory. The amount of memory dedicated to buffer headers can only grow with time, subject to the limit of *BUFHWM*. By decreasing *NBUF* (and allocating fewer buffers at a time), you force the system to allocate buffers more often, decreasing efficiency. Increasing *NBUF* (allocating buffers in larger groups) increases the number of unused (and perhaps never used) buffer headers taking up space in memory.

HASHBUF (V.2), *NHBUF* (V.3, V.4)

> The number of "hash buckets" to allocate for the buffer cache. This is the number of hash-table entries to use for searching the cache. Increasing it will make cache searches more efficient. It must be a power of 2 and is usually roughly one-quarter the number of buffers.

BUFHWM (V.4)

> The maximum amount of physical memory, in kilobytes, that can be used by I/O buffers. This value limits the number of buffers that can exist at any time. If the buffer hit ratio is low (see *sar -b*), increase *BUFHWM*. If the system spends a lot of time paging, try reducing *BUFHWM*.

S52KNBUF (V.3)

The number of buffers for block I/O on filesystems with a 2-KB block size. The ability to support a 2-KB block size may be an optional facility on your system. If you increase this parameter, you may want to decrease *NBUF* to compensate. (See also *S52KNHBUF* and the *RFS* parameters.)

S52KNHBUF (V.3)

The number of entries in the hash table used to search the filesystem buffers. This parameter applies only to filesystems with a 2-KB block size. This value must be a power of 2 and is usually roughly one-quarter of *S52KNBUF*. Increasing *S52KNHBUF* should make buffer searches more efficient.

MOUNTS (V.2), *NMOUNT* (V.3)

The maximum number of mounted filesystems. This figure includes the root filesystem, local filesystems, and all filesystems mounted via NFS or RFS. For the sake of efficiency, the size of the filesystem table should be as small as reasonable. However, you should allow for some expansion—when this table is full, you cannot mount additional filesystems. V.4 does not place a limit on mounted filesystems.

INODES (V.2), *NINODE* (V.3, V.4)

The size of the inode table. This is the maximum number of inodes that can be in use at any time. It is related to (but not the same as) the maximum number of open files. Opening a file always allocates an inode entry, but there are many other activities (opening a pipe, for example) that allocate inode entries without opening a file. Therefore, the inode table must be larger than the file table. When the table is full, you will get a warning message on the system's console. For V.4, *NINODE* only counts inodes for System V ("old-style") filesystems. V.4 maintains a separate inode table for BSD ("fast") filesystems; see *UFSNINODE*.

NS5INODE (V.3)

This parameter must be greater than or equal to *NINODE*. The two parameters are usually equal.

UFSNINODE (V.4)

The size of the inode table for UFS ("Berkeley") filesystems. This limits the number of files that can be open at one time in UFS filesystems.

NDQUOT (V.4)

The number of "quota" structures for UFS ("Berkeley") filesystems. If quotas are in effect, this value should be greater than the maximum number of users that can be logged in at any time times the number of UFS filesystems that are mounted. If quotas are not in effect or if you do not use the UFS filesystem, you can set this parameter to zero.

FILES (V.2), *NFILE* (V.3)

The size of the file table. This limits the maximum number of files (system-wide) that can be open at any time. Its value must be less than or equal to *NINODE*. When the file table is full, calls to *open* will fail and a warning message will be printed on the console.

NOFILES (V.3)

The maximum number of files that any process can open. This is independent of *NFILE* (the system-wide file table). The per-process file limit does not affect kernel size. The default is large enough to handle most applications, and changing it may be dangerous. In some implementations, the number of files per process is hard-coded into the run-time libraries. System V.4 doesn't place a limit on the number of files per process.

LOCKS (V.2), *FLCKREC* (V.3, V.4)

The maximum number of records that can be locked by the system.

BDFLUSHR (V.3), *FSFLUSHR* (V.4)

The system's flush rate in seconds. This controls the frequency with which the system will run the daemon that flushes data from the filesystem's buffer cache to the disk. Increasing the interval will improve performance but decrease the filesystem's reliability. The default value (1) runs the flush daemon every second.

NAUTOUP (V.3, V.4)

The age, in seconds, at which a buffer will be flushed to disk the next time the flush daemon runs. Increasing this limit will improve performance but decrease the system's reliability. For example, setting *NAUTOUP* to 15 seconds means that buffers that haven't been used in 15 seconds will be flushed to disk when the flush daemon runs. Setting *NAUTOUP* to zero means that all buffers in use will be flushed to disk.

ULIMIT (V.3)

The size of the largest file that a user can write, in 512-byte blocks.

ROOTFSTYPE (V.4)

The type of the root filesystem. By default, this is *s5* for the old-style System V filesystem. It may also be *ufs* if you want to use the BSD-style filesystem for the root. We have heard that this feature does not work properly.

RSTCHOWN (V.4)

Controls who is allowed to issue the *chown* command: 0 (System V.3 behavior) allows the owner of a file to change its user and group ownership arbitrarily, and 1 (BSD/FIPS/POSIX compatibility) means that only the superuser can change ownership; a file's owner can change its group membership, provided that the owner is member of the new group. Setting *RSTCHOWN* to 1 greatly improves system security.

NGROUPS_MAX (V.4)

The maximum number of groups to which a process may belong, assuming that you use BSD/FIPS/POSIX-style group ownership.

Process Management Parameters

The process management parameters determine how the system runs processes: how many it can run, how many shared libraries they can accesses, etc. If your system runs a small number of large jobs, you may be able to reduce these parameters significantly. However, memory savings will probably be relatively small. Table 8-2 lists the process management parameters. After the table, we will discuss each parameter briefly.

Table 8-2: Process Management Parameters

Name	Set In	Size Per Entry	Typical Value
V.2 Parameters:			
PROCS	xenixconf	72	100
REGIONS	xenixconf	42	300
MAXPROC	xenixconf	*	25
TEXTS	xenixconf	16	75
CALLS	xenixconf	12	100
CLISTS	xenixconf	70	660
V.3 Parameters:			
NPROC	stune	276	100
NREGION	stune	36	210
MAXUP	stune	*	25
SHLBMAX	stune	*	2
MAXSLICE	stune	*	2
NCALL	stune	16	30
NCLIST	stune	64	120
V.4 Parameters:			
NPROC	kernel	212	200
MAXUP	kernel	*	25
SHLBMAX	kernel	*	2

Name	Set In	Size Per Entry	Typical Value
NCALL	kernel	16	60
NCLIST	kernel	*	0
ARG_MAX	kernel	*	5120
INITCLASS	kernel	*	TS

PROCS (V.2), NPROC (V.3, V.4)

The size of the process table. The maximum number of simultaneous processes that the system can run. You should allow for at least two processes per user (this is an *absolute* minimum; five processes per user would be a more reasonable value), one process per terminal, and a dozen (or more) processes for system daemons.

REGIONS (V.2), NREGION (V.3)

The number of program regions that can be active at any time. Each UNIX process has at least three regions (text, data, and stack). Some processes may have two or more of each region. Different invocations of the same executable normally share the same text segment and, less commonly, the same data segment. *NREGION* is usually three times *NPROC*. Some versions of V.2 have a *texts* parameter instead of a *regions* parameter.

MAXPROC (V.2), MAXUP (V.3, V.4)

The maximum number of processes that any user (i.e., any user ID number) can have at one time. It must always be less than *NPROCS* but is usually relatively high—as much as 90 percent of *NPROCS*. By default, *MAXUP* is usually half of *NPROCS*. There is no reason to reduce *MAXUP*, except to provide some protection against runaway shell scripts or possibly as a desperate way to reduce CPU load. Some applications may require extremely large values for *MAXUP*. If many users log in with the same name (as may be the case in transaction processing applications), the total of all their processes must fall under this limit.

SHLBMAX (V.3, V.4)

The maximum number of shared libraries that any process can use at one time. For V.4, this limit applies only to processes with *COFF* executables. For more about *COFF* format, see the Nutshell Handbook *Understanding and Using COFF*.

MAXSLICE (V.3)

The maximum time slice (in clock ticks) for which any program can run uninterrupted. That is, the scheduler is guaranteed to run every *MAX-SLICE* ticks of the clock, at which time it may schedule some other process. The clock period is system-dependent. Playing with *MAXSLICE* is likely to be dangerous because changing its value may prevent daemons and other important processes from getting enough attention. If you increase *MAXSLICE*, interactive performance is likely to suffer. If you want to experiment, you could theoretically make a system that runs many compute-bound jobs more efficient by increasing *MAX-SLICE*. For V.4, you can configure different time slices for each priority level by using the *dispadmin* command.

TEXTS (V.2)

The number of text segments that can be active simultaneously. This parameter limits the number of processes with different executable files that the system can run at one time. Every process has at least one text segment; however, invocations of the same program normally share their text segments. The value of *TEXTS* is usually smaller than the value of *PROCS*. Some implementations of XENIX support the *REGIONS* parameter, which accomplishes a similar function.

CALLS (V.2), *NCALL* (V.3, V.4)

The number of entries in the callout table. This is the number of timer operations (most commonly used by device drivers but also available to users) that the system can handle. If the callout table is too small, the system will crash with a "panic" message on the console.

CLISTS (V.2), *NCLIST* (V.3, V.4)

The number of *clist* structures in the kernel. These are character buffers used for terminals and other low-speed I/O devices. AT&T recommends five to ten *clists* per terminal. If there are not enough *clist* buffers, the system will start to lose characters typed at the terminal. The *CLIST* parameter isn't used in Release V.4, although AT&T notes that there may be vendor-specific exceptions.

ARG_MAX (V.4)

The maximum length, in bytes, of the argument string that can be passed to the *exec* system call. This is effectively the length of a command's arguments plus all environment variables and their definitions. The default value (5120) is a good minimum value. If you need to execute commands with longer argument lists or with more environment variables, you may increase *ARG_MAX*. The value of *ARG_MAX* should not be more than one-eighth of *SSTKLIM*.

INITCLASS (V.4)

> The process class used to run *init*. Because all shells are children of *init*, this parameter controls the process class for all user processes. It should be *TS* (time sharing). Making the default user process type *RT* (real time) is unwise in most circumstances.

Memory Management Parameters

The memory management parameters control the paging and swapping algorithms. By changing these parameters, you can control the point at which your system begins paging and prevent the system from running seriously short of memory. Table 8-3 lists the parameters that control the virtual memory system. After the table, we will discuss each parameter briefly.

Table 8-3: Memory Management Parameters

Name	Set In	Size Per Entry	Typical Value
V.2 Parameter:			
MAXPROCMEM	*xenixconf*	*	
V.3 Parameters:			
AGEINTERVAL	*stune*	*	9
VHANDFRAC	*stune*	*	16
GPGSLO	*stune*	*	25
GPGSHI	*stune*	*	40
VHANDR	*stune*	*	1
MAXPMEM	*stune*	*	0
MAXUMEM	*stune*	*	2560
MINARMEM	*stune*	*	25
MINASMEM	*stune*	*	25
SPTMAP	*stune*	8	50
V.4 Parameters:			
GPGSLO	*kernel*	*	25
MAXPMEM	*kernel*	*	0
MINARMEM	*kernel*	*	25
MINASMEM	*kernel*	*	25
SPTMAP	*kernel*	8	100

AGEINTERVAL (V.3)

 The point at which any page of memory becomes subject to a page-out.
 The paging algorithm avoids paging-out memory that has been used
 recently because any memory that has been used in the recent past is
 likely to be used in the near future. Paging-out memory that will be
 needed almost immediately is worse than useless. It increases disk
 traffic without any long-term increase in the amount of memory that's
 available. A page may be paged-out after *AGEINTERVAL* clock ticks,
 where there are *HZ* clock ticks per second, and *HZ* is a constant defined
 in the file */usr/include/sys/param.h* (usually 100). Increasing
 AGEINTERVAL is probably a good idea if you run a lot of large programs that make scattered references throughout memory.

VHANDFRAC (V.3)

 The point at which the paging daemon starts to run, as a fraction of the
 total free memory available. If the amount of free memory falls below
 the greater of *GPGSHI* and *memory/VHANDFRAC*, the system starts to
 run the paging daemon *vhand*. Paging doesn't actually start until the
 amount of free memory drops below *GPGSLO*.

GPGSLO (V.3, V.4)

 The point at which page-outs start. The paging machinery starts to execute page-outs when the amount of free memory drops below *GPGSLO*,
 which is called the "low-water mark." Once started, page-outs continue
 until the free memory rises above *GPGSHI*. If you increase this value,
 page-outs will start earlier, possibly preventing the system from incurring a serious memory shortage. If you decrease this value, the system
 may not start paging until it is too late to avoid a serious shortage.
 GPGSLO must be less than *GPGSHI*.

GPGSHI (V.3)

 The memory "high-water mark," in 4-KB pages. Once the *vhand* daemon has started stealing pages to add to the free list, it will continue
 stealing pages until the free list is longer than *GPGSHI* pages. If you
 increase this value, the system will spend more of its time paging. If
 you decrease this value, the system will stop paging sooner but may
 have to start paging again very soon. *GPGSHI* must be greater than
 GPGSLO.

VHANDR (V.3)

 The rate at which the paging daemon runs. The *vhand* daemon wakes
 up every *VHANDR* seconds to inspect memory and decide whether or
 not to perform any page-outs. Increasing *VHANDR* thus decreases the
 system's overhead but lessens its ability to recover memory quickly
 under load. *VHANDR* also implicitly sets the amount of time that a
 page can be "untouched" before it becomes subject to paging (usually

2*VHANDR). Longer values of *VHANDR* means that a page can be unused for a longer time before the system will consider paging it out.

MAXPROCMEM (V.2), *MAXUMEM* (V.3)

The maximum amount of memory that will be used to run a process. For V.3, this parameter limits a process's virtual address space.

MAXPMEM (V.4)

Specifies the amount of physical memory to use, in pages. The special value 0 means "use all of physical memory." I don't understand why anyone would want to use less, unless perhaps the memory system has been damaged.

MINARMEM (V.3, V.4)

The number of pages of physical memory that are reserved for use by the data and text segments of user processes.

MINASMEM (V.3, V.4)

The number of pages of memory and swap area that are reserved for use by the operating system. Together, *MINASMEM* and *MINARMEM* prevent the system from getting hung because it cannot find memory to run important processes. If you see the message "swapdel - too few free pages" on the console, increasing *MINASMEM* may help the problem.

SPTMAP (V.3, V.4)

Controls the size of the page table map for system processes. You almost never want to adjust this value. However, increasing *SPTMAP* is necessary if you see the message "rmfree map overflow" on the console.

STREAMS Parameters

This section discusses the STREAMS facility, which is System V's modular interface between application programs and device drivers. It is commonly used to implement network protocols but can be used for other purposes. Table 8-4 lists the parameters that control the STREAMS facility. After the table, we will discuss each parameter briefly.

Table 8-4: STREAMS Parameters

Name		Set In	Size Per Entry	Typical Value
NQUEUE	(V.2)	xenixconf	36	96
NQUEUE	(V.3)	stune	36	96
NSTREAM	(V.2)	xenixconf	52	32
NSTREAM	(V.3)	stune	52	32
NSTRPUSH	(V.2)	xenixconf	*	9
NSTRPUSH	(V.3)	stune	*	9
NSTRPUSH	(V.4)	kernel	*	9
NSTREVENT	(V.2)	xenixconf	12	256
NSTREVENT	(V.3)	stune	12	256
MAXSEPGCNT	(V.2)	xenixconf	*	1
MAXSEPGCNT	(V.3)	stune	*	1
NBLKn	(V.2)	xenixconf	*	varies
NBLKn	(V.3)	stune	*	varies
STRTHRESH	(V.4)	kernel	*	2000000
STRMSGSZ	(V.2)	xenixconf	*	4096
STRMSGSZ	(V.3)	stune	*	4096
STRMSGSZ	(V.4)	kernel	*	0
STRCTLSZ	(V.2)	xenixconf	*	1024
STRCTLSZ	(V.3)	stune	*	1024
STRCTLSZ	(V.4)	kernel	*	1024
NLOG	(V.2)	xenixconf	12	3
NLOG	(V.3)	stune	12	3
NLOG	(V.4)	log	12	16
NSTRPHASH	(V.4)	sad	4	64
NAUTOPUSH	(V.4)	sad	44	32

NQUEUE (V.2, V.3)

The number of STREAMS queues that the system will support. Two queues are required for every module that is pushed onto a stream. Therefore, the value of NQUEUE must always be even and should equal (roughly) the number of streams times the average number of modules per stream times two. The number of modules per stream is almost always 2. Therefore, NQUEUE should usually be 4*NSTREAM.

NSTREAM (V.2, V.3)

The maximum number of streams that can be open at any time. An appropriate value here depends entirely upon how heavily your site uses the STREAMS facility. You may need to increase *NSTREAM* and *NQUEUE* if your site has developed or purchased applications built upon STREAMS. On many System V implementations, the network software, including the X window system, uses the STREAMS package. Therefore, the more you rely on X or NFS, the more streams you will have. The typical configuration shown above is very small and probably insufficient for most applications running X.

NSTRPUSH (V.2, V.3, V.4)

The number of modules that can be "pushed" onto a stream. That is, the number of different modules that can process data between a stream head (the application end) and a stream device driver. The default (9) is very generous. So far, no commercial applications are known that require more than four stream modules.

NSTREVENT (V.2, V.3)

The number of "stream event cells" to configure into the kernel. Additional event cells may be allocated as needed. However, *NSTREVENT* should be large enough to handle the system's load under all but the worst cases. Stream events are used when a process makes the *poll* system call. To arrive at an appropriate value for *NSTREVENT*, estimate the number of processes that might be using *poll* simultaneously. Multiply this by the number of streams being polled. To this figure, add the total number of processes that are using STREAMS.

MAXSEPGCNT (V.2, V.3)

The maximum number of additional pages of memory to allocate if more event cells are needed. Once allocated, this memory cannot be freed. *MAXSEPGCNT* should usually be set to 1, and *NSTREVENT* should be large enough to handle all but the heaviest loads. This strategy prevents the STREAMS facility from gradually allocating more memory until it starves the rest of the system.

NBLKn (V.2, V.3)

The number of data blocks and data buffers of size n. The STREAMS facility also uses these parameters to allocate message blocks and buffers. The number of message blocks of size n is roughly 1.25 times the number of data blocks of size n. Therefore, the memory requirements for any block size size is 2.25 times the block size. The typical values shown above, which are the 386/ix defaults, are only appropriate for systems that are not heavy network users. If your system uses STREAMS-based networking heavily (particularly the X window system), you may want to increase some of the *NBLK* parameters. Check block utilization by looking at *netstat -m*.

STRTHRESH (V.4)

In V.4, the data structures and tables for STREAMS are allocated dynamically. Therefore, you don't need to specify the number of streams, the number of queues, and so on. However, you do need to restrict the amount of memory that STREAMS can acquire for itself to prevent it from starving the rest of the system. This parameter limits the total amount of memory that STREAMS can allocate. It should be one-quarter to one-half of the system's total physical memory.

STRMSGSZ (V.2, V.3, V.4)

The maximum amount of data that any stream message can carry. One stream message should be able to accommodate the largest maximum packet size used by any of your system's stream modules. Making *STRMSGSZ* too large leads to inefficiency. For V.4, the special value of 0 means the amount of data that one message can carry is unlimited.

STRCTLSZ (V.2, V.3, V.4)

The maximum size of a stream message's control portion. This parameter is not particularly critical to performance; the default (1024) should be sufficient for all situations.

NLOG (V.2, V.3, V.4)

The number of minor devices that are available for system-wide error logging, using the "clone" interface to */dev/log*. This is a limit on the number of processes that can use the logging facility simultaneously.

NSTRPHASH (V.4)

The size the STREAMS's module's hash table. This table's size should never need to be changed on any system with a reasonable number of device drivers. Systems with an incredibly large number of drivers may need to increase it.

NAUTOPUSH (V.4)

The number of devices that can be pushed automatically onto a stream.

Message Facility Parameters

This section discusses the message facility, which is part of the interprocess communications package. Table 8-5 lists the parameters that control the message facility. After the table, we will discuss each parameter briefly.

Table 8-5: Message Facility Parameters

Name		Set In	Size Per Entry	Typical Value
MSGMNI	(V.2)	*xenixconf*	52	50
MSGMNI	(V.3)	*stune*	52	50
MSGMNI	(V.4)	*msg*	52	50
MGSMAX	(V.2)	*xenixconf*	*	2048
MGSMAX	(V.3)	*stune*	*	2048
MGSMAX	(V.4)	*msg*	*	2048
MSGMNB	(V.2)	*xenixconf*	*	4096
MSGMNB	(V.3)	*stune*	*	4096
MSGMNB	(V.4)	*mag*	*	4096
MSGTQL	(V.2)	*xenixconf*	12	40
MSGTQL	(V.3)	*stune*	12	40
MSGTQL	(V.4)	*msg*	12	40
MSGSSZ	(V.2)	*xenixconf*	*	8
MSGSSZ	(V.3)	*stune*	*	8
MSGSSZ	(V.4)	*msg*	*	8
MSGSEG	(V.2)	*xenixconf*	*MSGSZ*	1024
MSGSEG	(V.3)	*stune*	*MSGSZ*	1024
MSGSEG	(V.4)	*msg*	*MSGSZ*	1024
MSGMAP	(V.2)	*xenixconf*	8	100
MSGMAP	(V.3)	*stune*	8	100
MSGMAP	(V.4)	*mag*	8	100

MSGMNI (V.2, V.3, V.4)

 The maximum number of message queues the system can support.

MSGMAX (V.2, V.3, V.4)

 The maximum size of a message.

MSGMNB (V.2, V.3, V.4)

 The maximum length of a message queue, in bytes. The length of a message queue is the sum of the lengths of all the messages in the queue.

MSGTQL (V.2, V.3, V.4)

 The maximum number of outstanding messages, system-wide. That is, the total number of messages waiting to be read, across all message queues.

MSGSSZ (V.2, V.3, V.4)

   The size of the message segment, in bytes.

MSGSEG (V.2, V.3, V.4)

   The maximum number of message segments. The kernel reserves a total of *MSGSSZ*MSGSEG* bytes for message segments. The total amount of memory reserved must be less than 128 KB. Together, *MSGSSZ* and *MSGSEG* limit the total amount of text for all outstanding messages.

MSGMAP (V.2, V.3, V.4)

   The number of elements in the map used to allocate message segments.

Shared Memory

This section discuss the shared memory facility, which is part of the interprocess communications package. Table 8-6 lists the parameters that govern shared memory. After the table, we will discuss each parameter briefly.

Table 8-6: Shared Memory

Name		Set In	Size Per Entry	Typical Value
SHMMAX	(V.2)	*xenixconf*	*	524288
SHMMAX	(V.3)	*stune*	*	524288
SHMMAX	(V.4)	*shm*	*	130172
SHMMIN	(V.2)	*xenixconf*	*	1
SHMMIN	(V.3)	*stune*	*	1
SHMMIN	(V.4)	*shm*	*	1
SHMMNI	(V.2)	*xenixconf*	112	100
SHMMNI	(V.3)	*stune*	112	100
SHMMNI	(V.4)	*shm*	112	100
SHMALL	(V.2)	*xenixconf*	*	512
SHMALL	(V.3)	*stune*	*	512
SHMSEG	(V.2)	*xenixconf*	*	6
SHMSEG	(V.3)	*stune*	*	6
SHMSEG	(V.4)	*shm*	*	6

SHMMAX (V.2, V.3, V.4)
> The maximum size of any shared memory segment, in bytes.

SHMMIN (V.2, V.3, V.4)
> The minimum size of any shared memory segment, in bytes.

SHMMNI (V.2, V.3, V.4)
> The maximum number of shared memory segments the system will support.

SHMALL (V.2, V.3)
> The maximum number of shared memory segments that can be in use simultaneously.

SHMSEG (V.2, V.3, V.4)
> The maximum number of shared memory segments that can be attached to any given process at one time. This parameter is present but ignored by V.4.

Semaphore Configuration Parameters

This section discuss the semaphore facility, which is part of the interprocess communications package. Table 8-7 lists the parameters that govern semaphores. After the table, we will discuss each parameter briefly.

Table 8-7: Semaphore Configuration Parameters

Name		Set in	Size per entry	Typical value
SEMMAP	(V.2)	*xenixconf*	8	10
SEMMAP	(V.3)	*stune*	8	10
SEMMAP	(V.4)	*sem*	8	10
SEMMNI	(V.2)	*xenixconf*	34	10
SEMMNI	(V.3)	*stune*	34	10
SEMMNI	(V.4)	*sem*	34	10
SEMMNS	(V.2)	*xenixconf*	12	60
SEMMNS	(V.3)	*stune*	12	60
SEMMNS	(V.4)	*sem*	12	60
SEMMSL	(V.2)	*xenixconf*	12	25
SEMMSL	(V.3)	*stune*	12	25
SEMMSL	(V.4)	*sem*	12	25

Name		Set in	Size per entry	Typical value
SEMVMX	(V.2)	_xenixconf_	*	32767
SEMVMX	(V.3)	_stune_	*	32767
SEMVMX	(V.4)	_sem_	*	32767
SEMOPM	(V.2)	_xenixconf_	8	10
SEMOPM	(V.3)	_stune_	8	10
SEMOPM	(V.4)	_sem_	8	10
SEMMNU	(V.2)	_xenixconf_	8*(_SEMUME_+2)	30
SEMMNU	(V.3)	_stune_	8*(_SEMUME_+2)	30
SEMMNU	(V.4)	_sem_	8*(_SEMUME_+2)	30
SEMUME	(V.2)	_xenixconf_	8*_SEMMNU_	10
SEMUME	(V.3)	_stune_	8*_SEMMNU_	10
SEMUME	(V.4)	_sem_	8*_SEMMNU_	10
SEMAEM	(V.2)	_xenixconf_	*	16384
SEMAEM	(V.3)	_stune_	*	16384
SEMAEM	(V.4)	_sem_	*	16384

SEMMAP (V.2, V.3, V.4)

  The number of entries in the table used to allocate the memory reserved for semaphores.

SEMMNI (V.2, V.3, V.4)

  The maximum number of semaphore sets (system-wide). Semaphore sets are almost always shared by two or more processes. This parameters limits the number of unique sets that can be in use.

SEMMNS (V.2, V.3, V.4)

  The maximum number of semaphores (system-wide).

SEMMSL (V.2, V.3, V.4)

  The maximum number of semaphores per set.

SEMVMX (V.2, V.3, V.4)

  The maximum value of a semaphore.

SEMOPM (V.2, V.3, V.4)

  The maximum number of operations that a single call to _semop_ can execute. _semop_ is the system call performs operations on semaphores.

SEMMNU (V.2, V.3, V.4)

  The maximum number of "undo" structures, system-wide.

SEMUME (V.2, V.3, V.4)

The maximum number of "undo" entries per process.

SEMAEM (V.2, V.3, V.4)

The maximum "adjust-on-exit" value.

System V.4 Process Limit Parameters

System V.4 supports BSD-style hard and soft limits on file size, CPU time, and virtual memory requirements, etc. A group of kernel parameters set default hard and soft limits. These parameters are all set in the configuration file *kernel*. They have no effect on the kernel's memory requirements. The special value 0x7fffffff means that no limit is applied.

Table 8-8: System V.4 Process Limit Parameters

Name	Default	Description
SCPULIM	0x7fffffff	The soft limit on CPU time (user plus system), per process.
HCPULIM	0x7fffffff	Hard limit on CPU time.
SFSZLIM	0x100000	The soft limit on the size of any file that a process creates.
HFSZLIM	0x100000	Hard file size limit.
SDATLIM	0x1000000	The soft limit on a process's data segment size.
HDATLIM	0x1000000	Hard data segment limit.
SSTKLIM	0x1000000	The soft limit on a process's stack segment size.
HSTKLIM	0x1000000	Hard stack segment limit.
SCORLIM	0x100000	The soft limit on the size of a core dump file that a process can create.
HCORLIM	0x1000000	Hard core dump size limit.
SFNOLIM	0x18	The soft limit on the number of files a process can have open at one time.
HFNOLIM	0x400	Hard open file limit.
SVMMLIM	0x1000000	The soft limit on the size of a process's virtual address space.
HVMMLIM	0x1000000	Hard virtual address space limit.

A

Real-time Processes in System V.4

Real-time and Time-sharing Processes
Manipulating Priorities with priocntl (V.4)
Scheduler Configuration Tables

System V.4 adds an important new element to UNIX: *real-time* processes. At this time, relatively little is known about real-time processes. The discussions in the official V.4 reference manuals are sketchy and systems that actually run V.4 are scarce. In this appendix, we try to discuss real-time processes and other changes to the V.4 scheduling mechanism as concretely as possible in the absence of better information. Our discussions are based on the official V.4 manuals, general knowledge of real-time programming, and educated guesses at how real-time UNIX will behave. Please let us know if you have any concrete suggestions about how to use real-time processes, or the additional time-sharing configuration features, to your advantage. At this point, a body of useful lore and general knowledge just doesn't exist.

A.1 Real-time and Time-sharing Processes

Standard UNIX processes are *time-sharing* processes. The system tries to split the processor fairly between the different processes, subject to priorities. This means that high-priority processes get more attention than low-priority processes but even the lowest-priority processes still get some attention. Real-time processes throw fairness out the window. Applications that need real-time processes require the computer to keep up with something that's happening in the real world. For example, consider a robotics application: the computer must keep up with data arriving from sensors so that it can correctly steer a robot. If the computer is too slow, the robot will run into a wall before the computer has figured out the wall is there. To prevent such disasters, a real-time process is guaranteed immediate, low-latency service. A real-time process:

- Is scheduled as soon as it is runnable. It doesn't have to wait for other processes.

- Runs until it can't do any more work or until a higher-priority real-time process is runnable.

Obviously, there's some danger involved. A CPU-bound real-time process can easily take the machine hostage: since it never does I/O, it never needs to wait. A real-time process in a tight loop will crash the system. You won't be able to stop it because you will never be able to execute the *kill* command: by default, interactive shells run as time-sharing processes and don't get access to the machine while a real-time process is running. Furthermore, real-time priorities can even push system processes out of the way so important daemons and other system services won't run. Even if nothing drastic goes wrong, the memory used by real-time processes is immune from paging. This means that real-time processes can quickly gobble up all of the system's memory.

The actual picture is a bit more complicated than this but the bottom line is that real-time processes preempt other processes. Running real-time processes will hurt your interactive performance and may hurt it drastically. Never use real-time processes to solve general performance problems: they are a solution to one very specific problem. If one group of users is complaining that they can't get enough work done, don't let them make their jobs real-time—even if the group that's complaining purportedly owns the system. We guarantee that the rest of your users will complain, and vocally. Once the owners have commandeered the system, they will probably kill off each other because they still won't be able to get work done, since they will always be preempting each other. You don't want any part of this battle.

If you need real-time processes for data collection, cybernetics, computer animation, or some other application, then you're stuck. The system's other users will suffer. In the best of all worlds, real-time processes should only be used on systems that are dedicated to a particular task, and not on general purpose computers.

A.2 Manipulating Priorities with priocntl (V.4)

System V.4 provides the *priocntl* command to manipulate priorities and scheduling classes. It works with time-sharing and real-time priorities—you don't need to worry about global priorities unless you are configuring your system. Unfortunately, the *priocntl* command is complicated and tries to do too many things. We'll show its most valuable features.

The simplest *priocntl* command is:

```
% priocntl -l
```

This command shows you the names assigned to the real-time, system, and time-sharing classes and the range of priority values that is configured for each class. Why is this interesting information? It is also possible to build systems without the real-time or time-sharing classes. We suspect that systems built without real-time processes will be fairly common. It is also possible to rename the system class (by default, named *SYS*), though nobody knows why you would want to do this. *priocntl -l* will resolve any ambiguities about what classes exist and how they are set up.

To make a process real-time, log in as superuser and enter the command:

```
# priocntl -s -c RT -p prio -i pid n
```

The *-s* option says that you want to set the priority, *-c RT* means that you want a priority in the real-time class, *-p prio* assigns the new priority level (0 by default if this option is omitted), and *-i pid n* says you want to change the priority of the process whose ID number is *n*. Real-time priorities range from 0 to 59. Assigning a process a greater priority means that it will run before all other processes with lower priorities. (A refreshing breath of fresh air! Priorities that mean what you think they do!) You can also use this command and the other commands in this group to change the priority of a real-time process.

You can omit *-p prio* from the command. This sets the priority to the default real-time priority (0).

If you want to make an entire process group real-time, use the command:

```
# priocntl -s -c RT -p prio -i pgid n
```

where *n* is an identifier for a process group. You can make all of the processes owned by any user real-time with the command:

```
# priocntl -s -c RT -p prio -i uid n
```

where *n* is the user's ID number. This command is a bit more dangerous than the others. The user's shell will become a real-time process, meaning that any new programs that the user starts will also be real-time. Real-time shells are dangerous.

To start a real-time process, give the command:

```
# priocntl -e -c RT -p prio real-time-job
```

where *real-time-job* is the command you want to execute in real-time. Again, you may omit *-p prio* if the default priority (0) is acceptable.

To make a real-time process into a time-sharing process, give the command:

```
# priocntl -s -c TS -p prio -i pid n
```

Again, *n* is the ID number for the process you want to change and *prio* is the time-sharing priority (or the *nice* number) you want to assign to the process. If you omit *-p prio*, UNIX assigns the default time-sharing priority (*nice* 0) to your process.

To change the priority of a time-sharing process, give the command:

```
% priocntl -s -c RT -p prio -i pid n
```

You must be superuser to increase a process's time-sharing priority.

A.2.1 Configuring the Scheduler (V.4)

System V.4 allows you to configure the kernel's scheduler. The simplest thing you can do is configure your system without one class or the other. As we've said, there are some good reasons to avoid real-time processes. They are an extremely important solution to a particular class of problems, but they are not appropriate for general use. If you don't need real-time processes, it is both safe and healthy to configure your system without them.

Likewise, you could also do without time-sharing processes if your system will be dedicated to real-time applications. Aside from freeing a bit of memory, there's no good reason to do without real-time processes. You probably want this facility around for casual editing and so on. You can do without it if you like, but we don't recommend it.

System V.4 also allows you to fine tune the real-time and time-sharing schedulers. By using the *dispadmin* command, you can modify the amount of time the scheduler gives to processes at any priority and the way time-sharing processes move between priorities. We will discuss *dispadmin* shortly, but first, in order to configure the scheduler intelligently, you must have a basic understanding of how the global priority system works. Under V.4, there is a single set of "global priorities," which are divided into three classes: real-time, system, and time-sharing.

All three classes are given a range of global priorities numbers, as seen in Figure A-1.

The constant *TSMAXUPRI* defines the range of time-sharing priorities, which are equivalent to *nice* numbers. It can be changed during configuration, but the default value is 20. By default, there are 60 time-sharing priorities, 40 system priorities, and 60 real-time priorities. The number of priorities in each class can be changed as part of the configuration process, but we recommend that you avoid these details.

In the diagram above, each priority class occupies a distinct range of global priorities. Whenever the scheduler runs, it picks the first process that is runnable in the highest global priority class. Therefore, system and time-sharing processes only run when the system can't run any real-time processes. To prevent any one job from hogging the CPU, the time-sharing scheduler can move jobs from high priorities to low priorities and vice versa. The real-time scheduler never moves jobs between priorities; it gives the CPU's devoted attention to the highest-priority job around.

Note that the *nice* numbers only control a process's initial global priority and, further, that the range of *nice* numbers is not necessarily the same as the number of time-sharing slots in the global priority scheme. When you start a process at a certain time-sharing priority, the system computes an initial global priority in the range assigned to time-sharing processes. Once the process has started, its time-sharing priority varies according to how much CPU time the process is getting, how much time it is spending in queues, and other factors.

The command *dispadmin* can be used to modify the real-time and time-sharing priority structures. To make permanent changes to the real-time and time-sharing priorities, place *dispadmin* commands in one of the */etc/rc2.d* startup scripts. This strategy lets you change the system's default parameters without building a new kernel.

The *dispadmin* command is used as follows:

```
# dispadmin -l
# dispadmin -g -c class
# dispadmin -s file -c class
```

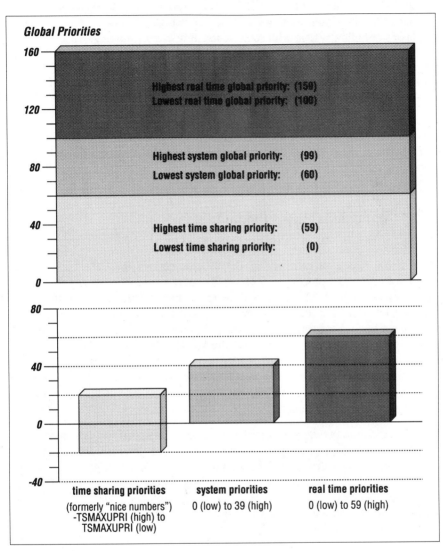

Figure A-1. Global priority scheme

The first form of the command (*-l*) lists the system's scheduling classes. This command will show you whether someone has changed the names of the scheduling classes or built a system with some scheduling classes missing.

The second form (*-g*) reports (gets) the scheduling table for the given class. For example, *dispadmin -g -c TS* gets the scheduling table that is currently applicable to the time-sharing (*TS*) class. We discuss the format of these tables below.

The final form (*-s*) reads the given *file*, which contains a scheduling table, and uses it to redefine the priorities for the given *class*. *class* may be either *RT* or *TS*, for real time or time sharing. We discuss the format of real-time and time-sharing scheduling tables below.

A.3 Scheduler Configuration Tables

When UNIX runs a process, it lets the process control the CPU for a certain amount of time. The process may use up its entire chunk of time, at which point the kernel's scheduler takes over and decides which process to run next (maybe the same one, but may not), or it may only use a part of this chunk and go to sleep, most likely because it has started an I/O operation and has to wait for that operation to finish before it can do anything else. For example, the kernel may give a process a 200-millisecond chunk of time. But if the process needs to read data from the keyboard when it is only 10 milliseconds into this chunk, it gives up the rest of its time slot. It can't do anything else, and there's no reason for the CPU to sit around doing nothing.

Setting scheduling parameters is primarily a matter of specifying how much time a process gets at each priority level. For time-sharing processes, there are some added complications that control how a process is rescheduled once it loses control of the CPU. For the purposes of scheduling, the fundamental unit of time is called the *quantum*. The quantum is set by a "resolution" line in the file that defines the real-time and time-sharing priority systems. A typical resolution line might say:

```
RES=1000
```

This means that the resolution, or time quantum, is 1/1000 of a second. Note that real-time and time-sharing processes may have different quanta, since each file can define a different resolution.

The time quantum has nothing to do with the system's hardware clock rate and only little to do with the actual resolution of the system's timers. The actual timing resolution is set by the preprocessor constant *HZ*, which is usually defined in the header file */usr/include/sys/param.h* and cannot be changed. A typical value of *HZ* for System V is 100, which sets the time resolution to 1/100 of a second (10 milliseconds). Here's the appropriate line:

```
# define HZ    100         /* 100 ticks per second of the clock */
```

If process in a given priority class is given *n* quanta of time, these quanta are rounded up to the next multiple of the actual timing resolution. For example, assume that a process has been given 42 quanta, where the quantum unit is 1/1000 of a second. This time period is rounded up to the next multiple of 10 milliseconds (the timer resolution defined by *HZ*), or 50 milliseconds.

A.3.1 Real-time Scheduler Table

A real-time scheduler table sets scheduling parameters for real-time processes. It defines the real-time quantum and the number of quanta given to processes at each priority. A reasonable real-time scheduler table might look like this:

```
# definition of real-time priority
# first, define time resolution (to be 1/RES seconds)
# then one line per priority level, defining the time quantum
# as a multiple of RES
#
RES=10000
#
600 # priority 0
590 # priority 1
580 # priority 2
 ...
 10 # priority 59
```

The *RES* line says that the resolution is 1/10000 of a second. That is, the time quantum is 1/10 of a millisecond. This isn't the clock's actual resolution—it may be much higher (or perhaps much lower).

After the *RES* line and any comments, there is one line for each priority level. The first line describes real-time priority 0 (the lowest real-time priority). It consists of one field: the number of time quanta for which a priority 0 process can run without interrupts. The second describes real-time priority 1, and so on, up to real-time priority 60 (the highest real-time priority). If a process uses up this time slice before "sleeping," the scheduler interrupts it and looks to see whether or not a higher-priority process is ready to go.

For example, the file above states that a priority 0 process can run for 600 quanta (60 milliseconds, subject to rounding) without disturbance. If the process is still running when its 600 quanta are used up, the system will look to see whether or not it can run a higher-priority real-time process. Similarly, a priority 1 process can run for 590 quantum units, and a priority 59 process (the highest priority) only runs for 10 units.

Note that higher-priority processes are guaranteed smaller slices of the CPU's time. This seems highly counterintuitive but is appropriate. It does not mean that the system spends less time running high-priority processes. After all, a priority 58 process that uses up its 20 milliseconds will almost certainly get to run again: only a a priority 59 process can preempt it. The chances are very good that any real-time process will get to run again after its time slice expires. It does mean that lower-priority real-time processes, when they get to run, are allowed to do more computation before the system checks the scheduler. This reflects a balance that is inherent in real-time processes. By definition, real-time processes deal with real-world of events and are therefore I/O-bound. The higher a real-time process's priority, the more it should be driven by external events and the less computation it should require per event. Ideally, no real-time process should run to the end of its time slice.

A.3.2 Time-sharing Scheduler Table

A more complex file controls scheduling for time-sharing processes. It also starts with a "resolution" line, which defines the quantum of time for scheduling time-sharing processes. After the *RES* line, this file has one line for each priority level between 0 and 59, the highest time-sharing priority. The first line describes global priority level zero (the lowest priority), the second describes global priority level one, and so on. Each line has the format:

run-time expired-level sleep-level wait-time wait-level

which are defined as:

run-time   The amount of time, in time-sharing quantum units, that a time-sharing process is allowed to run without interruption. If it uses up its entire allotment, the process is put on the *expired-level* queue and the scheduler gets a chance to schedule another process. The *expired-level* should be a lower priority; this means that CPU-bound processes gradually migrate to lower priorities and are prevented from monopolizing the system. As with real-time processes, higher-priority processes typically have a shorter time slice.

expired-level Specifies the priority to assign to a process if it uses up its entire *run-time* time allotment. This is usually a lower-priority level.

sleep-level   Specifies the priority level to assign to the process if it "sleeps" of its own accord (for example, waits for I/O to complete) before using up its entire *run-time* allotment. The *sleep-level* is usually equal to or higher than the current priority level. Processes that tend to be inactive (i.e., that tend to spend a lot of time waiting) migrate to higher-priority levels, letting them run more often.

wait-time   Specifies the maximum amount of time the process is allowed to wait at this priority level without being executed. If a process waits in at the current priority level for *wait-time* or longer, it is automatically moved into the queue given by *wait-level*.

wait-level   If the job waits at this priority level longer than *wait-time*, it is placed on the *wait-level* queue. The *wait-level* queue usually has an equal or higher priority. Processes that aren't getting run (i.e., that spend a lot of time waiting for the scheduler to give them a chance) eventually migrate to higher priorities, where they are more likely to be run quickly.

For example, consider the file below:

```
# definition of time-sharing priority
# first, define time resolution (to be 1/n seconds)
# then one line per priority level, defining the time quantum
#
RES=10000
#
600   0    2    200    2 # priority 0
590   0    3    200    3 # priority 1
580   1    4    200    4 # priority 2
570   1    5    200    5 # priority 3
  ...
 10  90  100  10000   59 # priority 59
```

Look at the definition of priority 3. This means that a process that has priority 3 can run at most 570 time quanta (570/10000 seconds or 57 milliseconds, with whatever rounding your system applies) before the UNIX kernel tries to reschedule it. If a job uses its entire time slice, it is reassigned to priority level 1 (a lower priority), where it waits. This makes sure that other jobs get a chance to run. But if the program does not manage to use up its entire time allotment—if the job waits for a user to type at a terminal or if it sleeps for any other reason—it gets put on a higher-priority queue when it can run again. The process is rewarded for giving up its time slice before it has to. Processes are allowed to wait in the priority 3 queue for at most 200 time quanta (200/10000 seconds, or 20 milliseconds). If a process doesn't get to run within this time limit, the kernel moves the process to the priority 5 queue. In other words, the process gets promoted to a higher queue because it has spent so much time waiting in line. The entire table is really a mechanism for moving jobs that spend a lot of time waiting to higher priorities, while moving jobs that do a lot of CPU-bound computation to lower priorities. By shuffling priorities in this way, UNIX attempts to distribute CPU time fairly among the time-sharing processes. If you consider a typical editor, which spends most of its time waiting for a user to type keystrokes, you will see how this scheme preserves interactive response without compromising the system as a whole. An editor will eventually gravitate to the highest priority: it spends most of its time waiting for I/O and rarely uses up its entire time slice. But when the editor has some work to do (i.e., when you type some keys), it will get to run very quickly. It won't have to wait behind other processes, yet because it is usually idle, it won't interfere with the rest of the system.

Note that these priorities are not *nice* numbers. They are the kernel's global scheduling priorities which, for time-sharing processes, begin at zero. The *nice* priority is used to assign an initial scheduling priority to a process.

To implement the priority schemes above, create the files *rt_table* and *ts_table* to hold the real-time and time-sharing scheduling tables. Then place the commands:

```
dispadmin -s rt_table -c RT
dispadmin -s ts_table -c TS
```

into one of your */etc/rc2.d* initialization files.

B

A Performance Tuning Strategy

This book has covered a lot of territory. Much of it was not easy to digest. In this appendix, we'll try to boil the book's contents down into a simple performance strategy, or checklist, that should help you analyze many problems.

We can't stress too much the importance of beginning your analysis before you have performance problems. We assume that you already know what load average is typical for your system at different times of the day, what jobs most users are likely to run, and other general information about your system.

If your system is having performance problems, the best overall approach is:

* Make general measurements of the CPU's load.

* Check for memory problems.

* If memory is OK, check for disk I/O problems.

* If disk and memory are OK but your system is in trouble, your problem is CPU overload (not enough cycles in the day).

In our summary, we assume that you are running BSD UNIX or SunOS. If you are running System V, we'll give the equivalent commands in parentheses.

B.1 Preparation: Setting Up Record Keeping

To set up the BSD accounting system, take these steps:

- Make sure that the command */etc/accton /usr/adm/acct* is in the system's */etc/rc* startup script. (For SunOS, use the command */etc/accton /usr/adm/pacct* instead.)

- Make sure that the */usr* filesystem is under 95 percent full.

- Run *sa -s* periodically to compress the accounting records. Add one of the following entries to the *cron* database:

```
0 0 * * 0 root /etc/sa -s > /dev/null    # BSD version
0 0 * * 0      /usr/etc/sa -s > /dev/null # SunOS version
```

Remember: With BSD UNIX, you edit */usr/lib/crontab* yourself. With SunOS, as with System V, you use the command *crontab -e root* to edit the root *crontab* file.

- Use the command *sa* to generate reports. The command has many, many options for different kinds of reports.

To set up the System V accounting system, take these steps:

- Link */etc/init.d/acct* to */etc/rc2.d/S22acct*. This file should contain the command */usr/lib/acct/startup*. If it doesn't, add it.

- Add these entries, or your own variations, to the *crontab* file for root:

```
# generate daily accounting reports (1 a.m.)
0 1 * * * /usr/lib/acct/runacct
# update disk usage statistics weekly (2 a.m. Sunday)
0 2 * * 1 /usr/lib/acct/dodisk
# manage accounting file size hourly (on the half-hour)
30 * * * * /usr/lib/acct/ckpacct
# generate monthly summaries (2 a.m. on the 1st of the month)
0 2 1 * * /usr/lib/acct/monacct
```

These entries will generate reports automatically. The reports are placed in the directory */usr/adm/acct* and its subdirectories.

- Use the command */usr/lib/acct/prdaily* to get a set of accounting reports.

To set up the System V *sar* utility, take these steps:

- Link */etc/init.d/perf* to */etc/rc2.d/S21perf*. This file initializes the system statistics databases whenever the system boots.
- Put the following entry, or a variation of it, into the *crontab* file for root:

```
0 * * * * /usr/lib/sa/sa1
```

This command collects statistics on an hourly basis.

B.2 Before the Problem Strikes

Regular monitoring when your system is healthy is the key to understanding its behavior when it is sick. Here are a few suggestions that will help you to understand and manage your system's behavior:

- Make performance agreements with your major users, and check regularly to make sure that your system is meeting these goals.
- Now that you've installed the accounting system, use it. Make sure you know the system's five most CPU-intensive programs, the five most I/O-intensive programs, and the five most memory-intensive programs.
- Run *iostat* (*sar -du*) regularly to see how I/O operations are distributed and how much time the CPU spends idle.
- Run *vmstat* (*sar -rwd*) regularly to see how the memory system is holding up under a normal load.

B.3 When the Problem Strikes

If you have been monitoring your system's health, you will probably know when performance is bad, before users even get a chance to complain. And you will probably have some good ideas about how to manage your problems. Here's a checklist of questions you should ask:

- Ask yourself: "What program am I running, and how am I running it?" If you are accessing files across the network, realize that network performance may be part of the problem. If you are running the program with significantly different input, realize that the program may just be slow because the data has changed.

- Run *uptime* (*sar -q*) and look at the load average. Is it increasing or decreasing? Is it high or low?

- Run *ps -aux* (*ps -el*) and ask these questions:
  - Are there any processes waiting for disk access or for paging? If so, check the I/O and memory subsystems.
  - What processes are using most of the CPU? This may help you distribute the workload better.
  - What processes are using most of memory? This may help you distribute the workload better.

- Give the command *iostat 5* and let it run for a while (*sar -u*).
  - Is the CPU spending a lot of time in the system state (over 50 percent)? If so, suspect I/O problems. If you have access to the source code, make sure that your applications are doing I/O efficiently.
  - Is the CPU spending a lot of time idle (over 10 percent) even though the overall load is high? If so, suspect I/O problems or memory problems.
  - Is the idle time always 0, without letup? It is good for the CPU to be busy, but if it always busy 100 percent of the time, work must be piling up somewhere. This points to a CPU overload.
  - Do you see highly unbalanced disk activity? (*sar -d* if your system supports it.) If so, try to distribute your I/O workload more evenly.

  If none of these are true—if further analysis of the memory system and the I/O system don't turn up anything—then the CPU is overloaded.

Here are some approaches to general CPU overload. It is a difficult problem to detect, largely because CPU overload really falls into a crack between memory problems and I/O problems.

- Eliminate unnecessary daemon processes. *rwhod* and *routed* are particularly likely to be performance problems, but any savings will help.

- Get users to run jobs at night with *at* or any queueing system that's available always helps. You may not care if the CPU (or memory or I/O system) is overloaded at night, provided the work is done in the morning.

- Use *nice* to lower the priority of CPU-bound jobs will improve interactive performance.

- Use *nice* to raise the priority of CPU-bound jobs will expedite them but will hurt interactive performance.

- However, using *nice* is really only a temporary solution. If your workload grows, it will soon become insufficient. Consider upgrading your system, replacing it, or buying another system to share the load.

B.4 Detecting Memory Problems

If your system has a lot of idle time under heavy load, or if *ps* shows that jobs requiring a lot of memory are running, you have the right to suspect memory trouble. Here are some steps that will help to confirm or disprove your suspicions:

- Run *vmstat 5* (*sar -wpgr*). For SunOS, *vmstat -S 5* is preferable.

  - Are page-outs occurring consistently? If so, you are short of memory.

  - Are there a high number of address translation faults (System V only)? This suggests a memory shortage.

  - Are swap-outs occurring consistently? If so, you are extremely short of memory. Note: Occasional swap-outs are normal; BSD systems swap-out inactive jobs. Long bursts of swap-outs mean that active jobs are probably falling victim and indicates extreme memory shortage. If you don't have *vmstat -S*, look at the **w** and **de** fields of *vmstat*. These should ALWAYS be zero.

  - Does *ps* or the accounting system show that your system is running many memory-intensive jobs? Look for jobs with a large resident set (**RSS**) or a high storage integral.

Here are some remedies for memory problems:

- Reduce the size of the buffer cache, if your system has one, by decreasing *BUFPAGES* (BSD), *NBUF* (V.3), or *BUFFERS* (V.2, XENIX). The buffer cache is not used in System V.4 and SunOS 4.X systems. Making the buffer cache smaller will hurt disk I/O performance.

- If you have statically allocated STREAMS buffers, reduce the number of large (2048- and 4096-byte) buffers. This may reduce network performance, but *netstat -m* should give you an idea of how many buffers you really need.

- Reduce the size of your kernel's tables. This may limit the system's capacity (number of files, number of processes, etc.).

- Try running jobs requiring a lot of memory at night. This may not help the memory problems, but you may not care about them as much.

- Try running jobs requiring a lot of memory in a batch queue. If only one memory-intensive job is running at a time, your system may perform satisfactorily.

- If your applications are "home grown," check to see that they use memory efficiently. Using out-of-core solvers or algorithms that maximize locality of reference will help. Make sure that programs obey any data alignment restrictions that are applicable to your computer. Virtually all systems will perform better if 4-byte data are located on addresses that are multiples of 4.

- Try using shared libraries to reduce memory requirements.

- Try to limit the time spent running *sendmail*, which is a memory pig, or configure your network so you can run *sendmail* on another system.

- Get users to switch from *emacs*, which is a memory pig, to another editor. Look into public domain *emacs* versions, some of which are less memory-intensive.

- If all else fails, buy more memory.

B.5 Detecting Disk I/O Problems

If your system spends a lot of time idle, even under heavy load, you have the right to suspect disk I/O problems. Remember that memory problems and I/O problems are often related. Here are some steps that will help to confirm that your system is suffering disk problems:

- Run *iostat 5* (*sar -d*, if your system supports it). Compare the results with your "healthy system" data. Is disk activity much higher than normal?

- Is disk activity distributed fairly among the system's disks?

- If not, are the most active disks also the fastest disks?

- Run *sadp* (some System V, but not all) to get a seek histogram.

- Is activity concentrated in one area of the disk (good), spread evenly across the disk (tolerable), or in two well-defined peaks at opposite ends (bad)?

- Are you using NFS? Are users reporting slow file access working locally, or are they accessing a remote filesystem? If they are using remote files, look at your network situation. You don't have local disk I/O problems.

- Look at your memory statistics by running *vmstat 5* (*sar -rwpg*). If your system is paging or swapping consistently, you have memory problems, and they are undoubtedly making disk I/O worse than it would be otherwise. Attack your memory problems first.

If any of these tests indicates a problem, try these approaches:

- Reorganize your filesystems and disks to distribute I/O activity as evenly as possible.

- Use your fastest disk drive and controller for your root filesystem—this will almost certainly have the heaviest activity. Alternatively, if single-file throughput is important, put performance-critical files into one filesystem and use the fastest drive for that filesystem.

- Put performance-critical files on a filesystem with a large block size: 16 KB or 32 KB for BSD, 2 KB for System V.

- For System V.4, use UFS (BSD-style) filesystems instead of the System V (S5) filesystem.

- Increase the size of the buffer cache by increasing *BUFPAGES* (BSD), *NBUF* (V.3), or *BUFFERS* (XENIX, V.2). This may hurt your system's memory performance.

- Rebuild your filesystems periodically to eliminate fragmentation. System V.4 users can use *dcopy*; other System V and BSD implementations should do a backup, build a new filesystem, and restore.

- *dcopy* has some options to concentrate heavily used files at the beginning of the filesystems. If *sadp* indicates that you have a bad seek pattern (two distinct peaks, many long seeks), try using *dcopy* to fix the situation.

We've just outlined disk throughput problems and some possible solutions. Your system may also have disk capacity problems. Are you constantly running out of room in your filesystems? If so, here are some things to try:

- Write a *find* script that detects old core dumps, editor backup and auto-save files, and other trash and deletes it automatically. Run the script through *cron*.

- If you are running BSD UNIX or V.4, use the disk quota system to prevent individual users from gathering too much storage.

- Use a smaller block size on filesystems that are mostly small files (e.g., source code files, object modules, and small data files).

B.6 Detecting Network Problems

On networks of computer systems, the network or other computers on your network can affect your system's performance. Here are some suggestions for detecting network problems:

- You can suspect problems with network capacity or with data integrity if users experience slow performance when they are using *rlogin* or when they are accessing files via NFS.

- Look at *netstat -i*. If the number of collisions is large, suspect an overloaded network. If the number of input or output errors is large, suspect hardware problems. A large number of input errors indicates problems somewhere on the network. A large number output errors suggests problems with your system and its interface to the network.

- If collisions and network hardware aren't a problem, figure out which system appears to be slow. Use *spray* to send a large burst of packets to the slow system. If the number of dropped packets is large, the remote system most likely cannot respond to incoming data fast enough. Look to see if there are CPU, memory, or disk I/O problems on the remote system. If not, the system may just not be able to tolerate heavy network workloads. Try to reorganize the network so that this system isn't a file server.

- A large number of dropped packets may also indicate data corruption. Run *netstat -s* on the remote system, then *spray* the remote system from the local system and run *netstat -s* again. If the increase in UDP socket full drops (as indicated by *netstat*) is equal to or greater than the number of drop packets that *spray* reports, the remote system is a slow network server. If the increase of socket full drops is less than the number of dropped packets, look for network errors.

- Run *nfsstat* and look at the client RPC data.

  - If **retrans** field is more than 5 percent of **calls**, the network or an NFS server is overloaded.

  - If **timeout** is high, at least one NFS server is overloaded, the network may be faulty, or one or more servers may have crashed.

  - If **badxid** is roughly equal to **timeout** (same order of magnitude), at least one NFS server is overloaded.

  - If **timeout** and **retrans** are high but **badxid** is low, some part of the network between the NFS client and the server is overloaded and dropping packets.

- If your system has a STREAMS-based network implementation, run *netstat -m*. Are there enough STREAMS buffers?

Here are some hints for reducing network workload:

- Try to prevent users from running I/O-intensive programs across the network. The *grep* utility is a good example of an I/O-intensive program. Instead, get them to log in to the remote system to do their work.

- Reorganize the computers and disks on your network so that as many users as possible can do as much work as possible on a local system.

- Minimize the number of diskless workstations. If possible, eliminate diskless workstations.

- Use systems with good network performance as file servers.

- If you are short of STREAMS data buffers and are running SunOS 4.0 or System V.3 (or earlier), reconfigure the kernel with more buffers.

If there is a data integrity problem, your only solution is to find the faulty piece of hardware and replace it. You will find that a network analyzer is an indispensable piece of equipment for this task.

B.7 Terminal I/O

UNIX systems typically give very high priority to terminals, so problems with keyboard response should be rare. However, here are some steps to take if you suspect trouble:

- Does *ps* indicate that the system's *getty* processes are accumulating any time? If so, the terminal line for that *getty* process is "chattering." Disable the terminal line by editing */etc/ttys* or */etc/ttytab* (whichever file is relevant for your system).

- Are the users complaining about terminal performance using a terminal that is directly connected to the system, or are they using *rlogin*, a networked X terminal, or some thing else that involves the network? If so, suspect network problems rather than terminal I/O problems.

- Is interactive response poor? Solving general CPU performance problems will help. If you are running System V.2, V.3, or SunOS 4.0, you may have insufficient STREAMS buffers. Run *netstat -m* and see whether or not there are allocation failures for small data blocks (4 to 128 bytes). If so, build a new kernel with more small STREAMS buffers.

- Does the terminal "lose characters" from time to time? If so, increase the number of character lists (a kernel configuration parameter).

B.8 General Tips

Here are some tips that will help users to improve interactive performance. A comprehensive discussion of most of these tips appears in Chapter 3, *Managing the Workload*. Some are corollaries of "basic network etiquette," which is discussed in Chapter 6, *Network Performance*.

- Use *dirs* instead of *pwd*.

- Avoid *ps*.

- If you use *sh*, avoid long search paths.

- Minimize the number of files per directory.

- Use *vi* or a native window editor rather than *emacs*.

- Use *egrep* rather than *grep* or *fgrep*: it's faster.

- Don't run *grep* or other I/O-intensive applications across NFS.

- Use *rlogin* rather than NFS to access files on remote systems.

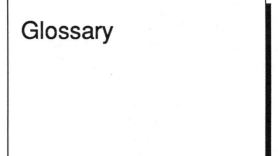

Glossary

aggregate disk throughput

    The rate at which a disk can service many unrelated data transfers, such as result from many processes accessing different files concurrently.

batch queue

    A mechanism for sequencing large jobs. A batch queue receives job requests from users. It then executes the jobs one at a time. Batch queues go back to the earliest days of data processing. They are an extremely effective, if uncomfortable, way to manage system load.

block size

    The largest amount of data that a UNIX filesystem will always allocate contiguously. For example, if a filesystem's block size is 8 KB, files of size up to 8 KB are always physically contiguous (i.e., in one place), rather than spread across the disk. Files that are larger than the filesystem's block size may be fragmented: 8 KB pieces of the file are located in different places on the disk. Fragmentation limits filesystem performance. Note that the filesystem block size is different from a disk's physical block size, which is almost always 512 bytes.

BSD UNIX

The versions of UNIX developed at the University of California, Berkeley. BSD UNIX has been dominant in academia and has historically had some more advanced features than System V: BSD introduced virtual memory, networking, and the "fast filesystem" to the UNIX community. It is also the system on which SunOS is based.

buffer cache

An area of memory in that mediates between application programs and disk drives. When a program writes data, it is first placed in a buffer cache and then delivered to the disk some time later. The disk driver can then perform I/O operations in batches, planning them to minimize seek time. In addition, future attempts to read this data can often use the version in the cache and avoid the disk completely. SunOS 4.0 and System V.4 have done away with the buffer cache.

callout table

One of the kernel's tables. The callout table is a table of timers. It is used primarily by device drivers, but is also used whenever any program sets a timer. When the callout table overflows, the system "panics," or crashes.

chatter

Random data generated by electrical noise or some other malfunction. Chatter usually appears on unused terminal lines that aren't terminated properly. Chatter can easily swamp a system because each meaningless character has to be processed.

clist

A small buffer that is primarily used for terminal I/O. The size of the *clist* table is an important configuration parameter. If the table is too small, the system will drop input characters under heavy load.

cron

A facility that allows system administrators (and other users) to execute certain programs automatically, at specified times. *cron* is essential to collecting system data and other aspects of system management.

daemon

A program that is invisible to users but provides important system services. Daemons manage everything from paging to networking to notification of incoming mail. BSD UNIX has many different daemons: without counting, I would guess that there are roughly two dozen. Daemons normally spend most of their time "sleeping" or waiting for something to do, so that they don't account for a lot of CPU load. However, some daemons can be a substantial load: in particular, *routed* and *rwhod*.

demand paging

A technique for starting a program running. The kernel sets up the program's virtual address space but does nothing to load the program into memory. It then transfers control to the program's first address. Because the executable is not in memory, this causes a page fault, and the paging mechanism brings the first page in from disk.

device controller

A piece of hardware that controls an I/O device: a disk drive, a tape drive, a network interface, a serial port, a parallel port, and so on.

device driver

A piece of software that interacts with a device controller to perform I/O. Device drivers are part of the UNIX kernel.

Ethernet

A communications medium that is very common at UNIX sites. Ethernet is a shared coaxial cable that provides raw data transfer rates of 10 megabits per second. The TCP/IP and XNS network protocols are commonly used to support Ethernet communications.

FDDI

A fiber-optic communications medium that will probably replace the standard 10-MB/second coaxial Ethernet within a few years. FDDI provides much faster transfer rates. FDDI hardware is now beginning to appear on the market.

fragment

In the BSD filesystem, a fragment is a portion of a disk block—usually one-eighth of a block, but possibly one-quarter or one-half of a block. If the last portion of a file doesn't occupy a full disk block, the filesystem will allocate one or more fragments rather than an entire block. Don't confuse "fragments" with "fragmentation." Fragments allow the BSD filesystem to use larger block sizes without becoming inefficient.

fragmentation

The tendency of an individual file to become physically scattered across a disk drive. When UNIX initially allocates space for a file, it will try to allocate a single contiguous area on the disk. However, it cannot always succeed. Furthermore, if you later expand a file, UNIX most likely will not be able to allocate new blocks that are contiguous with your old blocks. The term "fragmentation" is often applied to filesystems as a whole, referring to the tendencies of individual files to become fragmented. The System V filesystem is prone to fragmentation problems. The BSD filesystem is less prone to fragmentation but cannot eliminate it. The problem is really only solved by "extent-based" filesystems, which have been introduced by some UNIX vendors.

gateway

A system that belongs to two networks and can forward data from one network to the other.

hard limit

An absolute maximum limit that the C shell applies to some aspect of a process. For example, the C shell lets you place a hard limit on per-process CPU time. A process run by the shell cannot exceed the hard limit. See also **soft limit**.

HSC

A high-speed, parallel, point-to-point communications medium that supports transfers of 100 MB/second. It will probably replace standard coaxial Ethernet in some applications: for example, it is ideal for communications between a high-speed diskless workstation and file server or between very high-speed peripherals and a processor. HSC hardware is now beginning to appear on the market. For trademark reasons, HSC is now called HPPI.

inode

A data structure that describes a file. Within any filesystem, the number of inodes, and hence the maximum number of files, is set when the filesystem is created.

IPI-2

A disk drive interface that provides extremely high transfer rates and supports parallel transfer disks. IPI stands for *i*ntelligent *p*eripheral *i*nterface.

job

One UNIX command. It is easy to be sloppy and use the terms job, process, and program interchangeably. I do it, and I'm sure you do, too. Within UNIX documentation, though, the word "job" is usually used to mean one, and only one, command line. Note that one command line can be complex. For example:

```
pic a.ms | tbl | eqn | troff -ms
```

is one command, and hence one job, that is formed from four processes.

kernel

The part of the UNIX operating system that provides memory management, I/O services, and all other low-level services. The kernel is the "core" or "heart" of the operating system.

load average

A measure of how busy the CPU is. The load average is useful, though imprecise. It is defined as the average number of jobs in the run queue plus the average number of jobs that are blocked while waiting for disk I/O.

mbuf

A buffer used by the BSD network software. *mbufs* are medium-sized buffers. There is nothing you can do about tuning them. They are allocated dynamically, but once allocated they are never freed.

nice number

A number that is used to compute a process's scheduling priority. Low *nice* numbers yield high priorities; high *nice* number yield low priorities. UNIX does not let you set process priorities directly. Rather, you influence the priority scheme by selecting a *nice* number.

NFS

*N*etwork *F*ile *S*ystem. NFS allows UNIX systems and many non-UNIX systems to share files via a TCP/IP network. Subject to certain security restrictions, systems are allowed complete access to another system's files.

overlapping seeks

A capability of a disk interface or disk controller. Overlapping seeks means the ability to manage simultaneous operations by several disk drives that are connected in a chain. The disk controller handles data transfers from one disk drive while it is sending addresses and commands to other drives, waiting for them to move their heads into position, and so on. Most modern disk interfaces and controllers support overlapping seeks. However, not all disk drivers can take advantage of this capability.

paging

A technique that the UNIX kernel uses to free physical memory. The kernel looks for pages of memory that have not been accessed recently and copies them to a paging area on disk. It then reassigns the physical memory to some other function. A system begins paging when it is short of memory. Performance begins to degrade when paging starts, although the degradation may not be noticeable at first.

panic

UNIX jargon for a "crash." A panic is really a special kind of a crash. Panics occur when UNIX detects some irreconcilable inconsistency in one of its internal data structures. The kernel throws up its hands and shuts the system down before any damage can be done. As it is going down, it prints a "panic" message on the console.

partition

A portion of a disk drive. UNIX disk drives typically have eight partitions, although not all are in use.

per-process disk throughput

The rate at which a disk can service a sequence of large sequential data transfers, such as result from a single process accessing one file sequentially.

pipe

A UNIX mechanism for sending the output of one program directly to the input of another program, without using an intermediate file. All UNIX systems support pipes. System V and SunOS also provide "named pipes," which FIFO (first-in/first-out) buffers that have names and can be accessed via the filesystem.

priority

A number that determines how often the kernel will run a process. A higher-priority process will run more often and, therefore, will finish faster, than a low-priority process.

process

One stream of instructions using one set of system resources. Note how a process differs from a program. One program (i.e., one executable) can start a number of different processes.

real-time scheduling

A scheduling strategy that is often used in applications that require immediate response to external events. System V.4 includes real-time scheduling. Most previous UNIX releases have not supported real-time processes. Under V.4, real-time processes run to the exclusion of other processes.

resident set

The portion of a program and its data that is in the system's physical memory at any time.

retransmission

A network's way of guaranteeing that all data arrives correctly. If a packet of network data doesn't make it to its destination or if it is damaged enroute, the originator usually replaces the missing data by retransmitting the packet. Exactly who is responsible for requesting and generating a retransmission depends on the network protocol in use.

RFS

*R*emote *F*ile *S*haring. A facility developed by AT&T that allows cooperating UNIX systems to share each other's files. While there are some technical differences, RFS and NFS are functionally equivalent. The primary advantage of NFS is that is supported by almost all UNIX systems and many non-UNIX systems, while RFS is significantly less widespread and not supported by any non-UNIX systems.

SCSI

*S*mall *C*omputer *S*ystems *I*nterface. An interface standard that was developed for small, PC-style computers. While historically SCSI was limited to small, relatively slow disks and disk controllers, the most recent SCSI disk drives and controllers provide very high disk capacities and transfer rates. As a result, SCSI hardware should become increasingly common on large systems.

seek scheduling

An optimization performed by the disk driver to minimize total seek time. The disk driver groups disk operations into batches and computes the most efficient order in which to perform them. That is, the disk driver figures out how to perform the I/O operations in a way that minimizes the total distance the disk's read/write heads have to travel.

seek time

The time needed for a disk drive to move the heads from one track to another. Disk specifications usually include minimum, maximum, and average seek times.

segment

A section of an executable file or of a program's address space while it is executing. UNIX programs are divided into three segments: the text segment, which contains the instructions themselves; the data segment, which contains initialized data; and the BSS segment, which includes uninitialized storage.

shared text

A virtual memory technique that allows several invocations of one program
to use the same text segment while in memory. Shared text conserves physical memory because these invocations all share the same memory for their
text.

SMD

A disk interface that is very common on large systems. It supports very
large and reasonably fast disk drives, although the latest SCSI technology
has surpassed SMD. SMD stands for *s*torage *m*odule *d*evice.

soft limit

A limit to some aspect of a process, like CPU time or memory requirements. Programs that exceed their soft limit are notified and then get a
chance to raise their soft limit.

special file

An entity in the filesystem that accesses I/O devices. There is a special file
for every terminal, every network controller, every partition of every disk
drive, and every possible way of accessing every tape drive.

sticky bit

A bit that tells the virtual memory system to copy the program into the
swapping area and to leave the program's image in the swapping area after
it has finished executing. The sticky bit dates back to very early PDP-11
versions of UNIX. The sticky bit is obsolete on systems that support
demand paging, shared text, and paging from the filesystem's executable.
This includes most modern UNIX systems, but not all of them.

storage integral

The integral of a program's resident size over time. This is a measure of
how much load any program really places on the memory system. Programs that require a lot of memory for a lot of time have a much higher
storage integral than programs that require the same amount of memory but
only for a brief period.

STREAMS

An interface to device drivers that makes it easier to implement network
protocols. The most interesting characteristic about STREAMS is that it
allows you to structure I/O management as several independent subtasks
and to write an independent program to handle each of the subtasks. For
example, under STREAMS each layer of a network protocol can be written
independently. STREAMS is used by almost all modern System V implementations, SunOS, and a few other BSD implementations.

striping

A disk I/O technique that allows files to be spread across several disk drives. When programs read or write these files, all of the disk drives make transfers in parallel.

swapping

A technique that the UNIX kernel uses to clean up physical memory. The kernel moves entire processes from memory to disk and then reassigns the memory to some other function. Processes that have been idle for over 20 seconds may be removed from memory to save space. Swapping is also used to satisfy extreme memory shortages. When the system is extremely short of memory, active processes may be "swapped out."

System V UNIX

The version of UNIX that is under continuing development at AT&T. The most recent Release of System V is Release 4, known as V.4 or SVR4.

TCP/IP

A network protocol that is commonly used for Ethernet communications. TCP/IP is also called the "Internet protocol." It is also common to use TCP/IP over leased lines for long-distance communications.

time-sharing scheduling

A scheduling strategy that tries to divide the CPU's time fairly between the different processes that are running. UNIX systems have always supported time-sharing scheduling.

UDP

*U*niversal *D*atagram *P*rotocol. A part of the TCP/IP protocol suite. UDP is used by NFS. One important characteristic of UDP is that it does not guarantee successful delivery of a packet. The application program must make sure that each packet it expects is delivered. Likewise, the application program must request retransmissions as necessary to supply missing data.

virtual memory

A memory management technique provided by almost all modern operating systems.

XENIX

One of the first versions of UNIX to run on IBM PCs, and one of the few that will run on 80286 systems. XENIX descends from Version 7 UNIX, a version developed by AT&T in the late-1970s. It has many resemblances to BSD UNIX. Over time, XENIX has been rewritten as a variant of V.2.

zombies

Dead processes that have not yet been deleted from the process table. Zombies normally disappear almost immediately. However, at times it is impossible to delete a zombie from the process table, so it remains there (and in your *ps* output) until you reboot. Aside from their slot in the process table, zombies don't require any of the system's resources.

Index

About the Author

Mike Loukides is an editor for O'Reilly & Associates, with a focus on developing titles on UNIX utilities and system administration. He is the author of *System Performance Tuning* and *UNIX for FORTRAN Programmers*. Mike previously worked at Multiflow Computer, where he created all of Multiflow's documentation on programming languages.

Mike's interests are system administration, networking, programming languages, and computer architecture. His academic background includes degrees in Electrical Engineering (B.S.) and English Literature (Ph.D.). He is also a passable pianist—in fact, one of the few amateur pianists who even tries to play music by Olivier Messiaen.

Colophon

Our look is the result of reader comments, our own experimentation, and distribution channels.

Distinctive covers complement our distinctive approach to UNIX documentation, breathing personality and life into potentially dry subjects. UNIX and its attendant programs can be unruly beasts. Nutshell Handbooks help you tame them.

The animal featured on the cover of *System Performance Tuning* is a swordfish, a marine fish with a long, sword-shaped snout. The swordfish is distinguished from the marlin by its flattened snout, short, high dorsal fin, toothless mouth, and lack of scales. The fastest swimmer of all fish, a swordfish can grow up to 14 feet in length and weigh a thousand pounds or more. This combination of speed and size gives it strength and momentum—enough to drive its sword through the planking of a boat. The swordfish hunts by charging through schools of fish, striking to either side with its sword and then returning to collect its kill.

Edie Freedman designed this cover and the entire UNIX bestiary that appears on other Nutshell Handbooks. The beasts themselves are adapted from 19th-century engravings from the Dover Pictorial Archive.

The text of this book is set in Times Roman; headings are Helvetica; examples are Courier. Text was prepared using SoftQuad's *sqtroff* text formatter. Figures are produced with a Macintosh. Printing is done on an Apple LaserWriter.

SYSTEM
ADMINISTRATION

Books from O'Reilly & Associates, Inc.

Fall/Winter 1994-95

"Good reference books make a system administrator's job much easier. However, finding useful books about system administration is a challenge, and I'm constantly on the lookout. In general, I have found that almost anything published by O'Reilly & Associates is worth having if you are interested in the topic."

—Dinah McNutt, UNIX Review

TCP/IP Network Administration

By Craig Hunt
1st Edition August 1992
502 pages, ISBN 0-937175-82-X

A complete guide to setting up and running a TCP/IP network for administrators of networks of systems or lone home systems that access the Internet. It starts with the fundamentals: what the protocols do and how they work, how to request a network address and a name (the forms needed are included in an appendix), and how to set up your network. Beyond basic setup, the book discusses how to configure important network applications, including sendmail, the r* commands, and some simple setups for NIS and NFS. There are also chapters on troubleshooting and security. In addition, this book covers several important packages that are available from the Net (such as *gated*). Covers BSD and System V TCP/IP implementations.

"Whether you're putting a network together, trying to figure out why an existing one doesn't work, or wanting to understand the one you've got a little better, *TCP/IP Network Administration* is the definitive volume on the subject."
—Tom Yager, *Byte*

Managing Internet Information Services

By Cricket Liu, Jerry Peek, Russ Jones,
Bryan Buus & Adrian Nye
1st Edition December 1994 (est.)
668 pages, ISBN 1-56592-062-7

This comprehensive guide describes how to set up information services to make them available over the Internet. It discusses why a company would want to offer Internet services, provides complete coverage of all popular services, and tells how to select which ones to provide. Most of the book describes how to set up email services and FTP, Gopher, and World Wide Web servers.

"*Managing Internet Information Services* has long been needed in the Internet community, as well as in many organizations with IP-based networks. Although many on the Internet are quite savvy when it comes to administering these types of tools, *MIIS* will allow a much larger community to join in and perhaps provide more diverse information. This book will be a welcome addition to my Internet shelf."
—Robert H'obbes' Zakon, MITRE Corporation

Linux Network Administrator's Guide

By Olaf Kirch
1st Edition Winter 1994-95(est.)
400 pages (est.), ISBN 1-56592-087-2

A UNIX-compatible operating system that runs on personal computers, Linux is a pinnacle within the free software movement. It is based on a kernel developed by Finnish student Linus Torvalds and is distributed on the Net or on low-cost disks, along with a complete set of UNIX libraries, popular free software utilities, and traditional layered products like NFS and the X Window System.

Networking is a fundamental part of Linux. Whether you want a simple UUCP connection or a full LAN with NFS and NIS, you are going to have to build a network.

Linux Network Administrator's Guide by Olaf Kirch is one of the most successful books to come from the Linux Documentation Project. It touches on all the essential networking software included with Linux, plus some hardware considerations. Topics include serial connections, UUCP, routing and DNS, mail and News, SLIP and PPP, NFS, and NIS.

DNS and BIND

By Paul Albitz & Cricket Liu
1st Edition October 1992
418 pages, ISBN 1-56592-010-4

DNS and BIND contains all you need to know about the Internet's Domain Name System (DNS) and the Berkeley Internet Name Domain (BIND), its UNIX implementation. The Domain Name System is the Internet's "phone book"; it's a database that tracks important information (in particular, names and addresses) for every computer on the Internet. If you're a system administrator, this book will show you how to set up and maintain the DNS software on your network.

"*DNS and BIND* contains a lot of useful information that you'll never find written down anywhere else. And since it's written in a crisp style, you can pretty much use the book as your primary BIND reference."
—Marshall Rose, *ConneXions*

sendmail

By Bryan Costales, with Eric Allman & Neil Rickert
1st Edition November 1993
830 pages, ISBN 1-56592-056-2

This Nutshell Handbook® is far and away the most comprehensive book ever written on sendmail, the program that acts like a traffic cop in routing and delivering mail on UNIX-based networks. Although sendmail is used on almost every UNIX system, it's one of the last great uncharted territories—and most difficult utilities to learn—in UNIX system administration. This book provides a complete sendmail tutorial, plus extensive reference material on every aspect of the program. It covers IDA sendmail, the latest version (V8) from Berkeley, and the standard versions available on most systems.

"The program and its rule description file, sendmail.cf, have long been regarded as the pit of coals that separated the mild UNIX system administrators from the real fire walkers. Now, sendmail syntax, testing, hidden rules, and other mysteries are revealed. Costales, Allman, and Rickert are the indisputable authorities to do the text."
—Ben Smith, *Byte*

Essential System Administration

By Æleen Frisch
1st Edition October 1991
466 pages, ISBN 0-937175-80-3

Like any other multi-user system, UNIX requires some care and feeding. *Essential System Administration* tells you how. This book strips away the myth and confusion surrounding this important topic and provides a compact, manageable introduction to the tasks faced by anyone responsible for a UNIX system.

If you use a stand-alone UNIX system, whether it's a PC or a workstation, you know how much you need this book: on these systems the fine line between a user and an administrator has vanished. Either you're both or you're in trouble. If you routinely provide administrative support for a larger shared system or a network of workstations, you will find this book indispensable. Even if you aren't directly responsible for system administration, you will find that understanding basic administrative functions greatly increases your ability to use UNIX effectively.

Computer Security Basics

By Deborah Russell & G.T. Gangemi Sr.
1st Edition July 1991
464 pages, ISBN 0-937175-71-4

There's a lot more consciousness of security today, but not a lot of understanding of what it means and how far it should go. This handbook describes complicated concepts, such as trusted systems, encryption, and mandatory access control, in simple terms. For example, most U.S. government equipment acquisitions now require Orange Book (Trusted Computer System Evaluation Criteria) certification. A lot of people have a vague feeling that they ought to know about the Orange Book, but few make the effort to track it down and read it. *Computer Security Basics* contains a more readable introduction to the Orange Book—why it exists, what it contains, and what the different security levels are all about—than any other book or government publication.

"A very well-rounded book, filled with concise, authoritative information…written with the user in mind, but still at a level to be an excellent professional reference."
—Mitch Wright, System Administrator, I-NET, Inc.

Practical UNIX Security

By Simson Garfinkel & Gene Spafford
1st Edition June 1991
512 pages, ISBN 0-937175-72-2

Tells system administrators how to make their UNIX system—either System V or BSD—as secure as it possibly can be without going to trusted system technology. The book describes UNIX concepts and how they enforce security, tells how to defend against and handle security breaches, and explains network security (including UUCP, NFS, Kerberos, and firewall machines) in detail. If you are a UNIX system administrator or user who deals with security, you need this book.

"The book could easily become a standard desktop reference for anyone involved in system administration. In general, its comprehensive treatment of UNIX security issues will enlighten anyone with an interest in the topic."
—Paul Clark, Trusted Information Systems

PGP: Pretty Good Privacy

By Simson Garfinkel
1st Edition December 1994 (est.)
430 pages, ISBN 1-56592-098-8

PGP, which stands for Pretty Good Privacy, is a free and widely available program that lets you protect files and electronic mail. Written by Phil Zimmermann and released in 1991, PGP works on virtually every platform and has become very popular both in the U.S. and abroad. Because it uses state-of-the-art public key cryptography, PGP can be used to authenticate messages, as well as keep them secret. With PGP, you can digitally "sign" a message when you send it. By checking the digital signature at the other end, the recipient can be sure that the message was not changed during transmission and that the message actually came from you. The ability to protect the secrecy and authenticity of messages in this way is a vital part of being able to conduct business on the Internet.

PGP: Pretty Good Privacy is both a readable technical users guide and a fascinating behind-the-scenes look at cryptography and privacy. Part I of the book describes how to use PGP: protecting files and email, creating and using keys, signing messages, certifying and distributing keys, and using key servers. Part II provides background on cryptography, battles against public key patents and U.S. government export restrictions, and other aspects of the ongoing public debates about privacy and free speech.

System Performance Tuning

By Mike Loukides
1st Edition November 1990
336 pages, ISBN 0-937175-60-9

System Performance Tuning answers the fundamental question: How can I get my computer to do more work without buying more hardware? Some performance problems do require you to buy a bigger or faster computer, but many can be solved simply by making better use of the resources you already have.

"This book is a 'must' for anyone who has an interest in making their UNIX system run faster and more efficiently. It deals effectively with a complex subject that could require a multi-volume series."
—Stephan M. Chan, *ComUNIXation*

AUDIOTAPES

O'Reilly now offers audiotapes based on interviews with people who are making a profound impact in the world of the Internet. Here we give you a quick overview of what's available. For details on our audiotape collection, send email to **audio@ora.com**.

"Ever listen to one of those five-minute-long news pieces being broadcast on National Public Radio's 'All Things Considered' and wish they were doing an in-depth story on new technology? Well, your wishes are answered."

—*Byte*

Global Network Operations

Carl Malamud interviews Brian Carpenter, Bernhard Stockman, Mike O'Dell & Geoff Huston
Released Spring 1994
Duration: 2 hours, ISBN 1-56592-993-4

What does it take to actually run a network? In these four interviews, Carl Malamud explores some of the technical and operational issues faced by Internet service providers around the world.

Brian Carpenter is the director for networking at CERN, the high-energy physics laboratory in Geneva, Switzerland. Physicists are some of the world's most active Internet users, and its global user base makes CERN one of the world's most network-intensive sites. Carpenter discusses how he deals with issues such as the OSI and DECnet Phase V protocols and his views on the future of the Internet.

Bernhard Stockman is one of the founders and the technical manager of the European Backbone (EBONE). EBONE has proven to be the first effective transit backbone for Europe and has been a leader in the deployment of CIDR, BGP-4, and other key technologies.

Mike O'Dell is vice president of research at UUNET Technologies. O'Dell has a long record of involvement in data communications, ranging from his service as a telco lab employee, an engineer on several key projects, and a member of the USENIX board to now helping define new services for one of the largest commercial IP service providers.

Geoff Huston is the director of the Australian Academic Research Network (AARNET). AARNET is known as one of the most progressive regional networks, rapidly adopting new services for its users. Huston talks about how networking in Australia has flourished despite astronomically high rates for long-distance lines.

The Future of the Internet Protocol

Carl Malamud interviews Steve Deering, Bob Braden, Christian Huitema, Bob Hinden, Peter Ford, Steve Casner, Bernhard Stockman & Noel Chiappa
Released Spring 1994
Duration: 4 hours, ISBN 1-56592-996-9

The explosion of interest in the Internet is stressing what was originally designed as a research and education network. The sheer number of users is requiring new strategies for Internet address allocation; multimedia applications are requiring greater bandwidth and strategies such as "resource reservation" to provide synchronous end-to-end service.

In this series of eight interviews, Carl Malamud talks to some of the researchers who are working to define how the underlying technology of the Internet will need to evolve in order to meet the demands of the next five to ten years.

Give these tapes a try if you're intrigued by such topics as Internet "multicasting" of audio and video, or think your job might one day depend on understanding some of the following buzzwords:

- IPNG (Internet Protocol Next Generation)
- SIP (Simple Internet Protocol)
- TUBA (TCP and UDP with Big Addresses)
- CLNP (Connectionless Network Protocol)
- CIDR (Classless Inter-Domain Routing)

or if you are just interested in getting to know more about the people who are shaping the future.

Mobile IP Networking

Carl Malamud interviews Phil Karn & Jun Murai
Released Spring 1994
Duration: 1 hour, ISBN 1-56592-994-2

Phil Karn is the father of the KA9Q publicly available implementation of TCP/IP for DOS (which has also been used as the basis for the software in many commercial Internet routers). KA9Q was originally developed to allow "packet radio," that is, TCP/IP over ham radio bands. Phil's current research focus is on commercial applications of wireless data communications.

Jun Murai is one of the most distinguished researchers in the Internet community. Murai is a professor at Keio University and the founder of the Japanese WIDE Internet. Murai talks about his research projects, which range from satellite-based IP multicasting to a massive testbed for mobile computing at the Fujisawa campus of Keio University.

Networked Information and Online Libraries

Carl Malamud interviews Peter Deutsch & Cliff Lynch
Released September 1993
Duration: 1 hour, ISBN 1-56592-998-5

Peter Deutsch, president of Bunyip Information Services, was one of the co-developers of Archie. In this interview Peter talks about his philosophy for services and compares Archie to X.500. He also talks about what kind of standards we need for networked information retrieval.

Cliff Lynch is currently the director of library automation for the University of California. He discusses issues behind online publishing, such as SGML and the democratization of publishing on the Internet.

European Networking

Carl Malamud interviews Glenn Kowack & Rob Blokzijl
Released September 1993
Duration: 1 hour, ISBN 1-56592-999-3

Glenn Kowack is chief executive of EUnet, the network that's bringing the Internet to the people of Europe. Glenn talks about EUnet's populist business model and the politics of European networking.

Rob Blokzijl is the network manager for NIKHEF, the Dutch Insitute of High Energy Physics. Rob talks about RIPE, the IP user's group for Europe, and the nuts and bolts of European network coordination.

Security and Networks

Carl Malamud interviews Jeff Schiller & John Romkey
Released September 1993
Duration: 1 hour, ISBN 1-56592-997-7

Jeff Schiller is the manager of MIT's campus network and is one of the Internet's leading security experts. Here, he talks about Privacy Enhanced Mail (PEM), the difficulty of policing the Internet, and whether horses or computers are more useful to criminals.

John Romkey has been a long-time TCP/IP developer and was recently named to the Internet Architecture Board. In this wide-ranging interview, John talks about the famous "ToasterNet" demo at InterOp, what kind of Internet security he'd like to see put in place, and what Internet applications of the future might look like.

John Perry Barlow
Notable Speeches of the Information Age

USENIX Conference Keynote Address
San Francisco, CA; January 17, 1994
Duration: 1.5 hours, ISBN 1-56592-992-6

John Perry Barlow—retired Wyoming cattle rancher, a lyricist for the Grateful Dead since 1971—holds a degree in comparative religion from Wesleyan University. He also happens to be a recognized authority on computer security, virtual reality, digitized intellectual property, and the social and legal conditions arising in the global network of computers.

In 1990 Barlow co-founded the Electronic Frontier Foundation with Mitch Kapor and currently serves as chair of its executive committee. He writes and lectures on subjects relating to digital technology and society and is a contributing editor to *Communications of the ACM, NeXTWorld, Microtimes, Mondo 2000, Wired*, and other publications.

In his keynote address to the Winter 1994 USENIX Conference, Barlow talks of recent developments in the national information infrastructure, telecommunications regulation, cryptography, globalization of the Internet, intellectual property, and the settlement of Cyberspace. The talk explores the premise that "architecture is politics": that the technology adopted for the coming "information superhighway" will help to determine what is carried on it, and that if the electronic frontier of the Internet is not to be replaced by electronic strip malls, we need to make sure that our technology choices favor bi-directional communication and open platforms.

Side A contains the keynote;
Side B contains a question and answer period.

O'Reilly & Associates—
GLOBAL NETWORK NAVIGATOR™

The Global Network Navigator (GNN)™ is a unique kind of information service that makes the Internet easy and enjoyable to use. We organize access to the vast information resources of the Internet so that you can find what you want. We also help you understand the Internet and the many ways you can explore it.

In GNN you'll find:

Navigating the Net with GNN

 The *Whole Internet Catalog* contains a descriptive listing of the most useful Net resources and services with live links to those resources.

 The *GNN Business Pages* are where you'll learn about companies who have established a presence on the Internet and use its worldwide reach to help educate consumers.

 The *Internet Help Desk* helps folks who are new to the Net orient themselves and gets them started on the road to Internet exploration.

News

 NetNews is a weekly publication that reports on the news of the Internet, with weekly feature articles that focus on Internet trends and special events. The Sports, Weather, and Comix Pages round out the news.

Special Interest Publications

 Whether you're planning a trip or are just interested in reading about the journeys of others, you'll find that the *Travelers' Center* contains a rich collection of feature articles and ongoing columns about travel. In the *Travelers' Center*, you can link to many helpful and informative travel-related Internet resources.

 The *Personal Finance Center* is the place to go for information about money management and investment on the Internet. Whether you're an old pro at playing the market or are thinking about investing for the first time, you'll read articles and discover Internet resources that will help you to think of the Internet as a personal finance information tool.

All in all, GNN helps you get more value for the time you spend on the Internet.

 The Best of the Web

GNN received "Honorable Mention" for **"Best Overall Site," "Best Entertainment Service,"** and "**Most Important Service Concept**."

The *GNN NetNews* received "Honorable Mention" for "**Best Document Design**."

Subscribe Today

GNN is available over the Internet as a subscription service. To get complete information about subscribing to GNN, send email to **info@gnn.com**. If you have access to a World Wide Web browser such as Mosaic or Lynx, you can use the following URL to register online: `http://gnn.com/`

If you use a browser that does not support online forms, you can retrieve an email version of the registration form automatically by sending email to **form@gnn.com**. Fill this form out and send it back to us by email, and we will confirm your registration.

O'Reilly on the Net—
ONLINE PROGRAM GUIDE

O'Reilly & Associates offers extensive information through our online resources. If you've got Internet access, we invite you to come and explore our little neck-of-the-woods.

Online Resource Center

Most comprehensive among our online offerings is the O'Reilly Resource Center. Here, you'll find detailed information and descriptions on all O'Reilly products: titles, prices, tables of contents, indexes, author bios, software contents, reviews...you can even view images of the products themselves. We also supply helpful ordering information: how to contact us, how to order online, distributors and bookstores world wide, discounts, upgrades, etc. In addition, we provide informative literature in the field: articles, interviews, and bibliographies that help you stay informed and abreast.

 The Best of the Web

The *O'Reilly Resource Center* was voted "**Best Commercial Site**" by users participating in "Best of the Web '94."

To access ORA's Online Resource Center:

Point your Web browser (e.g., `mosaic` or `lynx`) to:
`http://gnn.com/ora/`

For the plaintext version, `telnet` or `gopher` to:
`gopher.ora.com`
(telnet login: `gopher`)

FTP

The example files and programs in many of our books are available electronically via FTP.

To obtain example files and programs from O'Reilly texts:

`ftp` to:

`ftp.ora.com`
or
`ftp.uu.net`
`cd published/oreilly`

Ora-news

An easy way to stay informed of the latest projects and products from O'Reilly & Associates is to subscribe to "ora-news," our electronic news service. Subscribers receive email as soon as the information breaks.

To subscribe to "ora-news":

Send email to:
listproc@online.ora.com

and put the following information on the first line of your message (not in "Subject"):
subscribe ora-news "your name" **of** "your company"

For example:
subscribe ora-news Jim Dandy of Mighty Fine Enterprises

Email

Many customer services are provided via email. Here's a few of the most popular and useful.

nuts@ora.com
    For general questions and information.
bookquestions@ora.com
    For technical questions, or corrections, concerning book contents.
order@ora.com
    To order books online and for ordering questions.
catalog@ora.com
    To receive a free copy of our magazine/catalog, "ora.com" (please include a postal address).

Snailmail and phones

O'Reilly & Associates, Inc.
103A Morris Street, Sebastopol, CA 95472
Inquiries: **707-829-0515, 800-998-9938**
Credit card orders: **800-889-8969**
    (Weekdays 6a.m.- 6p.m. PST)
FAX: **707-829-0104**

TO ORDER: **800-889-8969** (CREDIT CARD ORDERS ONLY); **ORDER@ORA.COM**

O'Reilly & Associates—
LISTING OF TITLES

INTERNET

!%@:: A Directory of Electronic Mail
  Addressing & Networks
Connecting to the Internet:
  An O'Reilly Buyer's Guide
Internet In A Box
The Mosaic Handbook for Microsoft Windows
The Mosaic Handbook for the Macintosh
The Mosaic Handbook for the
  X Window System
Smileys
The Whole Internet User's Guide & Catalog

SYSTEM ADMINISTRATION

Computer Security Basics
DNS and BIND
Essential System Administration
Linux Network Administrator's Guide
  (Winter '94-95 est.)
Managing Internet Information Services
Managing NFS and NIS
Managing UUCP and Usenet
sendmail
Practical UNIX Security
PGP: Pretty Good Privacy (Winter '94-95 est.)
System Performance Tuning
TCP/IP Network Administration
termcap & terminfo
X Window System Administrator's Guide:
  Volume 8
X Window System, R6, Companion CD
  (Winter '94-95 est.)

USING UNIX AND X

BASICS
Learning GNU Emacs
Learning the Korn Shell
Learning the UNIX Operating System
Learning the vi Editor
MH & xmh: E-mail for Users & Programmers
SCO UNIX in a Nutshell
The USENET Handbook (Winter '94-95 est.)
Using UUCP and Usenet
UNIX in a Nutshell: System V Edition
The X Window System in a Nutshell
X Window System User's Guide: Volume 3
X Window System User's Guide, Motif Ed.:
  Volume 3M
X User Tools

ADVANCED
Exploring Expect (Winter '94-95 est.)
The Frame Handbook
Learning Perl
Making TeX Work
Programming perl
sed & awk
UNIX Power Tools (with CD-ROM)

PROGRAMMING UNIX, C, AND MULTI-PLATFORM

FORTRAN/SCIENTIFIC COMPUTING
High Performance Computing
Migrating to Fortran 90
UNIX for FORTRAN Programmers

C PROGRAMMING LIBRARIES
Practical C Programming
POSIX Programmer's Guide
POSIX.4: Programming for the Real World
  (Winter '94-95 est.)
Programming with curses
Understanding and Using COFF
Using C on the UNIX System

C PROGRAMMING TOOLS
Checking C Programs with lint
lex & yacc
Managing Projects with make
Power Programming with RPC
Software Portability with imake

MULTI-PLATFORM PROGRAMMING
Encyclopedia of Graphics File Formats
Distributing Applications Across DCE and
  Windows NT
Guide to Writing DCE Applications
ORACLE Performance Tuning
Multi-Platform Code Management
Understanding DCE
Understanding Japanese Information
  Processing

BERKELEY 4.4 SOFTWARE DISTRIBUTION

4.4BSD System Manager's Manual
4.4BSD User's Reference Manual
4.4BSD User's Supplementary Documents
4.4BSD Programmer's Reference Manual
4.4BSD Programmer's Supplementary
  Documents
4.4BSD-Lite CD Companion
4.4BSD-Lite CD Companion:
  International Version

X PROGRAMMING

Motif Programming Manual: Volume 6A
Motif Reference Manual: Volume 6B
Motif Tools
PEXlib Programming Manual
PEXlib Reference Manual
PHIGS Programming Manual
  (soft or hard cover)
PHIGS Reference Manual
Programmer's Supplement for Release 6
  (Winter '94-95 est.)
Xlib Programming Manual: Volume 1
Xlib Reference Manual: Volume 2
X Protocol Reference Manual, R5: Vol. 0
X Protocol Reference Manual, R6: Vol. 0
  (Winter '94-95 est.)
X Toolkit Intrinsics Programming Manual:
  Volume 4
X Toolkit Intrinsics Programming Manual,
  Motif Edition: Volume 4M
X Toolkit Intrinsics Reference Manual: Vol.5
XView Programming Manual: Volume 7A
XView Reference Manual: Volume 7B

THE X RESOURCE

A QUARTERLY WORKING JOURNAL FOR X PROGRAMMERS
The X Resource: Issues 0 through 13
  (Issue 13 available 1/95)

BUSINESS/CAREER

Building a Successful Software Business
Love Your Job!

TRAVEL

Travelers' Tales Thailand
Travelers' Tales Mexico
Travelers' Tales India (Winter '94-95 est.)

AUDIOTAPES

INTERNET TALK RADIO'S "GEEK OF THE WEEK" INTERVIEWS
The Future of the Internet Protocol, 4 hrs.
Global Network Operations, 2 hours
Mobile IP Networking, 1 hour
Networked Information and
  Online Libraries, 1 hour
Security and Networks, 1 hour
European Networking, 1 hour

NOTABLE SPEECHES OF THE INFORMATION AGE
John Perry Barlow, 1.5 hours

O'Reilly & Associates—
INTERNATIONAL DISTRIBUTORS

Customers outside North America can now order O'Reilly & Associates books through the following distributors. They offer our international customers faster order processing, more bookstores, increased representation at tradeshows worldwide, and the high-quality, responsive service our customers have come to expect.

EUROPE, MIDDLE EAST, AND AFRICA
(except Germany, Switzerland, and Austria)

INQUIRIES
International Thomson Publishing Europe
Berkshire House
168-173 High Holborn
London WC1V 7AA
United Kingdom
Telephone: 44-71-497-1422
Fax: 44-71-497-1426
Email: ora.orders@itpuk.co.uk

ORDERS
International Thomson Publishing Services, Ltd.
Cheriton House, North Way
Andover, Hampshire SP10 5BE
United Kingdom
Telephone: 44-264-342-832 (UK orders)
Telephone: 44-264-342-806 (outside UK)
Fax: 44-264-364418 (UK orders)
Fax: 44-264-342761 (outside UK)

GERMANY, SWITZERLAND, AND AUSTRIA
International Thomson Publishing GmbH
O'Reilly-International Thomson Verlag
Attn: Mr. G. Miske
Königswinterer Strasse 418
53227 Bonn
Germany
Telephone: 49-228-970240
Fax: 49-228-441342
Email: anfragen@orade.ora.com

ASIA
(except Japan)

INQUIRIES
International Thomson Publishing Asia
221 Henderson Road
#05 10 Henderson Building
Singapore 0315
Telephone: 65-272-6496
Fax: 65-272-6498

ORDERS
Telephone: 65-268-7867
Fax: 65-268-6727

AUSTRALIA
WoodsLane Pty. Ltd.
Unit 8, 101 Darley Street (P.O. Box 935)
Mona Vale NSW 2103
Australia
Telephone: 61-2-979-5944
Fax: 61-2-997-3348
Email: woods@tmx.mhs.oz.au

NEW ZEALAND
WoodsLane New Zealand Ltd.
21 Cooks Street (P.O. Box 575)
Wanganui, New Zealand
Telephone: 64-6-347-6543
Fax: 64-6-345-4840
Email: woods@tmx.mhs.oz.au

THE AMERICAS, JAPAN, AND OCEANIA
O'Reilly & Associates, Inc.
103A Morris Street
Sebastopol, CA 95472 U.S.A.
Telephone: 707-829-0515
Telephone: 800-998-9938 (U.S. & Canada)
Fax: 707-829-0104
Email: order@ora.com

TO ORDER: **800-889-8969** (CREDIT CARD ORDERS ONLY); **ORDER@ORA.COM**